The Complete Idiot's Reference Card

tear here

The Right Equiptment

I. The right size racquet is very important so you do not develop tennis elbow.

Average racquet sizes are:

- ➤ Juniors   4
- ➤ Teens, Small Adults   4 $\frac{1}{4}$
- ➤ Large hands   4 $\frac{5}{8}$
- ➤ Average Man, Large Woman   4 $\frac{1}{2}$
- ➤ Average Woman, Small Man   4 $\frac{3}{8}$

II. The right shoes must have good arch support and the correct sole for the court surface you are playing. Running shoes, boat shoes, and walking shoes are not appropriate. Cross-trainers are all right, but shoes specifically designed for tennis are best.

III. The right balls. Do not be stingy, if you play with a can of balls more than three times, you run the risk of incurring tennis elbow. Most cans are pressurized so balls "go dead" after being open for a week, so keep a can of new balls on hand.

What to Bring to the Court

- ➤ Your racquet
- ➤ One can of new balls and some used balls in case you lose a new one
- ➤ Sweatshirt or warm-ups
- ➤ Hat, cap, or visor if playing outside
- ➤ Headband or hair band if you have flyaway hair
- ➤ Water bottle
- ➤ Sweatbands for your wrists, a must in hot weather
- ➤ Towel, in case the club doesn't provide one
- ➤ Bandages, safety pins, or a small first-aid kit
- ➤ Snack, like an energy or power bar
- ➤ Extra pair of socks to wear before and after playing
- ➤ Fresh shirt, or a second set of clothes if you sweat a lot
- ➤ Sunglasses if you are playing outside
- ➤ Sunscreen
- ➤ Aspirin/medication, in case you have a problem
- ➤ Pencil, pen, and paper to write down names and numbers of potential future opponents and/or partners

alpha
books

W9-BON-883

Scoring Within a Game

- ➤ Love: zero
- ➤ Fifteen: first point won
- ➤ Thirty: second point won
- ➤ Forty: third point won
- ➤ Next point won is game
- ➤ Deuce: when both players have forty points

Games won are scored as one, two, three until one player reaches six games which constitutes a set won. If score becomes five games–all, then set score can be seven games to five, as the set must be won by a margin of two games. If both players have six games, they can play out the set until one player wins by two games or play a tiebreaker, where a player must win seven points by a margin of two. The decision to play out the set, or play a tiebreaker, is decided before the match by the players or tournament. The more common decision, these days, is to play the tiebreakers.

April 10, 1998: The Good Friday Agreement is crafted.

May 22, 1998: The referendum accepting the Good Friday Agreement passes.

Rules

- ➤ Server always gets two serves.
- ➤ Always retrieve the balls and give them to the server.
- ➤ Take your time, but never more than 25 seconds between points.
- ➤ Relax between games. You change ends after every odd game. This changeover cannot take more than 90 seconds.
- ➤ Don't leave the court unless you are returning a ball or taking a bathroom break.
- ➤ Don't yell or throw your racquet.
- ➤ Play fair; call the balls as you see them.
- ➤ Server should call out the score before every point.

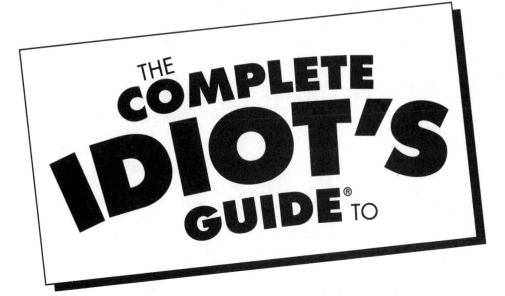

THE COMPLETE IDIOT'S GUIDE® TO

Tennis

by Trish Faulkner
with
Vivian Lemelman

alpha
books

A Division of Macmillan General Reference
A Pearson Education Macmillan Company
1633 Broadway, New York, NY 10019-6785

Contents at a Glance

Contents

Appendices

Foreword

I met Trish Faulkner when she came over from Australia to play the international tennis circuit in 1962. The top women players all went to the same events and we got to know one another rather well, both on and off the court. The tour was very different then as both the men and women played at the same venues and we all socialized and watched each others' matches.

I remember in the Spring of 1963 during the French Riviera Circuit, which was a series of four tournaments in Cannes, Menton, Nice, and Monte Carlo, Trish and I had asked for private housing. We were taken to an incredible villa on the hillside with a view of St. Jean Cap Ferrat. There were two other players there. We had a housekeeper and a cook at our disposal. We could walk out into the garden every morning and pick fresh grapefruit and oranges. We were in heaven. We didn't care if we even played tennis, let alone whether we won or lost. We found out our hostess was Gloria Butler, a very famous, wealthy lady who loved tennis. This was one of the nicest two weeks I have ever spent at a tennis tournament. Trish and I got to know one another very well and we have kept up our friendship for over 35 years. She was and is a great player. She is currently #2 in the world for her age group and #1 in the USA. Trish always impressed me with her passion for tennis.

Trish and I took different paths as we continued our interest in tennis. I chose to keep playing and was fortunate enough to participate in tennis during the Open era. I kept playing and winning money but more importantly, I achieved my dream—to win Wimbledon singles—and I did it in the Centennial year with royalty looking on. Trish chose to leave the amateur ranks and get married and have children. Her love for the game was too strong, however, and she soon became a teaching professional and then a top executive with the Women's Tennis Association.

Our love of tennis kept bringing us together for clinics, exhibitions, and charity tournaments. I think both of us enjoy spreading the magic of tennis to anyone who might want to watch or listen.

I can't think of anyone better to write this book. Trish has been on every side of the net. She was, and still is, an internationally ranked player. She is one of the most dedicated tennis teachers I have ever met. She understands the promotional side of the sport from her days as the marketing director for the Women's Pro Tour. She also knows all the big name players and she can share with you their strengths and weaknesses.

She has so much to share with you. Believe me, read this, follow her advice, and you will be playing good tennis in no time.

Virginia Wade

Introduction

In this book I guide you through a series of steps as if I just met you for the first time at my club, BallenIsles Country Club, in Florida. Many of my students of all ages ask if it's possible for them to learn tennis. I say, of course! And I take them on the same wonderful journey as you are about to experience.

How to Use This Book

Part 1, What Is This Game Called Tennis? introduces you to the game of tennis. I felt it important that you understand some of the history of tennis so that you would have a full appreciation of how far the game has come. I will also give you some of the basics of the sport, such as what you need to buy in terms of equipment and clothing.

Part 2, Play Ball!!! explains how to get ready to play, and gives you stretching and relaxation techniques that we also demonstrate. I also want to make sure you know how to choose the right professional. And I've included the rules and etiquette of the game.

Part 3, The ABCs of Tennis, takes you through the basics of tennis. I describe how to hold the racquet and how to swing at the ball. I also describe different serves. After reading this part, you should have some of the fanciest footwork in the game and understand some of the basic strokes.

Part 4, Your Advantage, informs you of the different ways you can make yourself a better, healthier, and injury-free player. I offer tips on cross-training, taking care of your nutritional needs, taking care of your skin, as well as tips for having a successful practice session.

Part 5, The Competitive Edge—Putting It All Together, assumes that you understand all of the basic shots and are now ready to play the game. I discuss how to be mentally tough and how you should approach a match. I also introduce you to the wonderful game of doubles—so different from singles it's worth another book!

Part 6, Different Ways to Enjoy Tennis, shows you how to enjoy tennis in different ways. I explore the interesting strategy of doubles (a whole game unto itself), how to get children involved, what to do if you start the game later in life, and playing wheelchair tennis. In this part I show you how to get started in leagues and tournaments, and how to learn from the pros. I also offer advice on how to choose a tennis camp or resort—plus, all you ever wanted to know about the pros.

At the end of book, you'll also find six appendices that offer some great information ranging from terminology and more reading to information on the top-ranked players.

Extras

Because we know how much you like variety and how easily we can all get bored with long paragraphs, you will find a number of interesting and easy-to-read boxes scattered throughout the book that will give you special tips, quotes from the pros, and some other invaluable information that we just couldn't fit anywhere else. The boxes look like this:

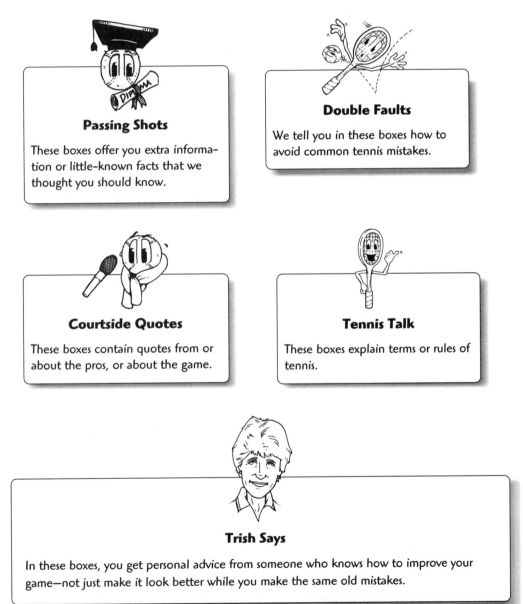

Passing Shots

These boxes offer you extra information or little-known facts that we thought you should know.

Double Faults

We tell you in these boxes how to avoid common tennis mistakes.

Courtside Quotes

These boxes contain quotes from or about the pros, or about the game.

Tennis Talk

These boxes explain terms or rules of tennis.

Trish Says

In these boxes, you get personal advice from someone who knows how to improve your game—not just make it look better while you make the same old mistakes.

Acknowledgments

Photographer - June Harrison, New York
BallenIsles Photographer - Vicki Fort, Florida
BallenIsles Tennis Professional Staff for their help and cooperation.
Secretary - Judy Moyses

Part 1
What Is This Game Called Tennis?

This is a pretty straightforward, no-frills introduction to the game. After all, you want to play tennis, not write a book on the subject (we've done that for you). Instead, we go right to the heart of the matter and teach you the who, what, where, and when of tennis to help you better choose your weapons and unravel some of the mysteries of the sport. Most importantly, you will learn how to get started and where to find a court. You will also find that age is no barrier to learning the basics of this wonderful sport. And what about fashion, you ask? We've got that covered, too. No Aussie jam shorts or muscle T-shirts for you.

In this chapter we show you how to dress for success and comfort, and tell you where to find all of those little essentials that no one talks about. I will also take you on a historical tour. Tennis has been around awhile, but the balls, racquets, and clothing have certainly seen some changes. You will meet up with some remarkable champions and learn how the sport evolved. Before you hock your new Rollerblades to fund this new adventure, you'll be delighted to discover that tennis is not really an expensive sport. In my native Australia, almost everyone is exposed to tennis at an early age. This is the main reason we have so many talented players. That and the great climate, nice beaches, friendly people...oh sorry, got a little homesick.

What you'll need to get started takes a small investment of money and time. By the end of Part 1, we'll have you looking good and ready for the thrill of a lifetime.

The Who, What, Why, Where, and When of Tennis

Tennis is one of the most popular sports in the world. The beauty of tennis is, it is inexpensive and yet is wonderful exercise. Not only can you burn calories, but you can have fun doing it. You don't have to be in tiptop shape to start playing. You can learn even if you are a klutz.

The sport allows you to play and improve at your own pace while still being able to enjoy the basic premise of the game: Get the ball over the net one more time than your opponent.

Forty-three million people play tennis worldwide. Seventeen and half million play in the USA. They are all shapes and sizes, and all ages. Tennis courts are now easily accessible thanks to many forward-thinking parks and recreation departments. There is even a tennis court at the White House that is used frequently by the staff and visiting dignitaries. George Bush played there many times during his term in office and invited pros to play charity events and exhibitions.

Tennis is one of the few sports where fans can watch their idols and then the very next day emulate them on the same courts and under the same rules. Young and old, male or female, all these spectators/players see themselves hitting serves just like Pete Sampras or volleys like Martina Navratilova. And you know what, they can!

Tennis is a game of skill and mental acuity. You have to plan and react, plan and react. It teaches you control, patience, teamwork, and character. After a hard day with the kids or a tough day at the office, there is nothing better than taking out your frustrations on the tennis court. Even changing into your tennis clothes gives you a rush of energy and excitement. Once you start running after your opponent's shots, slamming your serves, and hitting those winners, you begin to feel all the tension draining out of you. Then you can settle down and beat the pants off your friend on the other side of the net.

Tennis is not a dangerous sport. It is not a contact sport, unless you bump into your doubles partner. It is played in all climates, indoors and out. All over the world, people are playing tennis the same way you will be: with a racquet, balls, an opponent, and a game that can always get better.

In this chapter, I will help you take your first steps towards being a tennis player. I will share my passion and let you see why so many people love tennis.

Courtside Quotes

"Tennis seems innocently simple to those who are outside the fence looking in."
—Vic Braden, legendary tennis coach

Tennis Talk

A **tennis court** is a flat playing surface measuring 36 feet wide by 78 feet long.

What Is Tennis?

Tennis is a sport developed in the late 1800s and is played on a *court* which can be either indoors or outdoors.

The nice thing about tennis is that it isn't an expensive sport. In fact, the only real downside is that you need another person to play against. This should not be a problem unless you are totally without friends. And even if you are, you can look forward to cultivating a host of new friendships on the tennis court. (You can then go on to write *The Complete Idiot's Guide to Making Friends*.)

The basic premise of the game is to win points off your opponent who is on the other side of the net.

Going all out: Trish stretching for the ball.

Photo credit: June Harrison

The net is strung across the center of the court at a height of three feet. Your goal is to hit the ball over the net with your racquet and make your opponent run, stretch and gasp for air, all the while trying to force your opponent into making a mistake before you do! Meanwhile, your opponent is striving to do the same thing to you. In the above photo, my opponent certainly stretched me out here. Sounds like fun, doesn't it? It is, and you can easily play the game once you understand the basics.

You can hit the ball with the racquet when the ball is in the air or after it bounces. You can play aggressively or defensively. It is a game of skill with players making decisions as to how, when, and where to hit the ball.

Tennis singles, which sounds like a dating service, is two people on a court, each one on opposite sides of the net.

Four people on the court, with two on either side of the net makes a doubles game. Doubles positions vary during the point.

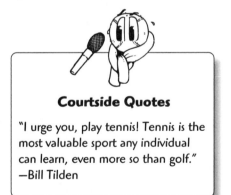

Courtside Quotes

"I urge you, play tennis! Tennis is the most valuable sport any individual can learn, even more so than golf."
—Bill Tilden

People at the net conversing.

Photo credit: Vicki Fort

Tennis singles: one on one.

Photo credit: June Harrison

Who Can Play?

Beginners are drawn to tennis because they have either seen the game played professionally or watched their friends play. Tennis is a wonderful sport because you can adjust your movements to suit your mobility and agility. If you were a jock in high school and have turned into a computer nerd, you can be saved. If you were not exactly a cheerleader, but you feel pretty good and you want to live another 50 years, tennis is your sport.

A doubles game: the more the merrier.

Photo credit: June Harrison

Anyone who can see a tennis ball and stand on two feet can learn to play tennis. Even this statement is not completely true; as you will see in my chapter on wheelchair tennis, you do not have to be able to stand to play. You just have to be able to swing a racquet. Racquets are made for all shapes and sizes, as well as pocketbooks. There is no excuse for not having one to swing.

Trish Says

I would encourage you to check with your physician before you start running around the court. Playing with a pro in a controlled lesson environment need not be too strenuous; but when left on your own, you may be caught up in the joy of playing and overdo it. Be cautious; check out your health before taking up the game.

The motto of the United States Tennis Association (USTA), the governing body for tennis in the United States, is "Tennis, a Sport for a Lifetime." There is no truer statement. Players who learned as children, but gave up the sport in adulthood, always seem to return to tennis in later years. As you can see from the next photo, young and less young can play together.

Fun at any age.

Photo credit: Vicki Fort

And even those who never learned as children are entering the game in later years as retirees who find themselves with time on their hands. They are the ones who are often eager to try new adventures. And believe me, tennis is an adventure. We are also finding many young professionals, who played football or baseball in their college days, taking to tennis as a sport that replaces their more strenuous youthful endeavors.

When I was teaching tennis in the 1970s, I had as a pupil a very well-known football player. He was nearing the end of his career and he was looking for other athletic endeavors to help keep him in shape. When he first started, he got very frustrated as he kept on over-hitting his shots. He was so strong and fearsome he thought he could force the ball to jump over the net simply by staring it down. Just because he was strong and athletic, however, didn't mean he was going to learn quickly how to play tennis well. Once he got over the fact that he couldn't simply muscle the ball over the net, and he learned the correct techniques to harness his power and strength, he became a good player.

So, as a beginner, don't worry if you are not strong. Don't be concerned if you feel you are too big and bulky to run around the court. And don't think you can do it without this book just because you were a star basketball player in high school. The beauty of tennis is the fact that there are so many levels and degrees of ability. You will, with my help, learn the game the right way and always be able to find an opponent or a partner.

Many sports do not require their champions to be big and strong. Tennis has stars of all shapes and sizes. Although I do have to admit the top men and women players of today are much bigger and stronger than we were twenty years ago. In a social, non-competitive situation, you do not have to worry about size and strength. You need to worry about fitness and finesse.

Strength isn't everything.
Photo credit: Vicki Fort

South American tennis star Guillermo Vilas was a master at tennis. He played as if he was painting a canvas or writing poetry, which he did often. He savored the art of maneuvering his opponent out of position so he could close in for his final shot. He was not very tall, but he had great legs for tennis, so he used them to his advantage to wear down his opponent.

Now that I have convinced you that anyone can play, and you are ready to pick up the racquet, you need to have somewhere to play. Let's find a court.

Where Do You Play?

The good news is that tennis courts are now relatively easy to find. Even the smallest towns have public tennis courts. They may not be in the best shape, but then again, you don't need the manicured lawns of Wimbledon to get you going. You will find out more about courts and court surfaces later in the book. Most outdoor courts are either soft or hard, depending on the geographic location. A soft court is clay, or a surface made up of layers of sand and a gritty clay blend. The hard courts are either cement or an asphalt base with a small amount of cushioning in the painted surface. When you first start, it doesn't matter what the court is like. It should have a net, and if possible, lines, but the net is the most important thing. A court is a court, so grab it.

No matter where you live, you can find public tennis courts, and they're usually free. But if the courts are supervised and have amenities, be prepared to pay a nominal fee. If you live in the U.S., particularly Florida, Arizona, Texas, or California, tennis courts are usually easy to find because tennis can be played year round due to the nice weather. However, in cold-winter-weather states like New York, Washington, and Maine, you may find fewer public courts. If you don't know where to go, or are unable to locate a court, call your local recreation department and ask for a listing of public tennis courts in your area. The recreation staff will also be able to tell you about lesson programs available to the public-court players.

Trish Says

I have a cousin whose family ran a local store in the Australian outback. Right next door to their store, they built an ant-bed tennis court. What is that, you might ask? In Australia, we have great big red ants that build 10-foot-high mounds as their homes. When they are finished with the mounds, people use the remains for the top surface of a tennis court.

For many years, tennis was considered a country club sport, and public courts were not easy to find. If you lived in a depressed area of town, you were not likely to find any.

This has slowly changed, and now you will find just as much tennis played on your local city courts as you will at the country clubs. Usually, the courts at the country clubs are in better shape than the public courts, but that really doesn't matter. As I said earlier, when you are first starting out, the condition of the court is not that important, but it should have a net. It is somewhat important that the net be around the right height, which is three feet at the center. If you are not in the habit of carrying a tape measure in your pocket, you can do one of the following. Give it the eye and hope that it is close to the right height. Or, stand your body next to it and try to imagine where three feet might come to from your feet up to your navel. Or, just make it higher than it should be, as it is a great way to learn how to lift the ball over the net.

Trish Says

Always bring a can of balls to the tennis court, especially at public courts where you're not likely to encounter a pro shop. If you are a country club guest where there is a pro shop, the shop might accept payment only on credit, not cash. If you are playing on a private court, it is good etiquette for you to supply the balls if your friend is supplying the court.

How do you make the net higher? A very good question. On most public courts, nets are nets, and you will not find the little handles needed to turn the crank on the net post to make the net go up or down. So you live with the height of the net and use your imagination if it is terribly out of line. At the club, the maintenance staff keeps control of the little widgets or cranks used to move the nets, but they will probably be on their coffee break when you need to change the height of your net. What is the moral of this? Don't concern yourself with the height of the net. If it is close to three feet, it will do.

If you are lucky enough to have a friend who owns his or her own tennis court, consider yourself in tennis nirvana. You will be able to practice to your heart's content and it won't cost you more than a few lunches and several cans of balls. Backyard courts are wonderful. My father built me one when I was 12 years old. It was the greatest gift he could have given me and the entire family. For one, my parents always knew where I was by the plop-plop sound of tennis balls. Secondly, the tennis court was a friend magnet. And I had lots of them. They came from near and far to play tennis on our court. From the perspective of the impact on our family, it shaped the future of each of our lives, particularly mine.

Why Do We Play?

No one ever called the King of Sweden a couch potato. He played tennis throughout his life and was still chasing tennis balls well into his 80s. The USTA has national championships for men and women 80 and over, as well as tournaments for juniors 10 and under. Why do all of these people play? Why should you play?

Tennis is a sport for mind, body, and soul. It is aerobically beneficial while challenging every muscle in your body, strengthening your heart, legs, shoulders, arms, and torso. You will quickly discover that tennis also tests and strengthens your mind and your psyche. Tennis will also improve your balance and your timing as well. While you may not be ready for the Bolshoi Ballet, you will find yourself walking, talking and thinking with more confidence. You will feel better, sleep more soundly, and smile often. All this because you are playing tennis—believe me, I see tennis changing people's lives every day.

Passing Shots

Monica Seles once said, "I want to play tennis for the right reason. The right reason is because I love the game." She is a true champion.

In my job at BallenIsles in Florida, I see many different types of tennis players. The ones I love best, those that capture my attention, are the ones that find the passion of tennis and thrill of learning. I can see it in their eyes and in the way they walk. If they are beginners, they often look scared. That may be because I have a reputation of being very demanding of my students. Being scared is good. This means they know they are facing a challenge and they are ready to tackle it. It also shows me they respect the game and know that it is worth the effort and sometimes the pain, as they learn new strokes and strategies.

I see women who have never done anything competitively before become tigers on the court. I watch them strive for perfection regardless of their level. My heart goes out to them when they think they have mastered a new stroke or spin in a lesson, only to have their hopes dashed as they try to apply their new techniques in a match setting. I watch men who have obviously been great athletes become frustrated as they try to learn tennis quickly. Playing good tennis takes patience and determination. Learning takes the same.

So, why do all of these people put themselves through all of this emotion? You won't know until you play tennis. You cannot have the feelings until you have placed yourself on the court. The elation you feel as you try to make the ball go where you want it to go so that you can beat your opponent is indescribable.

My parents made it possible for me to play tennis because they could see how much I loved to play. They knew then, even better than I, what tennis would mean to me in my lifetime. I also think they encouraged me because they knew it was a great door opener both in my adolescence and on into adulthood. (How did they get so smart?) In the years that followed, I met so many wonderful friends throughout the world with whom I continue to keep in touch. When I think of the long-term implications that tennis has had on my life, I realize that it is certainly more than just a game.

Trish Says

Ask any veteran player why they still play and they will tell you it's the camaraderie and friendships. Indeed.

Even junior players, those 18 years old or younger, will often tell you they play because they want to go to college or win Wimbledon.

When people first take up tennis, they don't do it with dollar signs in their eyes. Even young kids, the ones who have trophies and titles in their dreams don't think about tennis as a career.

Future champs.
Photo credit: Vicki Fort

People play because they get a thrill every time they walk out onto the court. Sure, some of the older juniors think about a college scholarship for tennis. The better junior players probably have the same dreams I had; playing at Wimbledon, winning a major tournament. I haven't ever heard someone say they took up tennis for money. Don't

Courtside Quotes

"Friendships born on the field of athletic strife are the real gold of competition. Awards become corroded, friends gather no dust."
—Jesse Owens, track star and gold medalist

misunderstand me, there is big money in pro tennis, but before you quit your day job and start shopping for the new Porsche, understand that very few tennis players reach this level. Most players are content to watch the superstars and then go back and hone their own game. This is one of the greatest aspects of the game of tennis. You can play your own game in the morning, and then drive to a major tournament in the afternoon and watch the pros show you how it's done. The next day, playing by all the same rules and on the same type of court, you can try to emulate all their great shots. Contrary to what your mother may have told you about practice making perfect, tennis is one sport where watching helps you learn. But, you'll still have to practice.

Be forewarned: Tennis can be addictive. Once you squeeze the grip on your first racquet and send that little yellow ball sailing across the net, you will be hooked—for life. And like all addictions, it creates a hunger that is insatiable. But don't rush off to your therapist's office just yet. This is one addiction that is actually good for you. Beginners are delighted to see how rapidly they improve and how easily they grasp the rules. Soon enough, you'll enter the next stage of development and realize that tennis is a real-life chess game, a game in which you are capable of learning the moves that will beat your opponent and leave him checked. Once this happens, there's no turning back. You will spend the rest of your life rising to all of the new challenges that tennis presents you, especially as your skills improve. Concerned about ever getting bored? Not to worry. There are more fascinating variables to this game than can be experienced in a lifetime.

When Can You Play?

Because tennis is a very physical sport, it is best played when you are in good condition and healthy. In other words, put down the Ben and Jerry's ice cream and haul yourself off to the doctor's office for a physical, especially if you have led a sedentary life and/or you're over 30. When the doctor gives you the okay, swing by your local gym and sign up for a fitness regimen—not a Baskin Robbins—to celebrate. No matter your physical condition, here's your chance to turn things around. What's more, you can have fun at the same time and discover positive, healthy ways to alleviate stress. Facing a not-so-rosy picture of your health now may be a little disheartening. You may have been very active in your early 20s, but once you went to work, you forgot to include exercise in your routine. Chin (or chins) up. Help is here.

Tennis will meet you wherever you are. In other words, it can be played to excess or can be eased into. If you're a beginner, I recommend cooling your jets a little and starting slowly. Get some good coaching, too. It will pay huge dividends in the long run. And before you take the court, make certain you are healthy enough to push your body even mildly. Stretch and test your flexibility to avoid unexpected injuries that can send you back to the couch. (Remember that place with all the potato chip grease stains?)

If you work during the day, you will probably be playing in the early evening or on the weekends. You will want to make certain you find courts that are lighted for night play. If you are lucky enough not to have any time restrictions, you will want to play during the coolest part of the day. The sun, the wind, and the rain will be your worst enemies—next to your opponent, that is.

Trish Says

Play catch with your child to help with motor skills. It will also help her hand-eye coordination.

Juniors will play most of their tennis after school or on weekends. Look for an active junior program for your child. Many clubs have restrictions on junior play, so find courts that allow juniors to have a fair share of court time. If you have a youngster, read through our chapter on junior tennis. It gives you a great deal of information for your next champion in the family.

Some people make the time to play tennis during their lunch hour. Even a beginner can get a good workout in an hour. Many stay-at-home mothers play as soon as the kids leave for school, so they can have the rest of the day for their families.

Ironically, tennis is one of the best sports for busy people. Unlike golf, it isn't time-consuming. Two sets of tennis, a great workout for players of all ages and abilities, can be played in under one and a half hours.

The Least You Need to Know

➤ Tennis will give you a good workout in just one hour.

➤ Tennis will tone your body, make your heart work better, and keep you flexible.

➤ Tennis will help you make friends all over the world.

➤ Tennis is a year-round sport that can be played by anyone from ages 5 to 95.

➤ Tennis is not expensive.

➤ You don't even need lines on the court when you first start to play.

➤ Tennis courts are easy to find, even in cold climates.

➤ Always carry a new can of balls.

Chapter 2

The Amazing History of Tennis: People and Places Throughout Time

In This Chapter

➤ Real Tennis, or is it really tennis?

➤ In tennis scoring, love means nothing

➤ Finally, the tiebreaker

➤ The champions of yesterday

➤ The club was the place to be

Oh, I am glad you didn't skip this chapter. I really did worry you might think this would be a chapter filled with a lot of boring dates and facts that would not be of any value to you. I even titled it "The Amazing History of Tennis: People and Places Throughout Time" in the hope of getting a few more readers for this chapter.

I tried to limit the number of dates I included, and there is no quiz later, so you don't have to memorize them. I gave you only the facts that were interesting, noteworthy, and fun.

This chapter may not improve your tennis game, but it should give you a better appreciation for the game of tennis and why it has become so popular. It may even help you answer a few questions next time you play Trivial Pursuit.

I promise it will be worth your while, so stop trying to skip to chapters where you can hit the ball. Take a little time for your history lesson.

What's in a Name

Where does the name tennis come from? Some say it came from the French word *tenez*, meaning take it, or from the French verb *tendere*, meaning to hold. In fact, nobody really knows the origins of the name, or for that matter, nobody really knows where the game actually came from.

Passing Shots

Rumor has it if you beat Henry VIII in tennis, you stood a good chance of being beheaded. Losing the #1 ranking doesn't seem so bad today.

Historians tell us that a game resembling tennis was played by the ancient Egyptians in a town named Tinnis. Then the Greeks got into the act and said, no, no, we started the game. Tennis devotees don't think the history of our game goes back that far, as there has never been any illustration or mention of the game during Greek and Roman times. So all of us who have shown a mild interest in the history are fairly certain that the French monks in the 12th century were the true pioneers. Tennis buffs have us believing that the monks would try to hit the ball and rebound it off the walls of their courtyards. This started Court Tennis, which then became Royal Tennis because so many members of royalty were playing. The name then changed to Real Tennis.

The basic game was called *jeu de paume*, which meant the game of the hand. The ball was made out of cloth wrapped around and around to form a solid ball. The courts were constructed both indoors and outdoors which made for interesting rules, as no two courts were the same. Eventually players got tired of using their hands, and paddles or racquets edged their way into the game. I think the kings and their courtiers were afraid of hurting their delicate hands, so they started hitting the balls with a paddle.

However, by the beginning of the 20th century, tennis had become a sport enjoyed by both men and women in all English-speaking countries. It continued to flourish as a sport that was challenging, athletic, graceful, and fashionable!

By 1922, it became apparent that tennis was no longer just a country club sport played by the elite. Tennis had been exposed to the masses. Spectators were clamoring to watch the matches. The sport had two dominant champions, and the fans were eager to pay to watch them play in tournaments. Bill Tilden and Suzanne Lenglen were virtually unbeatable. Although by tennis regulations they were still considered amateurs, both players received money that was supposed to be for "expenses." These fees often surpassed their legitimate expenses and the "shamateurism" of tennis was under way. They both made a lot of money by playing one-night stands for their "expenses." As you can see in the next photo, both Tilden and Lenglen had a commanding presence.

Prior to the beginning of the acknowledgement of paid professionals in the sport of tennis in 1968, the amateur and professional labels were a little fuzzy. Finally, tournament tennis as we know it today was born, allowing players to accept prize money above the table for their on-court performances and off-court endorsements.

Big Bill Tilden and the legendary Lenglen.

Photo credit: International Tennis Hall of Fame

Just like Tilden and Lenglen, and many others after them, the players were offered expense money, which frequently came to more than their expenses. We couldn't have survived if this didn't occur. I traveled the world for four years as an amateur tennis player. I played in all the major tournaments between 1962–1966. I even won a few here and there. Did I get more money if I won the tournament? Not really, but I got more expenses for the following tournaments because I had a good record and they knew I was a good player. I was able to pay my own way around the world to these tournaments many times over thanks to my expenses, or my hospitality allowance, as some tournaments called it. The really good players received much more in hospitality money than the journeymen. The lesser players maybe broke even at the end of the year after paying for everything. The bigger names were able to bank some of their expense money. They were really paid athletes but no one, particularly the tennis associations, wanted to admit it.

Where They Held Court

Major Walter Wingfield introduced tennis as it is today to the British in 1874. Tennis was promoted as being vigorous exercise suitable for both sexes and the game's popularity spread quickly.

Major Wingfield's rules did not state that the court had to be grass or turf, but the ground did need to be level. Because croquet was very popular, most of the spaces available for the new courts were lawns. Major Wingfield first designed a court that was

Passing Shots

In the 16th century, Paris was home to more than a thousand tennis courts, both indoor and outdoor.

shaped like an hourglass. As most of the play took place on the baseline area, this was designed to be wider than the net area. By 1877, the All-England Club, the current home of Wimbledon, staged their first tennis tournament, using a newly designed rectangular court and a scoring system more in line with what you will use today. In 1884, Wimbledon opened its courts for a Ladies Championship, as well as the Men's Championship. From that day forward, the club hosted both men's and women's events.

Our founder.

Photo credit: International
Tennis Hall of Fame

This new game was introduced to the United States in the summer of 1874. There is some doubt as to who actually pioneered the sport, but Dr. James Dwight of Boston became known as the father of American Lawn Tennis. The game quickly became popular and tournaments were held around the country. The very first official club was established in New Orleans.

In 1881, the US National Lawn Tennis Association was formed and it became, and still is, the governing body of tennis in America. Just as in Great Britain, the name "lawn" was not dropped from the name until late in the 1960s. The governing body of tennis in the USA is now called the United States Tennis Association.

Lawn tennis grew all around the world as more and more bluebloods took the game to the colonies. By the late 1880s, at least 25 countries boasted lawn tennis courts, clubs, and in many cases, championships for their respective countries.

In 1887, the Philadelphia Cricket Club hosted the first US Women's Championship.

Major Wingfield designed complete tennis game sets which, when boxed, contained a history of the game, the major's tennis rules, and instructions for erecting the hourglass shaped court, shown here in this diagram.

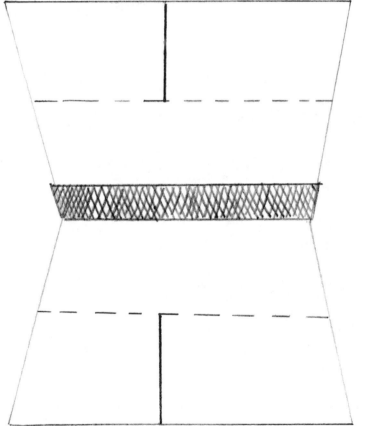

The first court.

Slowly the shape of the court changed as the courts were staked out. The hourglass shape became more of a rectangle and by 1877, the court looked pretty much as it does now.

For a number of years, the net height was adjusted according to the scores. If a game was too fast, the net was raised—too long and boring, then the net was lowered. I certainly have felt like doing that on some of my uncoordinated days. In 1882, the net height was finally set at 3 feet in the center and 3 feet 6 inches on the sides, which is the same today. In 1890, the rules were finalized, and apart from a few minor changes, they became the rules by which you will play.

Early Equipment

The monks in France used their hands to hit the ball. Royalty had soft skin so they knew that wouldn't work. Their craftsmen came up with a glove made of sturdy leather, probably a cross between a driving glove and a baseball mitt.

Gloves became paddles, which became racquets. They did not look much like your racquets today, and they were changed to keep up with the different balls and conditions.

Try playing with these.
Photo credit: Vicki Fort

As racquets changed, it was necessary for balls to change as well. The first balls had to be soft and were made mostly of wool and twine. Once paddles were introduced, they needed to be sturdy and so were made out of leather and filled with sawdust and sand. Finally, as the strung racquets came on the scene, the racquet makers found that a combination of leather and cloth and twine all bound together and sewn on the seams worked best. Balls were black or white, depending on the background of the courts. In 1845, the sport was revolutionized by the discovery that rubber could be made into balls. This and Major Wingfield's lawn tennis game started us into the modern era of tennis, and the equipment graduated, too.

This led to the necessity of formulating some rules for the game, including the size and length of racquets and rules for the composition of balls.

As the ball developed, so did the racquets. As the density, material, and weight of the ball changed, the ball got livelier. The racquets were designed with strings and the shape of the head changed.

Pressureless balls reappeared in the 1950s and were used for many years at major tournaments.

I can remember buying boxes of balls when I first started to play at home in Australia. They usually came in sets of six and, of course, were white. I remember when I played my first Wimbledon and they had a special Slazenger ball box with "made for Wimbledon" on the top of the box. It sent a chill through me—I felt that by finally playing at Wimbledon, I had fulfilled my dream.

Racquets started to be made in different colors other than wood grain and solid aluminum. My father was the general manager of the Australian Rugby Union Team that toured the world in 1959. He toured with them for almost six months. When he came back, he brought me a new racquet from England, made by Grays of Cambridge. It was white with blue decals. I had never seen a painted frame before. I had always played with a Dunlop Maxply, which came only one way, wood grain with clear lacquer. The trouble was that he only bought me one; not that I was ungrateful, but I liked it so much I never wanted to use it in case I broke it. I was not the most genteel of players.

In the last 30 years, racquets have been made from just about every material known to humankind. They now come in all shapes and sizes. You have every color choice. You can have them custom-made and custom-weighted. You can match the color of your strings to the color of the racquet.

What's the Score?

Sometimes when you are learning the game and trying to keep score, you wonder how on earth they came up with the scoring system that is in place today. One, two, three, four sounds much easier, but is very mundane. The French are never mundane, so we are stuck with 15, 30, 40 and deuce.

Tennis historians are very confused about the origins of tennis, but they are all in agreement as to how the scoring system came about.

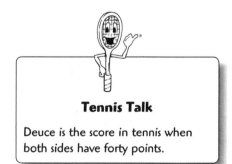

Tennis Talk

Deuce is the score in tennis when both sides have forty points.

The scoring terms are derived from French words. Love is from the word *l'oeuf,* meaning egg, or the shape meaning zero. Deuce is from *a deux,* meaning two or together. As a beginner, the scoring system never seemed to make sense. I realized quickly that all I had to do was memorize the point sequence—15, 30, 40, game. The French maintain the original scoring was derived from their early currency which came in these same increments. Who knows, and at this point, who really cares? Just learn how to keep score.

No-ad scoring is not used in major tournaments, but it is a great scoring system for social round robins and mixers. The points are scored one, two, three, and the game point is the winner of four points. Rather than having a game that goes on and on forever, the no-ad system means exactly that—no-ad. When the score gets to be three points all, the players play a final, "sudden-death" point. Whoever wins the fourth point wins the game. This allows all the matches played to finish in about the same period of time.

Trish Says

I remember the first time I played in a sudden-death tiebreaker. With the new rules, we knew we had to play the sudden death 9-point tiebreak. We all looked at one another and then at the chair umpire who didn't seem to know any more than we did. We didn't know who should serve and when to change ends. I am sure we didn't play the first one correctly.

The scoring innovation that Mr. Van Alen introduced changed the face of modern tennis. This is the tiebreaker. He unveiled it in Newport, Rhode Island, in 1965. The first one was called a 9-point *sudden-death tiebreaker* and was used in the U.S. Open from 1970 to 1974. This tiebreak plays a maximum of nine points; it is won by the first player who takes five points. The name "sudden death" comes from the fact that if the score is four points all, the ninth point decides the winner.

Another version, which Jimmie Van Alen called "lingering death", was the 12-point tiebreaker, which is the method now used in all tournaments throughout the world. In this system, one player, or team, must win seven points by a margin of two. Hence, the score could be 7 to 5, which accounts for the name 12-point tiebreaker. You do not have to play all twelve points. Once one player, or team, wins seven, that's the end of the tiebreak; however, it must be won by a margin of two. So the score cannot be 7 to 6. It must be 8 to 6, or even 10 to 8.

Let's face it. There is no need for you to remember all of this. Once you start swinging away, you won't care who designed Chris Evert's racquet, or who played the longest match before tiebreakers. You will always want to remember how to keep score. It helps to call out the score after each point. If unsure, give your opponent the benefit of the doubt.

I Haven't Got a Thing to Wear

While I am sure there is not much that can be written in our history about men's tennis fashions, there is a great deal to be said about women's tennis clothing. This photo depicts regulation tennis clothing from the 1890s.

Yes, they actually played in these outfits.

Photo credit: International Tennis Hall of Fame

Men wore your basic woolen trousers or knickers with leggings, long-sleeve shirts, ties, jackets, vests, and even hats. Women wore the same clothes as they would wear to high tea or an afternoon soiree. High-necked dresses, corsets, and, of course, all those petticoats, must have made it very difficult to move gracefully. The shoes were flat and made of brown or black leather.

Fashion was very important as tennis was often played at royal outings and garden parties. I cannot imagine what the guests felt like after playing a few leisurely games of tennis in all those clothes. Remember, they didn't bathe much in the Victorian era.

Finally, practicality ruled and the big hats were replaced by boaters. The ladies shed most of their petticoats and the new shoes had rubber soles with white canvas uppers.

The men took off their jackets and rolled up their sleeves. White flannel trousers, white shirts, white sweaters, and even white shoes made the players look very dashing and athletic.

In 1877, Lottie Dod won Wimbledon in a short skirt. This was not so scandalous as she was only 15 years old at the time. But the lady who changed women's tennis fashions forever was French superstar Suzanne Lenglen. She had an extraordinary style and flair both on and off the court. Her outfits of one-piece dresses, minus corsets and petticoats, shocked the conservative tennis world, but created great spectator interest. She gave women's tennis the boost it needed after the Great War.

By the time she finished playing in 1926, sailor suits, culottes, and even Bermuda-type shorts had become acceptable. Another player, American "Gorgeous" Gussie Moran made headlines with her hemlines, and more importantly, her lacy underpants.

Men's fashions did not change much, and even when shorts became acceptable, many players still chose to wear long pants. Maybe they had knobby knees.

English dress designer Ted Tinling, pictured below, took women's dresses to a new level of haute couture. Choosing his clients wisely, Tinling dressed only the big stars who could show off his clothes to their fullest. His materials, fashionable hemlines, and necklines made stars like Maria Bueno from Brazil seem even more graceful and formidable.

The one and only Ted Tinling.

Photo credit: June Harrison

I spent many an hour with Ted Tinling. In fact, in the late 1950s, he played doubles with my former husband in England. Ted was knowledgeable, talented, witty, urbane, and rather caustic on whatever topic he was embellishing. He did have an eye for fashion. Not only did he dress the champions, but he also dressed himself. You could pick out Ted at any tournament. First, he was 6 feet, 6 inches, with a shaven head. He loved scarves, and was always wearing a magnificent one, often purple, around his neck. When I ran some of the events on the women's professional tennis tour, I always invited him. He acted as liaison between the players and the press, introduced the players on center court, and generally held court himself whenever he had an audience. He was the most knowledgeable tennis trivia person I knew. He told the best stories about his clients and his 50 years in the tennis business.

Television helped bring tennis fashions into the present. Exposure brings sponsors, which means money, which means more players and they have to wear something to play in. This led to the advent of ready-to-wear, off-the-rack tennis clothes by a multitude of companies. Modern tennis had arrived, at least in a fashion sense.

The First Champions

Wimbledon in 1877 was just as prestigious as it is now. Spencer W. Gore won the first men's title, but he preferred the older game of Real Tennis, which is played on the indoor courts shaped like a courtyard. He did not play much competitive tennis after his win. Seven years later, they allowed the women in, and Miss Maud Watson became the first Wimbledon ladies champion. She actually played her sister in the finals.

In 1900, Dwight Davis introduced the notion of a team competition between the USA and Great Britain. This was the birth of the Davis Cup, which now boasts more than 60 countries in its competition each year.

The first true champions, those who won multiple titles and went into the record books, helped change the sport they played. Lottie Dod, pictured on following page, winner of Wimbledon at age 15, went on to win five titles.

May Sutton was the first American to win Wimbledon. Australian Norman Brookes, one of the world's best volleyers and a leftie, made his mark on the tennis world with his dedication and superb strokes. Each one brought with them a new stroke or style that inched tennis towards the hard-hitting, power sport it is today. As a player who has tried to follow in their footsteps, I believe there are no champions who should be forgotten. Some just had a greater impact than others.

Lottie Dod, Wimbledon winner at 15 years old.

Photo credit: International Tennis Hall of Fame

Elizabeth Ryan, an American, won an incredible 19 titles at Wimbledon, starting in 1913. This record was not broken until Billie Jean King surpassed her mark in 1979, when she won her 20th title with Martina Navratilova in doubles.

Ryan at one time partnered with a young French girl from Picardy named Suzanne Lenglen. Lenglen was perhaps one of the greatest players of all time, male or female. Certainly, she had the greatest impact on the sport next to Billie Jean King. She had only one face-off against another great player from the United States, Helen Wills. Wills was called Little Miss Poker Face because she never showed any emotion. She did, however, show her talent on the court by winning four Wimbledons and four U.S. Championships. Alice Marble, a beautiful, blonde, athletic player, was voted Woman Athlete of the Year in 1939 and 1940. She played a strong, aggressive net game and dominated the sport for a good eight years from 1932 to 1940. If her health had not been a problem, she would have been on top longer.

When it came to men's tennis, it took a 25-year-old, tall, outspoken, late developer named William Tatem Tilden to change the game. Tilden was an artist, a craftsman,

Courtside Quotes

"What a girl Alice Marble is, with everything the Venus de Milo has, plus two muscular, bare, sunburned arms, marvelously efficient."
—Arthur Brisbane, columnist for Hearst Papers

and a strong player with the ability to come back when he was down. Tilden won three Wimbledon's during the 1920s and 30s and he was ranked #1 in the United States for 10 years. He was banned at one point because he wrote about tennis, which violated the amateur rules; otherwise, he would have won more titles. Tilden went on to play as a professional to large crowds in Europe and the USA.

Tilden at his best.

Photo credit: International Tennis Hall of Fame

The Wightman Cup for women started in 1923. This brought the best British players against the Americans. This competition was the forerunner of the Federation Cup, which is the women's equivalent to the men's Davis Cup. Playing for one's country is somehow different from playing just for oneself.

The English and the Australians monopolized the major tournaments from 1900 to 1920, but then the French came to life. In 1925, they made a clean sweep of Wimbledon. Lenglen won the women's singles and, with Elizabeth Ryan, an American, won the women's doubles. She also won the mixed doubles with Jean Borotra of France. The men's final was a battle of two Frenchmen; Rene Lacoste defeated Jean Borotra. Henri Cochet, another Frenchman, fared well in reaching the quarterfinals. Another French player, Jacques Brugnon, also rose to the top. The four players representing France were known as the Four Musketeers.

Trish Says

I have played many matches, but the first time I played for Australia, I had an extra lump in my throat. It is almost impossible to describe the feeling I had when I looked up and saw my teammates cheering me on. It is a combination of team pride and camaraderie; it somehow makes you put forth that little extra effort—it all made me very glad that I was good enough to be able to experience all of those moments.

I could mention many more who contributed to the game of tennis. Englishman Fred Perry, who was a great tennis player and a gentleman, also lent his name to a stylish line of tennis clothing for men and women. American Don Budge, who was the first man to win the Grand Slam, accomplished the incredible feat of winning the singles in four major tournaments: the Australian, the French, Wimbledon, and the U.S. Championships all in the same calendar year. He also won the triple at Wimbledon, taking the singles, doubles, and mixed doubles all in the same year.

One cannot discount Bobby Riggs, who became known more for his betting than for his tennis. He did, however, win the triple at Wimbledon, and some say won more than $100,000 betting on himself. Riggs's match against Billie Jean King in the Battle of the Sexes did more to popularize tennis among the general public than any other single event in tennis history. (He lost, by the way.) Riggs, shown on the next page, hustled both on and off the court.

The two dashing Panchos—Pancho Gonzales and Pancho Segura—joined Jack Kramer, who did more for the professional side of the game after he won Wimbledon in 1947, on the pro tour.

Jack Kramer started a tour with the top male players. They played for money and mainly played one-night stands all over the USA. The two Panchos, Segura the scrambler, and Gonzales the powerhouse, became two popular regulars on the Kramer tour.

Bobby Riggs didn't lose often, on or off the court.

Photo credit: International Tennis Hall of Fame

Althea Gibson, the first black woman to win Wimbledon, showed us another form of serve and volley power tennis. All of us wonder how many titles Maureen Connolly could have accumulated if her tennis career had not been cut short by a riding accident. Little Mo, as she was known, was the first women's Grand Slam winner in 1952. Then came Maria Bueno, Margaret Court, Billie Jean King, Martina Navratilova, and Chris Evert. All of these post-war players came at a time when women's tennis was at its peak.

Billie Jean King, one of those one-of-a-kind athletes who transcends her sport, did more for women athletes than anyone. She had vision beyond herself and her sport. Her tennis record speaks for itself. Twenty Wimbledon titles, winner of the Battle of the Sexes Challenge, president and founder of World Team Tennis, co-founder of the women's tour, and spokesperson for the Women's Sports Foundation. No one has given back to his or her sport as much as BJK. No tennis book will ever be written without a tribute and photos of Billie Jean.

Courtside Quotes

"No man or woman in tennis has made such an extraordinary triple thrust as Billie Jean in advancing herself, women, and the game as a whole."

—Bud Collins, TV commentator and Boston Globe columnist

No one did more for tennis than Billie Jean King.

Photo credit: June Harrison

When I speak of giving back, I have to mention Arthur Ashe. For 12 years, he was in the men's top 10. He helped found the Association of Tennis Professionals, and served as a spokesperson for the men's game. He acted as an ambassador for the sport. A long-time opponent of apartheid in South Africa, Ashe lent his name and his money to help the less fortunate. He was a leader in the fight against AIDS and like BJK, he went beyond his sport by using his popularity and power to help the needy. Ashe died of AIDS in 1993.

Courtside Quotes

"Arthur Ashe was in the tradition of great leaders. He earned that status not by proclaiming it, but by living it."
—Jesse Jackson

The Australian Rat Pack: Frank Sedgeman, Lew Hoad, Ken Rosewall, Roy Emerson, Fred Stolle, Mal Anderson, John Newcombe, and the greatest of all time, Rod Laver, made a lasting impression on the sport and on their fellow players. Respected for their tennis talents, but loved also for their humor and fun-loving approach to tennis, these Aussies beat everyone in their path and then met them for a beer afterwards.

I can still hear Roy Emerson telling a group of rather staid south Florida tennis matrons his secret for playing winning doubles—first one to the net, first one to the pub. I think it shook them up, but they never forgot his advice and they have been rushing the net ever since. I am not so sure that they rushed to the pub after they won, however.

The great Arthur Ashe.

Photo credit: June Harrison

I was at Wimbledon the year my friend Virginia Wade won her title. How fitting for this superb English woman to win in front of the royal family and all of her British fans on the 100th anniversary of the Championships.

Virginia Wade, a great ambassador of the sport.

Photo credit: June Harrison

How do I do justice to the last four players in my historical review? Friends and foes, adversaries and co-hosts, John McEnroe, Jimmy Connors, Martina Navratilova, and Chris Evert: These champions took the game to new heights each in their own way. These four names are household words even if you don't play much tennis. For all their shenanigans, McEnroe and Connors delighted the crowds and kept them coming back for more, particularly in New York at the U.S. Open. Navratilova, winner of nine Wimbledon singles championships, and Evert, the player whom most young girls wanted to emulate, took the word rivalry to a new level. There may never be another two players who could command center court like Martina and Chris. Martina changed the face of women's tennis with her power game and fitness routine. Chris revolutionized the backhand with her two-handed weapon and showed the world how to lose and win with poise and grace.

These are the champions that I have either known or read about. These are the ghosts that float around in my dreams. If I could take all of their strokes, their keen minds, and their amazing athletic ability and put them into one person, this player would be unbeatable. Want to try?

Two of the greatest ever, McEnroe and Connors.
Photo credit: June Harrison

Evert and Navratilova, friends and rivals.

Photo credit: June Harrison

Clubs of the World

Although the game got started in France, it was the English who helped spread the word. The first club on record was at Leamington Spa at the Manor House Hotel. However, it was the first Wimbledon at the All-England Lawn Tennis and Croquet Club that helped get the media coverage in the late 1870s. These press reports urged English expatriates in France and Italy to form their own clubs.

Lawn was the surface of choice in England where beautiful rolled lawns were in favor for garden parties and royal games. However, in France and Italy courts were being built out of clay and cement. Most of these clubs opened in the late 1800s and early 1900s, and are still active tennis clubs today. The All-England Club pictured on the next page is over 100 years old.

The All-England Lawn Tennis and Croquet Club, home of Wimbledon for over 100 years.

Photo credit: June Harrison

In 1984, when I was head tour director for the Women's Tennis Association, one of my jobs was to oversee the French Open Ladies Event. The qualifying tournament, which accepts players who are playing for the eight spots kept for those players who come through the qualifying, was played at a very old club in the Bois de Boulogne close to Paris. The club was called *Tir aux Pigeons*. The first rounds went without any problems. The losers left to reexamine their game and their goals, the winners went on to play the next round. It was about 2 P.M. on a beautiful day and the club with all its gardens, ponds, and statues looked stately. I was roving, watching all eight courts to make certain all the players were dressed appropriately and not having any officiating problems. I stopped by Court One and was watching the two players who were having a very close singles match. Suddenly, the young New Zealand player at the far end jerked her body around to face the side fence and let out a squeal. She looked like she had been stung by a bee. I waited to see if she needed a trainer or an injury time-out. She walked around, glared at her opponent, who had no clue what was happening, swung her racquet a few times at an imaginary insect, and then got ready to receive serve again.

She hit the return, then let out another yelp and stopped play. She ran to the net and yelled to me on the far side. I could not see what her problem was, but she kept yelling for me to come on the court. Her opponent clearly thought she had gone mad. I walked out onto the court and she said, "Someone shot me." I said, "What!" She said, "I know it sounds crazy, but someone is firing pellets at me." Suddenly we both got hit with a volley of pellets. Now her opponent saw what was going on. I suspended the match and we all quickly vacated the court. I walked around the fence and saw about five very nicely dressed Frenchmen, shooting at clay pigeons. The decoys were being let go in the direction of the tennis courts. It was then that I realized what *Tir aux Pigeons* meant. We asked the club manager to please ask the shooters to redirect their targets, and hopefully their aim, away from the tennis courts. He shrugged and said something like, it has been this way for 100 years, but he did go and speak with the shooters. They did turn a little to the east. The girls resumed the match after all of us had a good laugh. The last time I was there, I noticed they had installed a very high mesh curtain above the regular tennis court fences. The shooters were still there and probably will be for another 100 years.

France wasn't the only country to build beautiful clubs. Tennis continued to spread through Scandinavia, Spain, the Netherlands, and Germany. Wales (home of Major Wingfield, the inventor of lawn tennis), Scotland, Portugal, and many other nations all got caught up in the new game.

The English spread their passion for this sport wherever they went. India, the USSR (as it was then), and other Eastern bloc countries built courts and formed clubs to encourage others to play. All the fashionable resorts built courts for their guests. It was still very much a sport for the wealthy and famous. In the British colonies, however, soldiers who were stationed there set up courts and started the local interest in Africa, Asia, and South America.

We haven't really mentioned the two countries that developed into the powerhouses of tennis. Australia and the United States became driving forces in the early 1900s. Funnily enough, the first club in the USA was established in New Orleans in 1876. The game spread across the United States and by 1890, there were organized tournaments and the colleges embraced the game. In Australia, far removed from all the other countries, the sport took off even faster. Each state formed its own association and had national championships before the 1900s.

It became a status symbol to have a tennis club in your hometown. Then you earned an extra feather in your tennis cap if you had a tournament at your club. Then it became prestigious to stage a national championship. Soon it was apparent that a governing body was needed. The International Tennis Federation was formed in Paris to help coordinate all of the international activity.

The sport of tennis, the players, the clubs, the tournaments, and the rules were now all coming together.

The Least You Need to Know

➤ In 1845, the rubber ball was first used to play tennis.

➤ The net is 3 feet high at the center and 3 feet 6 inches at the ends.

➤ Tennis was first played in its current form in 1874.

➤ The first lawn tennis club in the United States was formed in New Orleans in 1881.

➤ Wimbledon Championships have been played at the All-England Club since 1877.

➤ The Grand Slam of tennis means winning the championships of Australia, France, England, and the USA all in the same year.

Chapter 3

Hey Big Spender! What Kind of Equipment Should You Buy?

In This Chapter

➤ Carry a big stick—maybe even more than one

➤ Have a ball, you need at least three

➤ Do I really need all that? Tennis supplies

➤ Is it really string? No, it's probably synthetic gut

➤ New or broken in: how to choose your equipment

So, you've decided to make that next step and take up the game of tennis. Half the fun of starting to play tennis is buying your equipment and picking out your outfits. They don't have to be the latest or the best, but you do need to make sure you have the basics. In this chapter, I will focus on what kind of equipment you will need to get started. As mentioned before, tennis, unlike some other sports, does not require spending a lot of money on the equipment. In the beginning, you will need to have the basics: a tennis racquet, a bag, and a few essentials to keep in the bag. You could probably purchase all of these things for under $150.

That's all you need to start.

Photo credit: June Harrison

I once had a student who was about 12 years old. She decided on her own that tennis was the game for her. This was after she decided to take up horseback riding, ice skating, skiing, and art. Her parents, being very supportive, had invested in all of the above activities that she proceeded to lose interest in at the rate of every three months. Thus, when she came to tell them about her new passion, they were a little hesitant to go out and buy the equipment for it. Knowing that the racquet and other equipment would not be terribly expensive, I had suggested that they let her earn the money to buy what she needed to get started. I felt she may not drop tennis as quickly if she had to participate in buying the equipment. It took her three months of odd jobs, but she was able to save enough money for what she needed to buy. As a side note, it has been six years since she started to play and she never lost interest in the game. Now she has a college scholarship thanks to her tennis.

So cut a few lawns or give up dessert, and you will have enough money saved to buy everything you will learn about in this chapter.

Why Do They Carry All Those Racquets?

When you watch the professional matches the players come out onto the court carrying big racquet bags—six packs and they are not full of beer. Why do they need so many racquets? It is not to better the Jones', or the Sampras'.

At the professional level, it is not uncommon for a player to break strings in two or three racquets in one match. As it is necessary for top players to have all the racquets play and feel the same, the pros feel they need at least four to six racquets out on the court. If a string breaks or a racquet doesn't feel right, a player is not permitted to leave the court to get different equipment.

As a beginner or a social player, you do not need to carry many racquets. If you take care of your racquet and don't leave it in extreme temperatures, you can get away with only having one. As you become a better player, you will be more concerned about your racquet and how it feels in your hand. You will get fussy and find you get used to one kind. You don't play as well if you have to borrow someone else's. This is always a great excuse when you miss the ball. This is primarily psychological, but there is some truth to this as many racquets play differently.

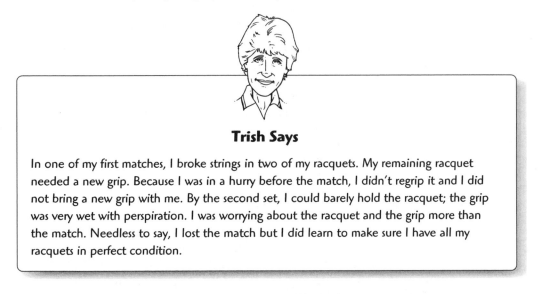

Trish Says

In one of my first matches, I broke strings in two of my racquets. My remaining racquet needed a new grip. Because I was in a hurry before the match, I didn't regrip it and I did not bring a new grip with me. By the second set, I could barely hold the racquet; the grip was very wet with perspiration. I was worrying about the racquet and the grip more than the match. Needless to say, I lost the match but I did learn to make sure I have all my racquets in perfect condition.

Racquets now come in all shapes and sizes. This was not true before 1960. Most racquets, including the handle, frame, and oval head, were made of wood. Although there was a steel racquet with steel strings manufactured in the 1920s, the wooden racquet reigned until French Hall of Famer, Rene Lacoste, conceived another steel frame that was made famous by both Billie Jean King and Jimmy Connors. Arthur Ashe used an aluminum frame shaped like a horseshoe to win Wimbledon in 1968. Other players followed suit and gave up their wooden racquets to try the new designs.

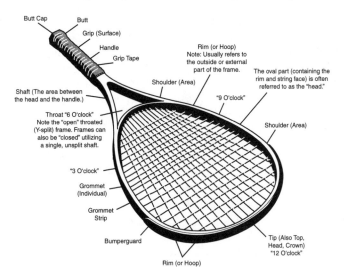

In 1976 Howard Head, ski designer and tennis enthusiast, revolutionized the tennis racquet industry with his oversized composition frame with a bigger hitting area. Following this, all sorts of materials were used—graphite, boron, fiberglass, and magnesium. Head sizes increased. Frames were lengthened. Racquet companies made so many models, the consumer and even the pros became confused.

Finally, in 1981, the International Tennis Federation made some rules governing racquets. It was then decided that the top of the head to the bottom of the handle should not exceed 32 inches, and overall width should not exceed 12.5 inches. The strung surface of the frame cannot exceed 15.5 inches in overall length and 11.5 inches in overall width. Racquet manufacturers have now come out with an entire menu of racquet shapes and sizes. Racquets like the Big Bang, the Weed, and the Wilson Stretch Limits are designed for small, non-powerful hitters. In order to maximize the point of contact, they have a large hitting area, or sweet spot, which is the part of the racquet face that most balls should hit.

As a beginner, you do not need to buy the best. You should, however, buy the best racquet for you. You can buy name-brand racquets from any reputable sports retailer or even a discount sporting goods store. You will get the best personal advice from a tennis pro shop which has knowledgeable staff on hand. These pros have probably play-tested all the racquets in the shop and are very familiar with all of their features. If you would prefer to go to a discount store and buy a cheap racquet to make certain you actually like the game—go ahead. I will guarantee two things—one, you will love the game, even if you are not very good the first few times you play, and two, you will have wasted $25. The racquet can hang in your garage as a momento or you can lend it to your mother-in-law when she comes to visit!

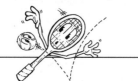

Double Faults

Do not rush out to buy a racquet. Try it out at least four different times before you buy it. Most pro shops will allow you to try out demo racquets.

If you are a female of average size, you will need either a $4^{1}/_{4}$ or $4^{3}/_{8}$ grip size. A normal-size male with average hands will take either $4^{3}/_{8}$ or $4^{1}/_{2}$. In the past, men used to play with grips sized $4^{5}/_{8}$ and $4^{7}/_{8}$, but the trend is now more towards manageable grips. The grip size is the circumference of the racquet handle. To measure your hand and check for the right size, take a ruler and measure the length from the tip of your middle finger to the middle of your palm. This measurement is your racquet size.

The actual racquet brand name and style will depend on your budget and your style of play. The racquet companies have specific features for each model; your decision will depend on your length of swing and need for power. Wilson Racquet Sports has a numbering system that makes it easy to select your racquet range. It has two top-of-the-line models—Hammer and Pro Staff. The Hammer series is weighted in the head, while the Pro Staff is more evenly weighted. You then need to seek advice as to whether you need regular length, stretch, or extra stretch. The only true means of selecting a racquet is to demo the ones recommended by your professional. Most stores will let you demo racquets for $5 that goes towards the purchase price. If you are a member of a private club, you can usually demo the frames without charge from your pro shop. Most shops stock the current frames in average hand sizes, $4^1/_4$ to $4^5/_8$. Smaller pro shops may have to order them from the supplier or a wholesaler, which does not take long. I would recommend buying from a store that will stand behind its sale.

Trish Says

Most professionals are very reluctant to try new racquets unless they are losing. I used a Wilson 2.7 Profile for almost seven years. I won many national senior titles and I was very happy with it. Wilson stopped making that model. How could they! I bought up as many of the old frames as I could find and played another two years with that frame before I finally switched to a newer model. Find a frame you like and buy a few just in case.

As you become more proficient and decide you want to move up a notch in the racquet department, you might be able to return your old racket, because some stores will donate it to a local tennis program and in return give you some reduction on your next racquet purchase. You may wish to keep the old racquet in the closet for a tennis-playing houseguest.

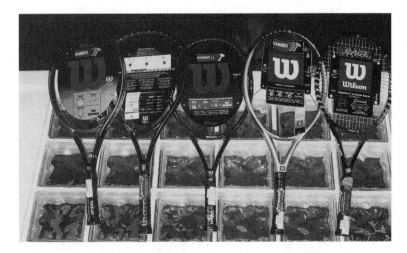

What's all the racquet?
Photo credit: Vicki Fort

Price isn't everything. Seek professional advice as some frames suit some players and not others. You do not have to buy the latest or the best unless it is the racquet recommended for you. An average price for a good racquet for a beginner is $75 strung. If you want to get the next level up, something a little more custom-fitted to your swing and power potential, you should expect to pay around $100 plus. Around $20 more will get it strung for you with good synthetic gut.

Passing Shots

Tennis balls were first white. Yellow balls were not manufactured until 1972. Wimbledon was the last major tournament to switch from the white balls.

Who Has the Balls?

Tennis balls have not changed that much over the years. When the game first started there were no pressurized balls. Balls were provided in a bag and were used many times over. Most of the time balls now come in a can, although there are still some balls that are packaged in a box. Prior to 1972, balls were all white. Nowadays, balls are yellow and standardized, except for slight difference in pressurization. The American ball is rather lively and the European ball is slower. The playing surface determines the outside covering, or nap, of the ball. Balls for grass are lighter with a short nap. For the U.S. Open, which is played on a hard court, the ball will have a longer, heavier nap. Indoor and clay court balls are the most widely used balls as they have a medium nap.

Let's have a ball.

Photo credit: Vicki Fort

I always have discussions with my club members about the price of balls. Members are constantly complaining that they can buy cans of balls about 50 cents cheaper at the discount stores. My answer to them is always the same. Either it is a very large chain and they buy in huge quantities (which lowers the price), or the store is using them as a teaser to get the shoppers in the store so that they will buy something else. Sometimes, the member gets home with the bargain balls and finds the balls are hard court balls and the member plays only on clay. Often the stores advertise the special low price and say that you can buy only six cans at this price. If it is worth saving 50 cents a can and driving three miles to the store, go ahead. Most players understand that the club pro shops charge a reasonable price for balls. The price should range from $2.50 to $4 a can. Balls with club logos or specialty balls will be slightly higher.

How many balls are in a can? Three usually, although Wilson Sporting Goods did come out with a new ball that will sell as four in a can. In Europe, you can still buy boxed balls that often come as a foursome. Why three? My theory is you need two to serve with so, just in case you lose one, you still have two! Some of the first men players actually held more than two balls in their hands when they were serving.

Even in a match, I hate playing with only three balls. You are constantly trudging from one side of the court to the other retrieving them for yourself or your opponent. If I am practicing, I will always take at least six balls to the court and often 12. This speeds up the practice and you are not always waiting to fetch the ball.

Passing Shots

There is a story about the famous Bill Tilden that claims he was so confident of his tennis abilities, he sometimes held four balls in his hand. One for each point of his service game so he never had to stop to retrieve a ball.

In tournament matches the officials usually give you one can of new balls to start and then, depending on the tournament rules, they may give you another new can if the match goes three sets. In major tournaments, three or four balls are used and the balls are often changed after 9 games and thereafter after 11 games. On grass or hard courts, or even on the slow red clay of Europe, the major tournaments may sometimes change balls after seven games and thereafter after nine games.

Because the balls are pressurized, it is best not to open the can until you are ready to play. Leaving them out of the can for more than two days will make them go flat and they won't have as much spunk. In rare cases you may open the ball can and not hear the "psssst" of the pressure being let out. This means the balls are dead or flat, and you should be able to get a refund from the store that sold you the can. The store should then be able to get a replacement from the ball company.

Trish Says

I had a student once who had just purchased a case of balls and thought it would be alright if she opened all the cans and practiced her serve with them and then used those balls for her game. By the next week, the balls had lost their pressure, and were not bouncing so well, and she had to buy a new case for her matches. It is, however, okay to use these low pressure balls for service practice.

There are very few internationally accepted balls. Most of the balls are made in the same factories (in Taiwan) and then stamped with the brand name of the company. The major companies are Dunlop, Wilson (the official ball of the U.S. Open and the USTA), and Penn (the official ball of the USPTA). Slazenger is used mainly in Europe. There are still some balls named Tretorn that come unpressurized in a box. They are very heavy and are usually not good for match play. Most tennis professionals buy balls in bulk for tournaments and use seconds or will use a special teaching ball when practicing. A conscientious professional who is concerned about tennis elbow and other injuries will change the teaching balls about every six weeks. Some pros use a multicolored ball to assist students in seeing the flight and spin of the ball in a lesson.

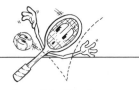

Double Faults

If you want to be a great tennis player, one of the first things you need to learn is to always bring a new can of balls to the court.

Except for special events like Halloween or New Year's, you should stick with the basic optic yellow ball approved by the USTA or the ITF.

There are products on the market now that are supposed to help revive old tennis balls by repressurizing them. You place the used balls into the canister and pump it up so it is repressurized. It may help prolong the life of your tennis balls for one more day. However, if you really want to be cool, use a new can every time.

The actual dimensions of the ball are not details you need to know but just in case you are playing Trivial Pursuit and it comes up—tennis balls are all $2^1/_2$ inches in diameter and 2 ounces in weight.

Trish Says

I used to play doubles with some friends who assumed that I got tennis balls for free because I was in the business. After about six weeks of using my balls, I didn't bring any for the next game. We played with used balls that were very dead and the game was not fun. After that, the other three players brought new balls to the game.

What's in Those Great Big Tennis Bags

When you watch the pros walk out onto the court at Wimbledon for the finals they have the men's locker room attendant carry their bags out onto the court. This is not because they need to save their strength for the match, although after watching some of those four-hour marathons, I wouldn't blame them. It is tradition, but it is also so that the players can bow to Royalty without falling over from all the stuff they carry. What do they carry anyway? What do you need to bring to the court?

It's in the bag.

Photo credit: Vicki Fort

I remember when my children first started to ski. We always left something behind and had to buy it when we got where we were going. The same thing happened when they started to go to tennis tournaments. They always forgot a shoe, socks, or something else that was important. I made them post a checklist on the back of their closet door and insisted they review it when they put their stuff together to play a match. It worked and they were able to pack for themselves.

Even if you are playing only social tennis, you need to be prepared. The first time you go out on the court you will want to make certain you have the following items:

➤ Your racquet—one is enough, two is better when you start playing more

➤ At least one can of balls, preferably two, in case one can is no good

➤ One towel in case the court does not provide them

➤ A water bottle in case the court does not have a fountain

➤ An extra pair of socks

➤ Two dry wristbands

➤ Three or four adhesive bandages—you may get blisters the first few times

➤ A hat or cap to protect yourself from the sun

➤ Sunglasses if you are playing in bright sunlight

➤ Hair or ponytail holder, or headband to keep your hair from flying around

➤ Sunscreen if you are playing outside, maybe even bug repellant if you are playing late in the day

➤ Money for sodas, guest fees, maybe even a little betting on the game

➤ Pencil and paper to write down players' phone numbers

➤ Your business card or phone number on pieces of paper

➤ A dry shirt so you can be comfortable on the way home, or a complete change of clothes if you need to shower afterwards

Double Faults

Check and replenish the items in your bag often so you don't arrive at the courts and have to purchase something like a hat because you don't have one in your bag.

As you progress there will be other items you will want to add to your bag, but the items I've listed will ensure you have everything you need to get started. You will also find many new friends because most new players will not have these items and you will be constantly lending your belongings to your disorganized partners. Just remember to whom you lent your favorite Wilson hat. Or who borrowed your sunscreen and forgot to put it back.

Be prepared.

Photo credit: June Harrison

At least once a month, and more often if you play more than twice a week, do an inventory and general clean out. If you don't, you will not be too popular as your bag will begin to smell a little like your old wet T-shirt. Wipe it out. Check your racquets to make certain the strings have not broken. Replenish the cans of balls. Replace the adhesive bandages you keep lending to your partners. Write down in your little black tennis book the names of your possible tennis buddies.

Bags come in all sizes. When you first buy your racquet, you will receive a cover that goes with the frame. This is very nice but it is useless because it holds only the racquet and maybe your keys. You will go to the court with your duffel bag and your new racquet in its cover and think you look great. Maybe you do! Sneak a look at the better players. What are they carrying? I would rather carry one bag that holds everything instead of two or three little bags.

Again, you will find you have a choice of sizes, colors, materials, and brands. You should try to buy a bag that is made by the same company that makes your racquet. You will be asked if you want a three pack, six pack, super six pack, pro tour bag, shoulder straps, or knapsack straps. It will sound like you are going to hike the Grand Canyon and bring all the beer. The numbers refer to the amount of racquets the bag can hold. My suggestion, unless you are going

Tennis Talk

Tennis bags need to have different pockets for wet clothes, dry clothes, and dirty tennis shoes. One big opening is not good.

to live out of your tennis bag, is to buy a three-racquet bag. This gives you ample room to stow your racquet, or racquets, as well as extra shoes, clothing, and all the other paraphernalia I've mentioned.

You are now ready for action. Oops, we forgot to string up your racquet.

String It Up

When you buy a racquet, you will have to decide whether to buy one already strung, or just the frame and then select your own strings.

Pre-strung is fine for your first purchase. I actually prefer factory-strung racquets. They are strung by knowledgeable stringers who do nothing but string racquets and they are always right on. Pre-strung will also be cheaper and the companies usually place decent strings in their mid-price racquets.

When you do come to select your strings, here are some of the things you need to know. You have two choices: gut and synthetic gut. Nylon used to be an option for cheaper racquets, but now the synthetic gut is so close to real gut and so much better than nylon there is no need to use nylon strings. Synthetic gut is reasonably priced at an average of $22 per string job. Real gut is very expensive and, because of its qualities, doesn't last very long. Top players who use real gut swear by it and would not use anything else. However, most of the professionals who use gut do not pay for their strings so they can afford to be selective.

String me along.

Photo credit: June Harrison

Gut strings are made from cow intestines. Synthetic strings are made from a combination of nylon and special filaments. Manufacturers now give players a choice of string styles; the higher the number, the thinner the gauge of the string. Consumers can choose 15-gauge, 16-gauge, 17-, 18-, and even 19-gauge strings (the lower the gauge number, the lighter the string). Strings also come in different colors.

Stringers can choose between a reel of strings or individual packages. The newer racquets need a longer string, so make certain your stringer has the right length and the new adapters needed to string the extra-length racquets. Lower gauge strings, like 16, last longer and are good for players who hit with a lot of spin. Better players like to use 17- or 18-gauge as this gives them more touch and feel.

The other fact you need to know about stringing is that you have a choice of tension. The required tension for most racquets is listed on the frame. The recommendations will be in a range of about 55 to 65 pounds. The tension is very important as it has a direct effect on your power and control. As a general rule, the looser the tension, say in the 50-pound range, the less control you have. The racquet acts more like a trampoline and the ball may fly off the strings and appear to have more speed. Tighter strings, say in the 60-pound range, will give you more control over the shot. The pros often string their racquets in the 70-pound range. This gives them a lot of control but the strings break faster. So, you need to experiment and find the best tension for you once you start stringing your frames instead of buying them pre-strung.

A stringer usually uses a stringing machine to string racquets. The stringing machines come in tabletop or freestanding models. Freestanding stringing machines do not take up a lot of space.

String it up.

Photo credit: Vicki Fort

Passing Shots

Most of the good stringers belong to the United States Racquet Stringers Association (USRSA), a national organization for stringers. Any stringer who displays their sign will be well-versed in the latest stringing methods and products. This is very important with all the oversize, different-shaped racquets now being strung.

Double Faults

Keep damp items away from racquet strings in your bag. Sweatbands and used hats should be stored in separate compartments of your bag to make sure the strings don't get wet and, therefore, last longer.

If you are interested in learning how to string, you need to contact the United States Racquet Stringers Association. It is a very good organization that services the stringing industry and its suppliers. Good stringers can earn $8 to $10 a racquet, plus the price of the strings. It takes about 20 minutes to string a racquet once you become proficient. Stringers at the U.S. Open and other major tournaments often string 50 racquets a day.

You do need to know what strings you like. Most good pros and stringers will be able to recommend the type and the gauge. Once you play, you will find you will have a favorite type of string. Each time your racquet is strung your stringer should place a label on the inside throat of the racquet listing the date and the tension. Stringing machines do vary, as do stringers. If you find a good stringer, stick with him or her. Good stringers will have your racquet back to you within 24 hours for a cost of around $22.

There are some products on the market that will save some wear and tear on your strings. There is a gut spray to help preserve the gut so it is not as susceptible to dampness and heat. There is a product called String-a-lings, which are plastic miniclips used to keep the strings in line. If you hit with a lot of spin, the strings move, so the String-a-lings stop them from getting out of alignment and breaking easily.

However you look at it, you will have to get your racquet re-strung at some point. Most beginners feel very pleased with themselves when they break their first string. It is as if they have taken a giant leap forward in the tennis world. If the strings break in the center sweet spot—maybe they have!

Used Equipment

Tennis is a sport that does not need a lot of equipment. Basically, if you have your racquet you can play. So, there is not much of a market for used anything in tennis.

Racquets tend to take a beating. Unless a player has progressed quickly out of one stage into another, or someone has to have the latest rage in racquets, you will not find used racquets in very good condition, as you can see in the photo on the next page.

There are a few decent frames at second-hand sporting goods outlets, but for the most part, they are not worth looking at. The best marketplace, if you wish to sell or buy, is an active country club or public tennis center. A club with many players will have a faster turnover in racquets.

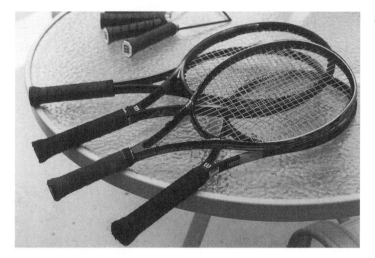

New may be better.

Photo credit: Vicki Fort

At my club in Florida, members are often looking to sell their old frames so that they can, in good faith, buy the newer models. You can get some good buys this way. Members ask the pro to keep an eye open for a prospective buyer, or if allowed, they place a note on the bulletin board saying "racquet for sale," listing the model and grip size.

Another way to buy used racquets is to speak to your tennis professional and see if he or she has any demos for sale. These are racquets bought at a low price and strung up so a customer can try, or demo, a racquet before actually purchasing a new one. Remember, I suggested you try a demo, if you can, when deciding which racquet to buy for yourself. Demos are played with a lot, but usually are taken good care of by the shop staff. Buying a demo is a good way to get a quality racquet at a reasonable price. Demo your demo before you buy.

Antiques in tennis are rare unless they are the players themselves.

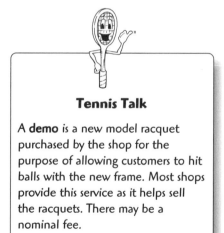

Tennis Talk

A **demo** is a new model racquet purchased by the shop for the purpose of allowing customers to hit balls with the new frame. Most shops provide this service as it helps sell the racquets. There may be a nominal fee.

The Least You Need to Know

➤ Even as a beginner, you should have two racquets. If one breaks, you will be able to continue playing with a racquet you like.

➤ Average racquet sizes for females are $4^1/_4$ or $4^3/_8$; for males, $4^1/_2$ or $4^5/_8$.

➤ Once you realize what you need to bring to the courts, you'll understand why it is necessary to have at least a three-pack racquet bag. Always carry two cans of new balls in your three-pack.

➤ Know your string type and tension in case you have to have your racquet strung by a different stringer.

➤ Keep an eye out for bargains on demo racquets.

Chapter 4

Dress to Impress: What You Should Wear

In This Chapter

➤ Feet first; your shoes are important

➤ Don't sell yourself short; what to wear

➤ Tuck in your shirt; how to look good

➤ Don't sweat it; warm-ups are great

One of the many things that attract people to the game of tennis is the attire. There is a standard to which tennis players adhere when dressing to play. Clubs that have been in existence for a long time have very stringent rules on proper attire on or around the tennis courts. In many clubs, the tennis attire on the court has to be all white. Other clubs stipulate such things as:

➤ Shirts must have collars

➤ Skirts must be a certain length

➤ Exercise outfits suitable for the gym are unacceptable on the court

As I discussed in Chapter 2, tennis fashions have come a long way. Clothes have become more comfortable. Ladies no longer have to play in long skirts and long-sleeve shirts with hats. Men do not have to play in long pants and shirts with ties. So, although there are rules for dress, the clothes today allow freedom of movement.

There are many different styles of tennis attire to choose from, so no matter what your shape, you should be able to find the style right for you.

Let's take a look at some of the choices you can make on your way to dressing to impress. *Remember, it's not just how you play, but how you look that counts.*

Looking good.
Photo credit: Vicki Fort

It's a Shoe In

Tennis shoes are a little like racquets. There is a style and a price to suit everyone. The first tennis shoes looked nothing like the high-tech, air-injected, lightweight miracles of modern engineering that the players wear today.

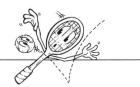

Double Faults

Make certain you check on the dress code if you have been invited to play at a new club. This will save you from embarrassment and possibly from having to buy a new outfit in the pro shop.

If you are a beginner without any major foot problems, you do not have to buy $150 Nikes. What you do need to look for is a shoe that looks like it will mold to your foot and support your arch. I would suggest you shop at a reputable sporting goods store or pro shop, because the staff will have the knowledge to fit you with the shoe you will need to get started.

It is not imperative that you buy new shoes. You may have an adequate pair floating around in your closet. If the tread is worn or the heel and toe are not in good condition, chances are you will injure yourself by slipping or falling as you begin to move on the court. Most shoe companies make special soles for the different court surfaces. You can play it safe and buy a cross-trainer that will allow you to wear the shoes for all activities.

Most tennis shoes are white with some trim. I would stay away from the fads and exotic-colored styles. You are probably paying for all that jazz anyway. Ask for a shoe that has some cushioning in the heel area. Make certain that it does not have a black sole or one that could possibly mark a court—it should not contain carbon black. Running shoes are not good for tennis because the weight transference is not the same. Tennis players need to be able to put more weight on the toes and balls of their feet. Runners need more of a heel-to-toe motion, so the toe section of a runner's shoe does not translate well to a tennis shoe.

Many of the new shoes on the market now have pressurized gas encapsulated within the urethane soles. This sounds like you will blast off at the first touch of a hot court. What it does is cushion the impact and save your feet, particularly in the heel area. The outside of the shoe is made from rubber. It will have various names, depending on the type of material used to help lighten or weight the shoes.

Shop clerks will start throwing words at you like blow-molded, nonslip sock liners, mid soles, out soles, dual pressure systems, medial and lateral supports. It will sound like you are buying a rocket ship, not a tennis shoe. You do not need to know all of the jargon. Buy a good pair of shoes with the cushioning needed for your feet. These shoes will not last forever, so when they wear out you can upgrade to another style or change manufacturers. Most shoes will last about six months unless you are playing on hard courts three or four times a week.

Passing Shots

Tennis sneakers are made with different treads for specific court surfaces. Unfortunately, they are not interchangeable and you will need a pair for every surface. However, if you're just beginning, you won't want to sink that much money into shoes, so, if you find that you'll be playing on different surfaces, you can resort to cross-trainers.

Different soles for different souls.

Photo credit: June Harrison

Trish Says

When playing a match, wear sneakers that you have broken in or worn before. I remember one of my first matches in England when I wanted to impress the people running the tournament. I had all new clothes, including my shoes. After a set and a half, I could barely walk because of my blisters. I was in agony. Next time, I broke in my sneakers by wearing them in practice before I wore them in a match.

Try the sneakers on in the store with a thick pair of tennis socks. Bring your own if you don't want to wear socks that have been on other people's feet. It is very important to do this, because the shoe fits differently without a thick sock. Walk around the store. Flex your feet. Go up on your toes and back on your heels to test the flexibility of the shoe. Take the shoe in your hand and see if it flexes at the center of the insole. If it is too inflexible, it will be too stiff for you to move around in. If it flexes too much, it probably doesn't have enough support.

Expect to pay at least $50 for a decent pair of sneakers. Canvas is acceptable, but it won't last long because of the sweat. Leather or synthetic leather is usually the material for the upper part of the shoe. Sometimes it will be combined with mesh. Most good tennis shoes come in two styles—regular or high top. The high tops are good if you have weak ankles because they do give extra support. High tops are heavier and do take a little getting used to.

Don't let the salesperson talk you into last season's style unless you are saving a great deal of money and the shoe is basically unchanged. Each year the technology in the shoe industry allows the top manufacturers to bring out better shoes with better supports. Pay a little more for the better brand names—it is worth it.

Sock It to Me

Don't laugh, but socks play a very important part in the life of a tennis player—pro or amateur.

In tennis, your nimble footwork will separate you from the klutzes. You will not feel like chasing down wide balls and deep lobs if your feet hurt. Not only wearing the wrong shoes, but also wearing the wrong socks can hold you back from becoming a player to reckon with.

Remember that I suggested you take a pair of your best tennis socks along with you when you buy your shoes. The socks will help cushion your feet as much as the shoes and they are much cheaper.

You need to look for a sock that is a combination of cotton, Lycra, microfiber, and nylon. One hundred percent cotton socks are OK, but the combination is much better because they will last longer and fit better.

Look for a sock label that says the sock is specifically designed for tennis, squash, racquetball, or it might just call itself a court sock. The best ones have what's called sculptured cushioning, meaning that you have extra cushioning in the heel area, in the Achilles tendon area, and on the ball of the foot, which is the area you are pounding most in tennis. You do not want a lot of padding or cushioning in the arch area. This would make the sock too bulky and uncomfortable in your shoe.

You also do not want a sock that is too thick on the top of the toe, although you do need some reinforcement so that you don't get the dreaded black toe. You get a black toe when your shoes are too tight and your big toe gets jammed up against the top of the shoe, giving you a big bruise. Look for the phrases "reinforced toe" and "cushioned heel" on the tag or the package of socks.

The Lycra and little bit of nylon added to the sock allow it to stretch and mold to your foot. It will also help keep the sock up and not allow it to droop. Good players do not have droopy socks. Socks should all be machine washable and dryable. The more expensive socks also have a material that helps the sweat rise to the surface of the fabric—Nike calls it Dri.F.I.T.

Short, long, or not at all.
Photo credit: Vicki Fort

Double Faults

Know when to throw your socks out. You don't want to be in the middle of a match and feel your toes coming out or the sock slipping down into your shoe. When socks are shot, out they go.

You can choose your sock length. Usually, the crew sock is the most popular. Some players like to wear the quarter length that does not give you a rollover portion at the top. Very few men or women like the ped (ankle) style for tennis because it often slips down into your shoe. Great for a suntan, but sometimes very irritating in a match. You have enough to worry about without having to be concerned about your socks.

A decent pair of socks will run you $3 to $5 a pair. If you find a style you like, buy a few pairs because manufacturers have a habit of changing styles frequently, and you may not be able to find them again.

Don't scrimp on your socks. Your feet will end up talking to you and you won't like what they are saying.

The Long and the Short of It

World-famous tennis designer Ted Tinling would turn over in his grave if he were to see a match between Andre Agassi and Pete Sampras, with their shirts outside their long, baggy pants. Stripes down the side of the shorts make them look more like surfers than two top-ranked tennis players duking it out for another major title.

Forget about the monks who played in their robes and kings and noblemen who played in all their finery. Forget the few ladies of the court—pun intended. You and I could barely walk down the street in what most of these early players wore to be suitably attired. When the players that I can relate to first played tennis, the men wore long, cream or white cotton pants, long-sleeved shirts, and the ladies wore dresses or shorts just above the knee. These outfits for women were a far cry from the early days when long dresses and long white stockings were in vogue. Take a look at the difference between the two photos on the next page. You will see how formal the outfits were compared to our current comfortable drip-dries.

Tennis Talk

All-white clubs are clubs where members and guests must wear clothing that is predominately white with only 10 percent colored trim allowed.

What caused the changes in attire to take place? Everyone looked very smart and the all-white or off-white seemed to make all the players appear regal. So, why did the men switch to shorts and the ladies to above-the-knee outfits? Obviously one reason was comfort and ease of movement. The game changed from a leisurely baseline rally to a net charging, hard hitting, competitive contest. It also became socially acceptable to show a little leg.

Players in the early 1900s.
Photo credit: International Tennis Hall of Fame

Much better.
Photo credit: Vicki Fort

Men first wore shorts in 1932. Women first showed a little leg in 1919 when Suzanne Lenglen gave up her French corsets to beat her opponents. Showing some thigh did not hurt the sport. In England, Wimbledon had to build a bigger center court. In the United States, Forest Hills stadium was built in 1923 to accommodate the increased interest. Let's just say that when the hemlines and pant legs went up the sport became more popular.

So, what should you buy? Forget the long white pants and long dresses. Let's go shopping. Right now, we are going to decide whether you are conservative or extroverted in your fashion choices. Believe me, there is an outfit for every type out there.

The new basic tennis shorts are made of cotton and poly-microfibers. This means the fabric breathes and, better yet, you can go without ironing it. Even if you are not planning to join a club that has an all-white dress code, go for light-colored shorts.

White shorts will not show the sweat as much and they are easier to match with your shirts. The downside of white is that it shows the dirt faster. Don't worry that you are expected to get dirty when you are playing tennis. You haven't played hard enough if you didn't get even a little sweaty. Did I say "sweaty?" Yes, you will get hot and the sweat will travel to your shorts. For men, you need to check the white shorts and make certain they have a liner; otherwise, you may show more than dirt!

For men's tennis fashions, the manufacturers have names for all the different shorts—structured, baggy, tailored, or form-fitting—and you can get very confused. You should choose baggy or fitted. If you are tall, you can get away with the baggy look. I would suggest you buy two pairs of shorts. One white, with a liner, and one navy. They should be pull-on with a fly front and an elastic waistband. I would get normal length, not baggy, and not extra long. Men's shorts also come in many price ranges. Stick to basic name brands and you will get shorts that will wash and wear well. You can get flashy once you know the brand and style you like. I am not worried that you won't like tennis.

For women, I would buy only one pair of white structured or tailored tennis shorts. Make certain they are for tennis. Golf shorts are longer than tennis shorts and will cut you on your quads, which are the muscles you will use the most. Many women players won't wear shorts because they are rather unflattering and they show sweat in some delicate places. Shorts were comfortable and acceptable tennis attire for women as early as the 1930s.

When trying on the shorts, remember that you will be stretching and lunging, so allow for freedom of movement and comfort at the waist. You will not want anything binding or distracting once you start to play.

Shorts are non-restrictive. Tennis star Alice Marble.

Photo credit: International Tennis Hall of Fame

How Not to Lose Your Shirt

Now that you have your racquet, balls, shoes, and shorts, all you really need is a tennis shirt. Chances are you already have something suitable in your closet.

Men's tennis shirts should have sleeves and be what is termed polo style with a collar. Women's shirts can be sleeveless, tank style, or polo style with sleeves and a collar. Women are lucky because we have many more styles to choose from, so it really depends on your personal preference.

Again, you need to remember you want comfort as well as style. One hundred percent cotton will be cooler and more desirable in warmer climates. But cotton shrinks, so make certain you buy the right size.

Shorts will last a lot longer than shirts, so you need to buy two shirts for every one pair of shorts. Even as a beginner, you should try to match your outfits. There is nothing worse than looking out onto a court and seeing players in inappropriate attire. You can be a rank beginner and miss every ball but if you look like you belong out there and you are trying your hardest, other players will help you and respect you.

I love T-shirts and there are some clever ones on the market, but they don't belong on a court where adults are playing tennis. T-shirts are suitable attire for kids on the court, but you should save them to wear to the fitness center or the pool.

In tennis, your appearance can win you a few points. Your opponents will give you credit for more shots than you have if you look like you can play well. So, go for the white shirt with the navy trim if you have navy and white shorts. Don't go for green just because it is your favorite color.

You will be safe playing at any facility if you have a plain white cotton polo shirt with a little color trim on the collar or on the sleeves. Save the fancy outfits for later when you know what you like to wear.

Double Faults

You are going to perspire even in cold climates, so look for outfits that are made out of 100 percent cotton or at least a cotton blend.

Double Faults

Always pack an extra shirt when getting ready for your game. Many clubs don't allow T-shirts, so save them for after the game. I always change my shirt after each match. There is nothing worse than the feeling you get when you are wearing a damp shirt. It's not good for your muscles or your health.

Courtside Quotes

"Confidence can make the difference between winning and losing...if a woman feels she looks better than her opponent, that is an edge."

—Ted Tinling

Let's Skirt Around the Issue

Women wore skirts to play tennis in the early days of the sport, but they had to worry more about ankles showing and leggings sagging than their backhands.

Double Faults

I always spill my coffee or my Allsport on my white shirt, so I suggest to everyone that they pack an extra shirt in their tennis bag.

Thanks to French star Suzanne Lenglen, women were liberated from wearing long skirts on the court. She let her racquet and her style speak for her. She was the first real tennis fashion icon.

Women players today have a myriad of choices when it comes to what to wear on the court. You can wear shorts, skirts, dresses, or even one-piece leotards, as sported by Ann White at Wimbledon.

Tennis skirts today are made out of microfibers, allowing the skirt to be lightweight. Waistbands are usually part elastic and part fitted to give you a good fit but not too snug. You want to be comfortable and fashionable.

Trish Says

Making a fashion statement is fine off the tennis court. Most tennis outfits are sporty, yet practical. I remember playing a match in France against a woman whose outfit was at least two sizes too small. Every time she served, she pulled down her skirt waist or pulled at the hem. She looked miserable in her beautiful tennis clothes, and I felt sorry for her. Almost sorry enough to lose the match.

Warm-ups, Sweatsuits, Sweaters, and Vests

One of the greatest inventions of modern day tennis is the warm-up suit. I have a closet-full, and if I could, I would wear them everywhere, even to black-tie functions.

This is one purchase that I would encourage you to shop around for and check out prices. You don't need a designer suit, but they are wonderful and often have the best fabrics. Discount stores get last season's merchandise and this will do just fine. You will see many different styles and colors. You need to try them on, because the leg length is important. Look for bottoms that have zippers rather than plain elastic in the cuffs. If you don't have a zipper, you will have to take off your shoes every time you want to take off the warm-up pants. Believe me, you will get tired of this routine.

I always put things in my pockets, so I look for a pair of pants with at least one side pocket. Many of the newer styles have zippered pockets; however, I prefer regular pockets so I can easily put balls in them.

Make certain the jacket has enough room in the arms and shoulders for you to swing a racquet. You may need to warm-up in your jacket if it is cool. Take a few practice service motions, as this is the biggest range you will need. You don't want a tight waistband, because you won't be able to stretch. I like a zip front instead of having to pull the top over my head. By the time I am ready to take off my jacket, I already have my hat on, so I don't want to take everything off again.

Many companies now sell jackets only, which is very smart. You can buy one pair of pants (back to my navy or white) and two jackets. Then it looks like you own two warm-up suits.

Ready to warm-up.

Photo credit: Vicki Fort

The major difference between a warm-up and a sweat suit is usually the material. Warm-ups are usually poly-microfiber or polyester. Sweats are often poly-cotton mixed or 100 percent cotton. Sweats are more casual and often have a pullover top or sweatshirt-style top. Warm-ups are not usually fleece lined, whereas sweats are. Sweats are great for training and stretching for tennis, or even just lounging around.

Double Faults

Make sure you dress for the weather. There is nothing worse than trying to play in an outfit that does not breathe. You will be uncomfortable and feel restricted, as well as very warm. You will not be able to concentrate on the game.

If you live in a warm climate, you may not want to stock up on warm-up suits. A good white sweater is the next best thing. Again, remember that there may be some clubs where you can wear only white, so you can never go wrong with a white, cable-knit, long-sleeve sweater.

Some players, particularly those with back problems, like to wear vests so that they get really warmed-up before they take them off. This is a great idea and will save you from injury.

You can even take your couch potato, lay-around, at-home outfit and use it for tennis. You may not look ready for *Vogue* or *GQ*, but the money you save on the warm-up can be used for lessons.

The Least You Need to Know

➤ A good pair of socks is worth the investment. You cannot play good tennis when your feet hurt.

➤ Look for a pair of tennis shoes that will give you extra support in the heel and arch area.

➤ A fashionable warm-up is a good investment, even if you don't play tennis.

➤ Don't have too many flashy outfits in your closet, because many clubs have a no-color rule for clothing on the tennis court.

➤ Your shirts will wear out faster than your shorts or skirts, so have a few extra styles and colors of shirts to match the bottoms.

Part 2
Play Ball!!!

Now you are all set. You know why we are all hooked on the game and whom we should thank for getting us to this point. You are dressed to the hilt and you look very imposing. The problem is, you don't know how to hit the ball. Well, after this section you still won't know all the shots—you are not quite ready yet. You need to know how to choose a professional, one who will guide you through the maze of learning this wonderful game.

You also need to know how to keep score and how to recognize the different court surfaces. Before you hit the courts in the next part, you need to make sure you are fit enough to run around and hit that little yellow ball. So, pay close attention to the chapters on flexibility and stretching. We don't want you sore and limping before you become your club champion. If nothing else, some of the techniques will relax you and help you become more limber. Read on.

Chapter 5

Ready, Set, Go! How to Get Started

In This Chapter

➤ What is a tennis court? Know your measurements

➤ On the surface; clay court, hard court, or what court

➤ Who you gonna call? Finding a good professional

➤ You're on candid camera; you'll look good on video

You have your tennis equipment, and you have a brand new tennis outfit. You are now ready to get started. Where do you go, you ask. Let's head over to a tennis court.

I would like to tell you that tennis courts come in all shapes and sizes, but that would be wrong. They do, however, come in all different surfaces. In this chapter, I will tell you why they do and how that affects your game. You will probably find that you prefer one surface over another. One might suit your style of play better because it is faster or slower. Even the pros have their favorite surfaces. I love playing on grass. I love the feel of it under my feet and the fact that the ball stays very low. I have had my best wins on grass.

Depending on where you live, you will find some court surfaces more readily accessible. There are different places to play: public parks, private clubs, and nicest of all, courts in someone's backyard. Courts are usually clay or hardcourt, but it depends on the location; courts west of the Mississippi are commonly hardcourt, which are, incidentally, cheaper to build.

The next very important step is finding a professional who can teach you how to play and enjoy the sport. I am going to share with you some of my secrets when it comes to tennis professionals, so that you can find one who suits you and your personality.

Court time is now in session; let's get started.

Courtside Quotes

"The customers get more for their money on clay. I always felt that on grass I was gypping them because the points were over quickly."

—Rod Laver, Grand Slam winner

What Is a Tennis Court?

From its not-so-humble beginnings as a royal court game, tennis has developed into a popular sport enjoyed by many.

Real Tennis Courts were first designed as indoor mazes. Then Major Wingfield designed his lawn tennis game.

The first courts were laid out on cultivated lawns. Thanks to the British, this tradition continues even today with the beautifully manicured lawns of Wimbledon, host to the world's most famous tennis tournament.

The court dimensions have not changed in more than 100 years.

Grass court.
Photo credit: Vicki Fort

Bigger Than a Bread Box

Unless you get completely hooked and plan on building your own court, there is no reason for you to memorize the dimensions of the entire court. It is helpful to understand the relationship and depth of the service box compared to the backcourt so that you can judge the length of your shots. Otherwise, let the court builders know the measurements. You need to concentrate on the game.

The lines serving as boundaries for the court and the interior lines all have specific names. The line at either end is called the baseline. The two lines that run the length of the court are called sidelines. In some countries, they are called tramlines. The space between the two sidelines is called the alley. Remember, the net is 6 inches higher in the alley, and you will need to remind yourself of this when you learn to hit down the line. The two lines that look as if they are cutting the court in half on either side are called service lines. The line running down the middle that forms a box with the service line is called the center service line. The box itself is called the service box. On either side, you have a right box and left box. Some players refer to the service boxes as forehand court (the right side) and backhand court (the left side). The small line that divides the baseline in half is called the hash mark.

The actual dimensions of a tennis court for every surface worldwide are shown in this diagram.

Double Faults

When building a court, be sure you leave enough room outside the perimeter of the court so that you can chase down balls without bumping into the fence. Standard space is at least eighteen feet back from the baseline to the fence and at least nine feet on the sidelines.

PLAN OF THE COURT

Court dimensions.

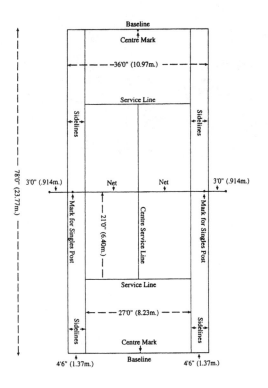

It is necessary to have some running room around your court. The court size you see in the diagram on the previous page does not include the outside perimeter. Unless you want to chase more balls than you hit, or unless you own a tennis ball company or have numerous children on hand to chase the errant balls, you will also need to install fencing all around the court. The end fences need to be at least 6 feet high, but 10 or even 12 feet is better so that the balls do not bounce over the fence. The side fences can be lower, but most private courts have high fences all the way around so that the balls stay inside the playing area. Clubs with multiple courts often do not have side fences. Some have mini fences to stop the most frequently hit shots from running onto your neighbor's court.

As clubs began to flourish, so did the tournaments. As the players became more well-known, spectator interest grew. In the late 1920s, when Suzanne Lenglen and Bill Tilden were on top of the game, they drew large numbers of spectators. Old clubs were forced to build new stadiums.

In the USA, the Westside Tennis Club moved to its current site in Forest Hills, New York. A new stadium, pictured here, was built to house the increased number of fans.

Westside Tennis Club, Forest Hills, New York.

Photo credit: June Harrison

Australia, France, Italy, and England all expanded their clubs to accommodate the growing interest in the game. Each one chose the surface that best suited the respective conditions of each country.

What's Beneath the Surface?

In Europe, red clay became prevalent, because it was readily available. In Australia, they build courts out of all sorts of materials. Bitumen, or asphalt, ant-bed, and regular clay were tried because the grass courts became too expensive for personal backyard endeavors. In the USA, grass courts were introduced on the East Coast, but the West

Coast could not maintain the grass, so they switched to cement. In the South, because of the heat and the rains, they came up with a surface that combined a clay top dressing with a porous foundation.

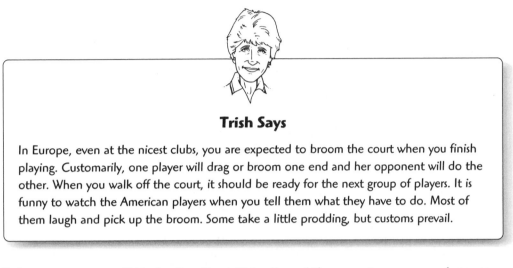

Trish Says

In Europe, even at the nicest clubs, you are expected to broom the court when you finish playing. Customarily, one player will drag or broom one end and her opponent will do the other. When you walk off the court, it should be ready for the next group of players. It is funny to watch the American players when you tell them what they have to do. Most of them laugh and pick up the broom. Some take a little prodding, but customs prevail.

Indoor courts sport all kinds of surfaces. This allowed the game to grow even faster as players in northern climates were now able to play all year round. From a cost standpoint, indoor courts were mostly hard courts. These were made out of a rubberized asphalt material that allowed for easy upkeep. These courts are hard on the legs and back, but are the cheapest to build and maintain.

The two most common surfaces are clay and hard courts. In Australia, the clay courts are more of a sand color. In Europe, the clay is red. In America, it is a green/gray color.

Taking care of business.
Photo credit: Vicki Fort

73

Clay courts are nice and soft underfoot. In order for the clay not to blow away, it needs to be broomed and watered on a regular basis. In the USA, clubs now have underground watering systems that help keep the courts moist all day long. The older clay court systems need to be closed down and watered at least once during the day. Late at night, the sprinklers need to be turned on either manually or electronically so that the top layer of clay does not blow away as it dries out.

Hard courts require very little maintenance. Occasional sweeping or blowing leaves and trash off the surface is about all that they need. Courts are usually painted with a textured, rubberized substance. The normal color is green or green with red surrounding the actual court. Sometimes you will find a blue court, but that is not the norm. States such as California, Arizona, and New Mexico have the added problem of dealing with earthquakes, which cause the courts to crack, or extreme heat, which also causes buckling of the painted surface. Indoor facilities tend to use this asphalt base when it does not have to deal with the elements.

Grass still reigns as the most respected surface. The inherent problems of grass are costs to maintain and playability. For your average club player, grass is a tough surface to use for social tennis. The ball does not bounce very high and you definitely have to bend your knees. Most clubs cannot afford to keep up with the costs of maintaining the courts. There are some clubs in the eastern United States which date back to the late 1880s. They have kept their grass courts and still host many national tournaments.

Other surfaces have been developed and are now being used because of cost and weather problems. Omni court is a synthetic grass surface that is being used worldwide. It is similar to a football field with sand added to the carpet. Some indoor facilities have a carpet that is basically a regular indoor/outdoor carpet with painted lines on it.

Some professional tournaments are played on a rubberized carpet that is rolled out onto a wooden or cement floor. This often is necessary when one major center court is required for exhibitions or major championships, such as the women's year-end Corel Champions Tournament in Madison Square Garden in New York City.

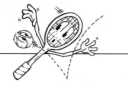

Double Faults

If you play tennis everyday, you should try to play on a soft surface because hard courts are very tough on knees and backs.

Double Faults

If you and your friends want to play on grass, wait for late morning because the grass is still very damp and slippery until the sun dries off the dew.

Trish Says

I once ran a women's professional tournament in Albuquerque, New Mexico. The courts belonged to the city and were in terrible shape. We agreed to resurface the courts so we could play the tournament at the public court site. The following year, when I arrived to inspect the courts for the event, I found that the elements and a small earthquake had created had a 2-inch wide, 20-foot crack right down the middle of our show court. I was shocked. The courts had been built on a fault.

Choose your surface. Hard or soft.
Photo credit: Vicki Fort

Where Should We Hold Court?

The tennis player's dream is to have a court in his or her own backyard. No more worries about whether you can get court time. No fighting traffic to get to the club. No more worrying if it is raining at the club even if it isn't raining at your house. Your only concern will be who your opponent will be each day.

The next best thing is to belong to a club close by, so that you can play tennis as often as possible. Memberships cost anywhere from $200 to $2,000 per year. Decide what you want in the amenity department and then pick your club. Proximity to home or business should be important. You will play more if you do not have to drive 30 minutes to get your game going. After you have experienced some of the different surfaces, you will definitely have a preference. Consider this when selecting your club. Also, take into account what sort of activities you are looking for from your club.

If you want lots of leagues, clinics, and activities, look for a club that is very busy. However, the busier the club, the harder it will be to get court time. If you are an avid player, or just an eager beginner, it will be much more fun to be at a club that offers you everything.

It is also important that you find yourself a good tennis professional to help make your club and your lessons enjoyable and worthwhile.

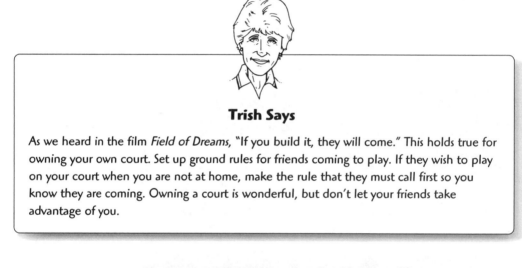

Trish Says

As we heard in the film *Field of Dreams*, "If you build it, they will come." This holds true for owning your own court. Set up ground rules for friends coming to play. If they wish to play on your court when you are not at home, make the rule that they must call first so you know they are coming. Owning a court is wonderful, but don't let your friends take advantage of you.

A nice slow surface.

Photo credit: June Harrison

Playing at home.

Photo credit: June Harrison

Who You Gonna Call?

You probably have done what most first-time players do—play without taking any lessons. This is OK, because it will give you a chance to see if you like the game of tennis. You might decide that chasing a little yellow ball around so that you can hit it back and forth over a net is a waste of time. Chances are you will realize that it is a game everyone can play once they learn the basics.

Choosing a tennis teacher is a little like choosing a hairdresser or a mechanic. There are good ones and bad ones. There are those who can help you, but only to a certain level of competency. In order for you to find the right professional, you first need to ask yourself some questions. How much time can you and do you want to spend on tennis? How often will you be able to play? How much money do you want to spend both learning and playing the sport? Once you have decided on your approach to the sport, you will be able to select the right pro.

Tennis professionals have a governing body just like golf professionals. The United States Professional Tennis Association (USPTA) is the organization that certifies and oversees tennis professionals. Unlike golf, where all golf professionals go through a school, the USPTA does not require that tennis professionals be licensed. There is also a second organization, the United States Professional Tennis Registry (USPTR), which offers teaching courses for those members wanting to be teaching professionals. Although it does not have as many members, the USPTR does a great job in training professionals. In time, one group will govern all tennis

Double Faults

Don't rush into signing up for a series of lessons with the first pro you find. Like a racquet, pros are different. Try a few until you find one that fits your personality.

professionals, but for now, only about 70 percent of pros are members of the USPTA or the USPTR. Of the two, the USPTA is dominant. Most professionals who work at reputable clubs are members and have gone through the test to be certified. This doesn't make them great pros, but it does mean they have the knowledge and the capabilities to teach someone how to play tennis. Is that someone you?

Trish Says

BallenIsles Country Club in Florida, where I am the director, has 22 courts and all four surfaces: grass, clay, red clay, and hard courts. There is something for everyone within our scope of member activities. The good thing about an active club is that you can always find players and meet new friends. The more players you have around you, the more you play, the more you improve, and the more you increase your circle of friends. Enthusiasm breeds more enthusiasm.

Let's go back to those questions you asked yourself. If all you want are the basics and you are not going to take the game to anything beyond a beginner level, it doesn't really matter who teaches you. If you have a strong personality, you may feel more comfortable with a teacher who is very honest and outspoken when it comes to breaking down your mistakes. If you are introverted and unsure of yourself, you may wish to work with a professional who has more of the "Mary Poppins" approach. It will be the job of the professional to bring out your best on the court. Just because a professional is, or was, a great player, does not make him or her necessarily a great teacher.

Courtside Quotes

"You must be joking; with my temper, no kid would be safe." —Ilie Nastase, volatile Romanian star, commenting on whether or not he was going to teach after retiring from competitive play.

You also need to ask yourself whether you will feel more comfortable with a male or female teacher. Tennis is a very physical sport, and in order for you to grasp some of the strokes, it will be necessary for the pro to do some hands-on teaching.

This is particularly true if you are not a student who learns from visualization. It may take you some time to make contact with certain shots. You will have a better chance of feeling the motion and understanding the swings if the pro guides your hand, arm, and racquet through the motions using the correct techniques. Sometimes a man will feel that a female tennis instructor will not have the power required to hit with him. Most women professionals have played a high level of tournament tennis, and are usually capable of beating the better male players at their respective clubs. This, of course, holds true of the male professionals, too. Many women players, particularly beginners, feel more comfortable with a female instructor because of the physical contact required during teaching. Many men feel the same way and want a male pro. Sometimes, the sexual preference works in reverse and the fact that the pro is of the opposite sex makes the lesson more fun. In most cases, the pro, male or female, is out there to teach you tennis, and to make sure you get your money's worth and have a great time.

Hands-on teaching.

Photo credit: Vicki Fort

It is more important to select the right instructor if you intend to spend a great deal of time, money, and effort in learning the sport. It is imperative that you learn the right way. It is very important that you select a pro who understands your goals and does not ignore your desires just because you will never make the pro circuit. Some professionals, young males in particular, underestimate older female students. Just because you are over 30 doesn't mean you cannot play local tournaments and achieve personal pride in reaching your own goals.

Trish Says

As a woman professional, I have to earn the respect of the better club players. When I first take a job at a new club, there is always the discussion as to whether their male club champion can beat me. After a discreet amount of time, I usually manage to find myself in a game where I can generally show him and the onlookers that I have a game to be reckoned with.

Any surface will work.
Photo credit: Vicki Fort

Passing Shots

A good way to cut down the cost of lessons is to take them with a friend of the same ability level.

The Benefits of Lessons

If you are a rank beginner, it will be more beneficial to take one-hour lessons until you have mastered the basics. If you are a good student and practice outside of your lesson time, this might only take six lessons. Once you understand the strokes, it is very important to play as much as possible. If you are on a limited budget and cannot afford to continue lessons at least once a week, then try to have your pro check you out for bad habits at least once a month. You can do this with one-hour lessons so that he or she can take a quick check on all your strokes. If you are playing regularly, it is important you have a monthly checkup so that poor swings and incorrect techniques do not result in injuries such as tennis elbow.

Good professionals will give you a game plan with a short-term and a long-term goal. You will want to sit down periodically and review those goals. If you have an injury, or you have learned a particular part of the game quickly, you may have to make some adjustments. If you practice a lot and have been diligent, you may even be able to jump a few plateaus.

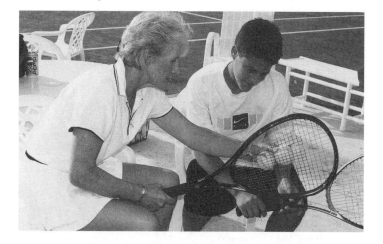

Strategic planning.
Photo credit: Vicki Fort

Many students learn well in a group setting. They have more fun, meet people to practice with, and it gives them a benchmark of their progress. It is also cheaper. If you feel embarrassed taking private lessons, or you cannot afford them, group lessons are great. Make sure that your ratio, student to teacher, is no more than six to one. Any more than that and you will be standing around for too long between each turn.

Groups are fun.
Photo credit: Vicki Fort

The most important reason for taking even a few lessons is to stop any bad habits that will lead to possible injuries down the road. Your funny grip on the serve might work now, but when you try to raise your game to the next level, or if you come out cold one day and swing just a little too hard, something may snap. Take the time. Spend the money and work out a lesson program that will suit your needs.

Teaching Aids

Some professionals do not use any materials or gimmicks to assist them in their teaching programs. Most, particularly those who teach young juniors, use ball machines, practice walls, rebound nets, cones, and targets, as well as other devices that help them make lessons more interesting. Some teaching aids simply emphasize what the pro is trying to demonstrate. Some really help show the point of contact between the racquet and the ball.

The robotic pro.

Photo credit: Vicki Fort

Many pros string a colored rope attached to two poles on the end of the net posts about three feet above the net. The students are then asked to hit over the colored rope. This helps the students learn topspin, depth, and consistency.

Cardboard cutouts of feet which you can place on the court help with footwork and movement. Jump ropes help with conditioning and footwork. Medicine balls are used by the pros to help with strengthening exercises and hand-eye coordination. Many good players travel with a short rubber cord that helps them stretch out when they cannot get to a gym.

One of the best teaching aids is the ball machine. It comes in all shapes and sizes. A ball machine costs between $250 for a small portable to $3,000 for a sophisticated, remote-control unit with capabilities equal to a good tournament player. You can use the ball machine by yourself or within a lesson. I like to book an hour on the ball machine and ask a friend to share the time with me. It can get boring if you do it all alone.

Some clubs use a ball retrieval system along with the ball machine. This makes it a little easier as you don't have to pick up balls all the time. The retrieval trough feeds the balls back into the ball machine.

My favorite teaching tool is the video camera. There is no substitute to watching yourself on film. I can tell my students to do one thing, and they think they are doing it, and they are not even close. It is so simple to show them and then comment and make suggestions.

Many players are afraid of the video camera and refuse to have the pro tape them in action. These students are wasting the best tool there is to help them improve their game.

If you want a video lesson, you will need to tell the pro ahead of time to make certain the camera is charged and ready for action. I always book an extra 30 minutes so the student can sit with me and watch the tape. This way I can analyze his or her mistakes and show the student how to fix them. The student also has permanent footage to learn from, or review, as he or she progresses.

I also like to have my students look at tapes of good matches. You will be amazed at how much you can learn simply by watching the best players.

Come on, let's get going. I know a great pro.

The Least You Need to Know

➤ Clay courts are easier on the body than any other surface.

➤ Grass courts are expensive to maintain, but soft underfoot to play on.

➤ Take your time choosing a professional. Your personalities must mesh.

➤ Don't be afraid of the video camera. It is your best teaching tool.

➤ Spend a little money on your lessons. In tennis, you tend to get what you pay for.

Chapter 6

Dos And Don'ts of Tennis

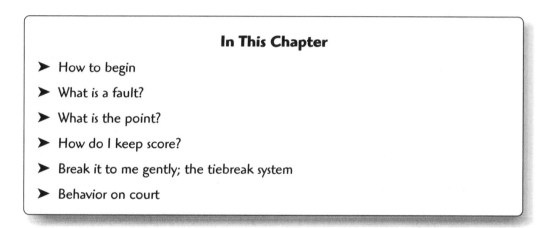

In This Chapter

➤ How to begin

➤ What is a fault?

➤ What is the point?

➤ How do I keep score?

➤ Break it to me gently; the tiebreak system

➤ Behavior on court

One of the best things about tennis is that you can go anywhere in the world, bring a racquet, and play tennis. The rules, which were set up by the Marylebone Cricket Club, the first club in England, have been in existence since 1875. Some have been revised by the All-England Club.

When I first started playing international tournaments, I was apprehensive. Knowing the customs were different, I reasoned perhaps there were differences in the way you played a match. The first tournament of the year was in Egypt. I had drawn a ranked Italian player. We had a French umpire and most of the spectators were Egyptian. As the match progressed, I realized that the only differences between this court and the more familiar Australian courts were the language and the sponsor signs and bill-boards. The Aussies prevailed.

In this chapter, my aim is to familiarize you with some of the basic rules of the tennis game. Knowing these rules will allow you to play the game. I also discuss how to keep score.

Trish Says

In one of my matches early in my career, I was a little nervous about the match. The stands were full and my opponent was the number-one seed in the draw. I had won the toss and elected to serve. I went to the baseline and without even looking up, I served what I considered a perfect serve. I stood there waiting for the return that never came. I looked up only to find out that my opponent had signaled that she wasn't ready to receive. Did I feel foolish! Plus, I had wasted a good serve.

Keeping score is not as straightforward as one, two, three. Different numbers are used, and you do not win by just winning four points. Oh, and love has something to do with the scoring, too. Perhaps that's why scoring is a little complicated and not so straightforward. But not to fear; like love, once you get the hang of it, it isn't that complicated.

In the second part of this chapter, I discuss the proper etiquette of the game. To go along with all of the rules of the game, there is a very definite way you should conduct yourself on or around the tennis court. Knowing the proper etiquette will add to your enjoyment of the game, as well as your opponent's.

Passing Shots

You don't have to throw your racquet on the ground to choose sides or serve. Just gently spin the racquet in your hand and cover the base of it. Let your opponent pick up or down (after spinning the logo on the base of the racquet will be up or down).

Unlike anything else in life, rules are not meant to be broken in tennis, so let me begin to explain them to you.

How to Begin

You now know where to play and what to wear. You have a nice tennis bag filled with a racquet and all the other paraphernalia that I told you about in Chapter 3.

You have taken some lessons with the club pro, and he or she has suggested that you may want to try to go out and play with another player who is about on your level. That sounds like a good idea to you, so you call up the player and plan to meet her at the court. Both of you show up on time, shake hands, exchange a few pleasantries, and now it is time to get started.

What do you do to begin? Whether you are playing the pro circuit or a social match, the rules you play by are the same. All matches begin with a 5-minute warm-up, and it is decided before the match who will be serving first and on what side. In the next photo, see the two women at the net, spinning the racquet to decide who starts and on what side.

A coin toss or a racquet spin gives the winner the option to choose which side to play and who serves first. The player who wins the toss can decide or he can leave one or both choices up to the other player. In plain terms, you have four choices and you can take only one.

The winner of the coin toss or racquet spin has four choices:

➤ choose to serve

➤ choose to receive

➤ choose which end of the court to play from

➤ forfeit the choice

Tennis Talk

The **service box** is the part of the court closest to the net that is designated as the correct target area of the serve.

Spinning for side and serve.

Photo credit: June Harrison

This choice can be important depending on weather conditions, or the strength or weakness of your serve. Then, if the winner chooses to receive (for example), the loser can choose which end of the court to play from.

Once it is decided who is serving and on what side, each player then walks to opposite sides of the net on the baseline, facing each other diagonally. Then the official warm-up begins. Once this is finished, all the balls should be sent to the side of the court where the player is serving.

The server serves first from the right-hand side of the court diagonally to the opposite side. The ball must land in the *service box* where the receiver is waiting to return the ball.

See the next picture and notice that I am standing behind the line to serve. See how I throw the ball in the air and hit it before it touches the ground?

First serve of the match.

Photo credit: Vicki Fort

As the server, you must wait for the receiver to be ready before you serve. The game is played to the tempo of the server, but the receiver does get 25 seconds to prepare, and 25 seconds between points.

Returning serve.

Photo credit: June Harrison

The receiver may stand anywhere he wants to on his side of the net. He must wait for the ball to bounce in the service box before hitting it back. As you can see in the second picture on the previous page, I am standing behind the *service line* to return the service.

If the ball is served somewhere in the service box, without it being a *let*, the receiver will return the ball, and the point is then played out.

This seems pretty simple, right? It is, but there are still a few more rules you have to know. Now let me tell you about faults.

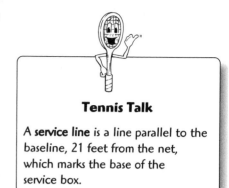

Tennis Talk

A **service line** is a line parallel to the baseline, 21 feet from the net, which marks the base of the service box.

Whose Fault Is It?

Unlike car insurance, in tennis, there is not a no-fault clause. There are times when either you or your opponent will get a fault called on you. This will happen when you are serving under the following conditions:

➤ If the ball lands outside the service box, it is a fault.

➤ If you miss the ball when serving it, it is a fault.

➤ If the ball bounces off something and lands in the correct service box, it is a fault.

Then there is my all-time favorite—the foot fault. Actually, it's my least favorite. A foot fault is called if you touch the baseline or go over it while you are serving. In the next picture, notice that my foot is over the line, meaning a foot fault has occurred.

It's my fault.
Photo credit: June Harrison

Trish Says

I was playing in a very important tournament in France, and had made it all the way to the semifinals. I really felt on top of my game. My serves were coming in like bullets. I had won the first set and was up in the second. I went to serve and all of a sudden, the umpire yells "foot fault." I couldn't believe it. I had been playing tennis for 20 years and I had never been foot-faulted. She then called me for delay of game, so I was penalized a point. I lost my concentration, my serve, and the second set. I had to play a third set to win the match.

If a fault is called on you after the first try, you get another chance. If a second fault is called, you have now *double faulted* and you lose the point.

Tennis Talk

During the service, a **let** is a ball that touches the net but lands in the proper court. The service is then re-taken.

Tennis Talk

A **double fault** is two faults in a row while serving.

After each point, the server moves to either the backhand or forehand side of the court for the next serve. This alternating service system continues until the game is over.

I just told you about the faults of tennis. Now I would like to tell you about the lets.

Let Us Entertain You

The lets are a little less ominous than the faults of tennis. It is sort of like a do-over, which is somewhat nice. Let me explain.

First, we have already mentioned a service let. This is a serve where a ball touches the net, but still lands in the proper service box. There is no penalty to the server, and there can be unlimited lets during a serve. Also, if the receiver is not ready, and the server serves, a let is called and the serve is taken over regardless of where it lands.

A let in all other cases is a situation where something disturbs the players and the point is just replayed. The disruption has to stop the player from completing his stroke or getting to the ball. For example, look at the following picture and notice the cup that fell on the court in the middle of the point.

Do over.

Photo credit: Vicki Fort

At this point, you can call a let and start the point over. Sometimes, the lets come at good times for you, and other times, the timing is better for your opponent. It is sort of just luck.

There is currently a new rule being considered by the tennis bigwigs that involves lets. Tournament players are being asked to continue play when the serve hits the top of the net. Instead of taking a do-over, as the rules states now, the players would continue to play without stopping. I think this is a good idea, as it will speed up play.

Did you have enough of lets? Then let's get to the point of it all.

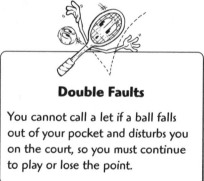

Double Faults

You cannot call a let if a ball falls out of your pocket and disturbs you on the court, so you must continue to play or lose the point.

What's the Point?

At this point, you are probably wondering what you have to do to win a point, not to mention how to win the match.

I am happy to say that the rules on how to win a point are pretty straightforward. They are as follows:

➤ If your *opponent serves a double fault,* you win the point.

➤ If your *opponent does not return the ball* after it bounces on her side of the net, you win the point.

➤ If the *ball bounces twice on your opponent's side* before she sends it over the net, you win the point.

➤ If your *opponent hits the ball outside of the line,* or *into the net,* you win the point.

➤ If you look at the following picture, you will notice the ball is outside the lines of the court. Although it is close, it is still your point.

That's my point.

Photo credit: Vicki Fort

➤ If your *opponent's racquet touches the net* or any part of the net while the ball is in play, it is your point.

➤ If your *opponent hits a ball while it is still on your side of the net,* it is your point.

➤ If your *opponent hits a permanent fixture* (other than the net or something attached to the net; for example, the umpire's chair) outside of the court, and the ball lands in the court on your side, it is still your point.

➤ If the *ball touches something other than your opponent's racquet* (something she is wearing or carrying), it is your point.

➤ If your *opponent deliberately carries the ball with her racquet,* it is your point.

➤ If your *opponent hits the ball more than once,* you win the point. This one is hard to prove. Your opponent is on the honor system here.

➤ If *your opponent does or says something to deliberately make you miss the ball,* it is your point. Once again, this is hard to prove and trying to prove it could result in a fight.

So you know how to score a point. Let me explain how to keep score.

Trish Says

I was in a very close doubles match for a national title. My partner and I were having trouble lobbing, because it was very windy. At 4–5 down in the second set, after losing the first set, we put up another weak lob. Our opponents both rushed in for the overhead. The ball held up in the wind and our opponent took a huge swing and put the ball away. The umpire called her for reaching over the net prior to hitting the ball. She got so upset, they lost the set and the match, because she never did regain her composure.

Who Is Keeping Score?

As I mentioned before, keeping score is not as easy as 1, 2, 3, 4, although you do win a game by getting four points.

The first point is called 15. If the server wins the first point, the score is called 15–love (love means no points). If the receiver wins the first point, the score is love–15. The second point is 30 and the third point is 40. If one player wins all four points, the game is won. If both players win three points, then the score is called deuce (40–all). The next point is called advantage.

If the server wins the advantage point, the score is called "advantage in" or "ad in." If the person receiving the serve wins the advantage point, the score is called "advantage out" or "ad out." If the player with the advantage wins the next point, that player wins the game. If the player not holding the ad point wins the next point, the score goes back to deuce. Once a game is at deuce, one player must win two points in a row to win the game.

After the first game, and after every odd-numbered game, the players change to the other side of the net. See the picture on the next page. You are allowed a 90-second break during the changeover. You can use this time to regroup and have something to eat or drink.

It takes 6 games to win a set and you must win by two games. If both players win 6 games each, they play what is called a tiebreaker. The usual tiebreaker played is called a 12-point tiebreak. The player or team who reaches 7 points first, winning by at least a margin of two, wins the tiebreaker. To start, the first player serves one point from the right side. Then the next player serves two points starting from the left side. Then the first player servers two points, and so on until one reaches 7 points. A tiebreaker could be 7–0. The match is won when one player wins the predetermined number of sets. It's called a 12-point tiebreak, but could be more or less. Nevertheless, it's still shorter than a non-tiebreak third or fifth set.

Double Faults

It is not worth your concentration to be distracted by fighting over what is a deliberate action to make you miss your shot. If your opponent continues, do not argue—simply call an umpire.

On the pro circuit, sometimes men's matches are the best of five sets. The winner must win three sets. There is only one event on the women's pro tour where they play best of five sets. Most social matches, for both men and women, are best of three. In many cases, players play until "duty calls." Fanatics play four or five sets until they drop or are kicked off the court by the next players.

Sometimes something happens during the match that may require a longer rest time. The rules allow for certain break times. Read on.

90 second pit stop.
Photo credit: June Harrison

Can I Catch a Break?

Most matches are played without an extended break. All players are allowed a 90-second period during a changeover. You are also allowed 25 seconds between points. Sometimes, circumstances exist when you may allow additional time.

If an injury occurs on the court, you are allowed one 3-minute suspension in play for treatment. If your mom forgot to remind you to go to the bathroom before your match, you are allowed two breaks during a match, but they cannot exceed 5 minutes each. If a break is taken during a changeover, you can add an additional 90 seconds. If you have a problem with your clothes or shoes, you are permitted to change clothes off the court. Six and one-half minutes are allowed.

In amateur matches, or in senior and junior tournaments, players are allowed a 10-minute rest period between the second and third sets. In professional matches, an official must accompany players who leave the court for clothing or bathroom breaks. This is to keep coaches from telling the player how to play his or her opponent.

So, here you have it in a nutshell: the rules, the scoring, and the breaks. But there is still one important element that I have left out. It is the unwritten rules of tennis. As I have said before, tennis has been around for many years and because of this, there are many traditions and codes of conduct that go along with the game. Let me tell you about a few.

A Gentleman's Game

Tennis is regarded as a gentleman's sport because good behavior is expected on the court. Bad behavior is not only looked upon as unfavorable, but it is even penalized.

Professional tennis has had a code of conduct since 1976. The code lists the penalty points that are given for racquet abuse, verbal abuse, and delaying the game. If bad behavior continues, the umpire can eject the player from the game.

Courtside Quotes

"Sportsmanship is the essence of the game."
—Rod Laver

Trish Says

I remember I was playing a very close match and my opponent got very upset because she double faulted a game away. Changing sides, she walked over to the chairs and banged her racquet. The racquet hit the chair and got stuck. She was penalized one point because she could not get her racquet out in the allowed amount of time for the changeover.

Most players are attracted to the game of tennis because of the sportsmanship that the game offers.

I have made a list of some of the unwritten rules that constitute good sportsmanship in the game of tennis. They are as follows:

➤ Leave the court in the same condition as you found it.

➤ Observe the dress code of the facility. This usually means no jeans, no cutoffs, and often, no T-shirts.

➤ Show up on time for your match, even if it is only a friendly game.

➤ Before the start of the game, be prepared to give your opponent a warm-up. This means hitting the ball to him or her, not practicing your passing shots.

➤ Always give your opponent the benefit of the doubt when a ball is close. Play it as good.

➤ At the end of a match, shake hands whether you win or lose.

Since 1875, when the Marylebone Cricket Club formulated the rules, men and women have been shaking hands to signify that the match is over and another game of tennis has been played and enjoyed. See the picture on the next page. There is a sense of accomplishment in both women's faces.

Trish Says

With the advent of modern technology, the cellular phone has been introduced to the tennis courts. There is nothing more annoying than being on a court or next to a court when the phone rings, and you are in the middle of a point. I knew a player once who carried her phone to league matches. Although she was warned many times to turn it off, she did not. Finally, the league penalized her a match when her phone rang during the game. She never brought her phone again.

Match is now over.
Photo credit: Vicki Fort

The Least You Need to Know

➤ You can go anywhere in the world and tennis will be played by the same rules.

➤ You are allowed certain breaks during match play.

➤ Tennis is a gentleman's sport and good behavior is expected from the players.

➤ The server is responsible for calling out the score when playing without an umpire.

➤ The tiebreaker was invented so matches did not go on forever.

Chapter 7

Let's Be Flexible

In This Chapter

➤ You need to be flexible

➤ Before and after; how to stay limber

➤ Don't just take a cold shower

➤ Relax, trust me

I wonder how many people have had my same high-school nightmare. You rush to the gym locker room to put on the ugliest outfit ever created by man, and you walk to the gym. Once in this large, unventilated sweat tank, you are subjected to 50 minutes of ridiculous stretches that even a contortionist could not do. All the while, the gym teacher is directing you to do these exercises, but she has yet to do one herself. You limp to the locker room feeling totally inadequate and totally uncoordinated. As you try to get dressed, your body is definitely talking to you. You make a vow that once you get that gym credit, you will never, ever enter another gym to do any stretching again. No, sir. The only kind of stretching you will ever do will be reaching for a cup of coffee. Does any of this sound familiar? If so, not to worry. You don't have to skip this chapter. I have compiled a simple set of stretches that anyone can do. These stretches actually have a purpose, and as you can see by the pictures, unlike the gym teacher, I have used and still do use them today.

These stretches will help your body limber up for your tennis game and improve your flexibility. So put down that cup of coffee and let's get started.

General Daily Stretches: Overall Flexibility

For social players, one of the most overlooked things is stretching. Many people rush on the court, hit a few ground strokes, and think their muscles are warm enough to start a match. Yet, these same people will spend many dollars on the right equipment and tennis lessons to improve their game. What is just as important, or actually more important, is to increase the flexibility of your body so that you cut down the chances of pulled muscles. Tennis is a sport that uses almost every muscle in your body—this is why it is a great game. But if you do not take care of your body, your body will not work for you.

That is what this chapter is all about. I will show you the proper stretching exercises to help you avoid muscle stiffness and pulls. These exercises are essential for the longevity of your tennis enjoyment. Let's face it, if you hurt the next day every time you go out to play a set or two, or, worse, if you pull a muscle, you will not enjoy the sport.

Trish Says

I once had a student who was very promising and who practiced very hard. After six months she had pulled just about every muscle in her body and injured her ankle. She decided tennis was too hard on her body. In fact, she had been too demanding of her body without giving it a chance to warm-up and cool down properly. If she would have stretched and toned her muscles, she could still be playing today.

During a tennis game you will bend backwards to hit serves and overheads, rotate your wrist and arm to hit the ball, extend your shoulders, back arm, hips, groin, and knees as your body fights to hit and maintain balance. This happens every time you go to hit the ball and it all takes place in just a few seconds.

With these requirements in mind, I have broken down by major muscle groups the overall stretching you will be using for tennis. You should stretch from the top down. First, stretch your neck, shoulder, and back, then your legs, arms, and feet. These stretches are good for you regardless of whether you play tennis or not. They will increase your general *flexibility*. By increasing your flexibility, you will improve your circulation and muscle tone, and reduce your risk of injury.

Stretching should be done when you go from being inactive to active. It should be done before and after the activity. Stretching reduces muscle tension and helps loosen up your muscles. Stretching should be done to the extent of your range of motion; do not try to over-stretch. If you feel pain while doing any of these stretches, do not continue.

I am going to concentrate only on stretches that will take care of the major muscles you use for tennis. A stretch a day will not turn you into a pretzel, but you will have a spring in your step.

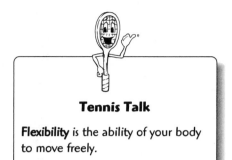

Tennis Talk

Flexibility is the ability of your body to move freely.

Trish Says

There are sometimes rain delays on the pro circuit, and one day, when I had to stop for rain, I was stretching in the locker room. My opponent was watching me, so I pretended to be extra flexible and took my stretch a little further than usual. I felt a little pull in my leg. I had pulled my hamstring. That taught me two things—don't show off and stretching is not a competitive sport.

So let's not stretch this introduction out anymore. Let's get your neck stretched.

Don't Stick Your Neck Out

When doing the neck stretch that I am demonstrating in the next photo, remember, do not jerk your neck. You should slowly drop your head to one side so that your left ear is leaning toward your left shoulder. Hold that position for 15 seconds, then slowly repeat the same motion on the right side.

Do this neck stretch three times on both the left and right sides.

Neck stretch.

Photo Credit: June
Harrison

Don't Shoulder the Burden

Although there are many shoulder stretches, the one I decided to demonstrate to you is the one with the racquet. It can also be done with a towel in place of the racquet. As you can see from this picture, I am holding the racquet grip with one hand over my shoulder, and I am holding the frame with the other hand straight back.

Another use for your racquet.

Photo Credit: June
Harrison

Watch Your Back

Back stretches are very important because most people spend a great deal of time sitting hunched over at a desk or bending to tackle their particular tasks. The back can be very strong, but it also cries out for attention. If you ever watch a dog or cat, you'll see that it automatically stretches out its whole body, particularly its back, before it gets up from lying down. We should all pretend we are large cats and do the same thing. Even before we get out of bed, we should do some preliminary back stretches. Something simple like bringing your knees up to your chest will do. Remember, one of the best ways to strengthen your back is to make certain you have strong stomach muscles. Crunches, crunches, and more crunches (and I am not talking about candy bars) will give you a strong back as well as flat abs.

Passing Shots

I have found that so many of my aches and pains can be relieved by stretching before I get out of bed, before going on the court, and after getting off the court.

The back is supported by a large group of muscles that are actively involved during all tennis swings. If these muscles are not properly warmed up and stretched, you have a greater chance of being injured due to the forces imposed on them while you rotate during a tennis swing.

In this picture, I am demonstrating a seated back stretch that can be done anywhere. As you can see, I am sitting down with my hands on one knee. One leg is bent and the other is straight out. Pull your right knee toward your body and twist your upper body toward your right side making sure to look over your right shoulder. Keep your back straight. Hold this for 15 to 30 seconds. Then repeat it on the other side. Do this three times on each side.

Back stretch.

Photo Credit: June Harrison

103

Get a Leg Up

Leg stretches are essential when you are a tennis player because this is the part of the body that takes the biggest beating. Strong *quadriceps* and *hamstrings* will help you save your knees and your hips.

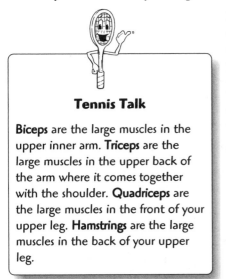

Tennis Talk

Biceps are the large muscles in the upper inner arm. **Triceps** are the large muscles in the upper back of the arm where it comes together with the shoulder. **Quadriceps** are the large muscles in the front of your upper leg. **Hamstrings** are the large muscles in the back of your upper leg.

In tennis, your legs take a pounding, because you will often be out on the court for two or three hours. If someone told you to stand on your feet for three hours, you would say it was some form of torture. In tennis, it certainly isn't torture. But if you do not take care of your body—particularly the legs—after playing a long match, you will feel like you have been on the rack. Everyone's legs are different, but you can all achieve a certain level of flexibility even if you don't have long slender limbs. In long matches, legs have a habit of cramping. This is mainly due to the loss of fluids, but if you have a tendency to cramp, it helps to have loose, flexible muscles to fight off the stiffening and tenseness that occurs with a cramp.

Thigh muscles generate an extreme amount of force during a match or even practice. Because tennis requires a frequent amount of stopping and starting, the thigh muscles take the brunt of this force.

In the following picture, I am demonstrating a quadriceps stretch. As you can see, I am standing on one leg, and holding onto the other ankle with my hand. I am gently pulling my heel toward my bottom. My knees are close together and my back is straight. Hold this stretch for 15 to 30 seconds. Then do the same with the other leg. Repeat the stretch on both sides.

Strong quads, strong legs.
Photo Credit: June Harrison

The next leg stretch you see me demonstrating is a hamstring stretch. This stretch is important because if the hamstring starts to tighten or cramp, you will not be able to continue playing. You use your hamstring just to walk, so it is imperative that you treat this muscle with respect. I have known players who, after pulling a hamstring, have had problems with them for many years after.

The hamstring acts to decelerate the body while running. For this reason, it is very important to make sure you stretch it out and warm-up correctly. It is one of the most common injuries among better players.

As you can see in this picture, I am flat on my back, my shoulders are relaxed, my lower back is pressed down, and I am gripping my leg behind my knee with both hands, pulling it gently toward my body. Do this two times for 15 to 30 seconds on both sides.

Stretch those hamstrings!

Photo Credit: June Harrison

The next leg stretch that is important is for the *Achilles tendon.* It is important to do this stretch because your tendon can snap at any time, even when you are warm. Women are particularly in danger when it comes to Achilles and Planterus injuries because wearing high heels shortens this part of the foot and back of the ankle and leg.

Even nonathletes should make themselves do at least one of these tendon stretches.

One simple stretch can be done by using a stair or a step. In this next picture, I am using a step, holding the stretch for at least 15 seconds. I have

Tennis Talk

The large tendon that connects the calf muscle to the heel is called the **Achilles** tendon. The **Planterus** is the long muscle that runs up along the back of the leg.

one leg that is tighter than the other because of an ankle injury, so I do 10 with my good leg and fifteen with my bad.

The step test.

Photo Credit: June Harrison

As you can see from the following picture, I am demonstrating this stretch with the use of a net. You can just as easily do this using a wall. I am keeping my knee straight and the heel on the floor. My front knee is bent slightly and I am leaning into the net. Repeat this on both sides and hold for 15 to 30 seconds.

Net stretch.

Photo Credit: June Harrison

The last leg stretch I am demonstrating here is the groin stretch. This is important because it is a very hard area to stretch, and yet, in tennis it is a very easy area to injure because you are stretching and lunging so frequently. Unfortunately, the groin muscles lag behind in strength because daily activities are usually straight ahead or backward, whereas tennis often requires quick lateral movements. It is important to hold these stretches so that you feel them, but not to the point of pain. The groin is a hard area to pinpoint when you have an injury. The injury often occurs during an overhead shot, so, again, stretch before and after you play to ensure you don't extend your body for the first time on the court.

As you can see, I have both of my hands on my hips. My toes are pointed forward and I am slowly bending one knee to the side until I feel the stretch in my groin area. Hold this stretch for 15 to 30 seconds and then repeat it.

When the pros are ready to start serving in the warm-up you will see most of them do the same thing on their first four or five service motions. The pros casually walk up to the baseline and without checking their position or worrying about which box they are serving to, they fire off a few very loose easy serves. This motion keeps them relaxed, carefully warms-up their shoulder area, and allows them to gently raise their arms over their head. They really don't have to practice their serves. It is too late for that. They are simply trying to stay limber and relaxed. Why don't you try it?

Groin stretch.

Photo Credit: June Harrison

Armed and Ready

I chose to demonstrate two arm stretches that I find particularly helpful. The first is for my triceps. As you can see, I am reaching behind my back with one arm over my shoulder and the other arm under while I am interlacing my hands. I will hold this stretch for 15 to 30 seconds, relax, and then repeat it again on the other side. Repeat this exercise three times.

Tricep stretch.

Photo Credit: June Harrison

The second arm stretch is a wonderful stretch that is good for both my arms and shoulders. As you can see from the following picture, I have one arm out in front of me and across my chest. With my other hand, I am pulling on the elbow of that arm. I will hold this stretch for 15 to 30 seconds and do the same on the other arm, then repeat it.

Arm stretch.

Photo Credit: June Harrison

Hand It to Me

The stretch that you see me demonstrating is for my forearms and hands. This is not an area you think about stretching. But when you play tennis for three hours and your hand has been gripping the racquet, you need to release all the tension in that area.

When you tighten your grip you tense up your forearm, and if you do it too often and your point of impact is incorrect, you will be well on the way to getting the dreaded tennis elbow.

As you can see, with my elbow straight and my palm up, I use my opposite hand to stretch my wrist back. I repeat on both sides twice, holding the stretch for 15 to 30 seconds.

Forearm and hand stretch.

Photo Credit: June Harrison

This stretch could also be done with a three-pound weight, curling the hand up and down while holding the weight. This will stretch as well as strengthen your hands.

Feet First

This is the last part of the body to stretch before you are all stretched out. As you can see from the next photo, I am lifting one leg up and gently moving my foot around. I repeat this with the other leg as well. Do this for 15 seconds, then change legs.

You can also do an easy heel/toe exaggerated walk motion to help stretch out this area.

Double Fault

Be sure you wear appropriate clothes to warm-up in. They should be loose-fitting, and their weight should suit the climate you are in.

109

Foot stretch and flex.

Photo Credit: June Harrison

Pregame Stretching and Warm-up

Believe it or not, before you do any stretching, you should warm-up. This is to get the blood flowing to your muscles. This can be only 5 to 10 minutes of a brisk walk, or perhaps a bike ride to the tennis courts.

Passing Shots

Martina Navratilova would prepare for her matches by either jumping rope or stretching, so that when her match was called she would be warmed-up and ready to go.

Some players like to ride a stationary bike or use the treadmill to get their heart rate up. Remember that you are exercising only to pump the blood so that you can begin your stretching. Stop the warm-up when you begin to perspire.

Try to stretch those areas of your body that feel tight and be sure you stretch both sides equally. Make sure that you don't force a stretch until it hurts. While stretching, don't jerk or try to increase the length of a stretch, as this could result in an injury.

After you have done some slow, deliberate stretching of all of your muscles, you are ready to play! Did I hear you say "finally"?

Post-Game Cool Down

After a match, you should shower immediately. Even though it feels wonderful to stand under a very hot shower, use cool water and let the water run on your entire body. You should then stretch all parts of your body again. These stretches should be done to ensure that your body does not get tight and inflexible. As muscles get fatigued, they will stiffen up. If you have an injury, now is the time to ice it. See Chapter 15 for more information.

Use the stretches illustrated in the earlier warm-up section of this chapter. They are just as appropriate for the cool-down period.

Relaxation Techniques

Tennis players get all pumped up when they play a match, so it is very important to find ways to relax after the game. I mean more than just packing up your gear and heading for the nearest pub, although the Aussies would tell you that this is the cheapest form of relaxation.

Many players do yoga, one of the oldest forms of exercise. It combines breathing techniques, stretching, balance, and meditation. It is one of the best forms of relaxation I know. You can do it in a group with an instructor, or you can find a quiet corner of the locker room or your home, and begin. Lay down a mat or a thick towel, turn down the lights, turn off the kids and the television, take the phone off the hook, and for at least 15 minutes turn off the world.

Yoga is excellent for people of all ages. It forces you to take time for yourself and to do something good for your body.

Tai chi is an ancient Chinese form of exercise that utilizes relaxation techniques along with breathing and balance. It is a wonderful and beautiful way to bring your mind and body into peaceful harmony.

Double Fault

When you are doing your cool-down stretches, remember you are already warm so you are probably more flexible than when you did the warm-up routine. You may be able to take each stretch just a little further so take it easy. Always hold, don't over-extend, and don't jerk or bounce.

Concentration of mind and body.

Photo Credit: Vicki Fort

Push Me, Pull Me

If I win the lottery, I am going to hire a massage therapist so that I can have a massage every day. This is my idea of heaven—at least as far as relaxation is concerned.

Double Fault

Drink plenty of water after any form of exercise, but particularly after a massage. You need to help rinse out your body and get rid of the toxins.

Massage is more important than you think. It isn't just a treat you give yourself after a hard week with the kids or a tough day at the office. Professional athletes will tell you that massage is absolutely essential to get your body back into shape after a tough game.

Good massage therapists will stretch and manipulate you so your muscles work all the bad toxins out of your body. It is very important after a good strong massage to drink lots and lots of water.

There are different kinds of massages. I happen to like a deep massage that allows the therapist to really manipulate deep into the muscle. Some people don't like a hard massage and would prefer the spa touch.

This is a "feel good" experience and believe me, we all need that every now and again. However, it does not help your tired, stiff, shortened muscles if they are not pushed and pulled just a little. Get a good sports massage.

Heaven.
Photo Credit: Vicki Fort

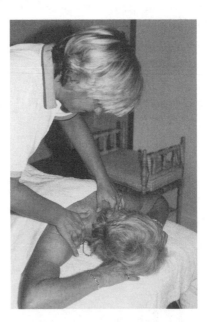

Even if you don't have time for a full one-hour massage, treat yourself to a shorter version or even take one of those 15-minute chair massages. I guarantee you will feel better immediately.

Your body will say thank-you in various ways. No more aching back, stiff neck, or pulsing headache as you allow the masseuse to work out the tension.

Let's Think About It

Even if you cannot do any of these forms of relaxation, try to meditate. If it is not too painful and stressful, try to imagine your match and replay some of the points. Use this as a positive tool as you visualize your good shots as well as your bad.

Sometimes it pays to be able to tune everything out even when you are on the court. When you play a tournament, the conditions are not always perfect. Planes fly over, trains go by, babies cry, and sometimes your opponent grunts loudly on every point. You need to be able to train yourself to focus on the job at hand. You do not, however, want to go into a dreamy meditative state. Otherwise, before you know it, you will be shaking hands with your opponent. You do need to be able to block out life and concentrate on the ball and the score, and visualize what you need to do to win. I will tell you more about this when we get to the mental side of tennis.

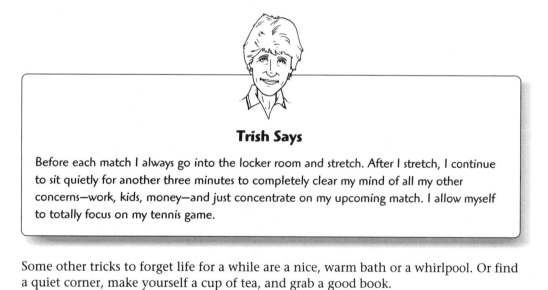

Trish Says

Before each match I always go into the locker room and stretch. After I stretch, I continue to sit quietly for another three minutes to completely clear my mind of all my other concerns—work, kids, money—and just concentrate on my upcoming match. I allow myself to totally focus on my tennis game.

Some other tricks to forget life for a while are a nice, warm bath or a whirlpool. Or find a quiet corner, make yourself a cup of tea, and grab a good book.

Remember, deep breathing is your cheapest and easiest form of relaxation. Peace and quiet around you also allows you to unwind.

Relax, you deserve it.
Photo Credit: June
Harrison

Props for Staying Flexible for Tennis

Most of the pros travel with a Sportcord or a long piece of rubber tubing which can be used for stretching when they are on the road and unable to get to a gym.

These can be purchased at any sporting goods store. They come in different lengths, but a basic stretch tube should be about 3 to 4 feet long. They often come with a set of simple exercises that are for stretching and, in some cases, rehabilitation of an injured body part. Don't try to do this without getting instructions from a physical therapist.

Just one more.
Photo Credit: Vicki Fort

Small hand weights are also useful when trying to stretch and tone. Depending on your goals, you will need different exercises and weights. I suggest you speak with a personal trainer who can give you tips on special exercises and personalize your training routine. Personal trainers are worth the cost. I recommend that everyone who wants to get into a regular exercise routine should book at least six half-hour sessions with a personal trainer.

Knowing you must be at the gym for an appointment makes you get up and go. The trainer will show you how to work all the machines and free weights. The trainer will also evaluate your body type and tell you where you need work. Trainers are great for motivation and encouragement.

It takes a lot of time off the court to keep your body in shape not just for tennis, but for living. It's worth it—keep it up.

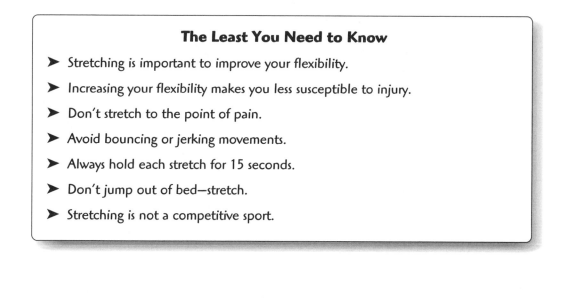

The Least You Need to Know

➤ Stretching is important to improve your flexibility.

➤ Increasing your flexibility makes you less susceptible to injury.

➤ Don't stretch to the point of pain.

➤ Avoid bouncing or jerking movements.

➤ Always hold each stretch for 15 seconds.

➤ Don't jump out of bed—stretch.

➤ Stretching is not a competitive sport.

Part 3
The ABC's of Tennis

OK, you are ready to hit the ball. Get into your best outfit, grab your racquet and balls, and hightail it off to the courts.

Don't forget everything else you have read. Stretch first, check all of your equipment, and remember to look confident.

Take the right grip, some fancy footwork, and listen to everything your pro has told you and you will be just fine.

You will begin to understand what the fuss is all about. I know that once you step on that court and begin to hit the ball you will get the bug. Take your time and don't expect to learn it all at once. Just as I have taken you step by step up to this point, I will continue to make certain you have all the knowledge you need to make you into a better player.

You will learn how to serve, hit spin, and even lob your way out of trouble. Unfortunately, you will also now come up against an opponent. If you're lucky, you will find a friend who is better than you are to practice with and play against. This is the best thing that you can do right now—practice with and play against someone who is a level above you.

Now comes the hard part: doing it until you get it right!

Let's proceed. You still have a lot of lessons to learn.

Chapter 8

Let's Hold On—Learning How to Hold the Racquet

In This Chapter

➤ Watch your grip; how to hold on

➤ Two hands are better than one; double-handed shots

➤ Oh no, a southpaw; left-handers are tough opponents

➤ No frying pans here; bad grips cause injuries

When I was first started taking lessons in Australia, my coach was not world-famous and he did not teach at a large club with lots of members. His name was George Filewood and he had a court in his backyard. This was not unusual in Australia. There were plenty of private courts, and many good players were brought up on these courts.

Mr. Filewood was a stickler for form and technique. He made me practice without a ball for at least 10 minutes at the start of every lesson. He would make me grip the racquet over and over again without looking at it so that I could feel the right grip. The right grip then was the continental grip. This grip was made popular by the great Australian players in the 1940s and 1950s.

I was eight when he first started coaching me and I wanted to hit the ball any way I could. He wouldn't let me. Everything had to be perfect and he was very hard on me. He made me practice on the practice wall every day after school before I could play with the older kids. He emphasized the grip, the grip, always the grip.

Trish Says

All my students know that when they take a lesson from me they will always hear me saying, "watch your grip." I am a firm believer in insisting on the correct grip. I have actually lost students because they did not want to change their grips and they felt I was too demanding. I see them later in their tennis lives and they have not progressed as far as they should have because they were unwilling to make changes early on.

Over the last 20 years, the innovative designs and new materials used in the racquets have changed tennis. Grips and swings had to adjust to the newly found power. Apparently, none of the newer players had Mr. Filewood because they came out with all sorts of grips. But they all worked. Bjorn Borg looked like he was going to shovel something off the court when he started his swing. He did—usually he shoveled his opponents off to the locker room. Monica Seles did it her way using both hands on both sides. Many of the clay-court specialists had a grip that was more Western than John Wayne, but they managed to hit the ball with incredible topspin.

So, which grip is the right grip for you? I am not sure, so let's learn together.

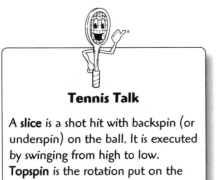

Tennis Talk

A **slice** is a shot hit with backspin (or underspin) on the ball. It is executed by swinging from high to low.
Topspin is the rotation put on the ball by swinging from low to high.

Which Hemisphere

This is a strange title for a paragraph on grips but they really are referred to as "Eastern" and "Western." The most important part of your first tennis lesson will be the grips. So, read carefully as I show you how to hold the racquet and why some grips are better than others.

The grip that I was taught to use for everything, the continental, worked very well when we hit everything flat or with a *slice*. Now when you need to hit with topspin to control the ball, this grip doesn't work as well. All of us, who were tournament players prior to the 1970s, did not use a lot of *topspin* so we were able to get away with the continental grip. This is not true now.

I am going to show you how to grip the racquet first as a right-hander. Take the racquet at the throat in your left hand. Then put your right hand just below it on the throat and slide the right hand down towards the grip going all the way to the end of the racquet. Your right hand should be slightly to the right of the center of the racquet as you look at it from the top. Take a look at the photo and see where I am holding my right hand. This is an Eastern forehand grip.

Double Faults

Make sure you buy the right size grip to prevent injuries and maximize your stroke. Check our tear-out reference card for your racquet size.

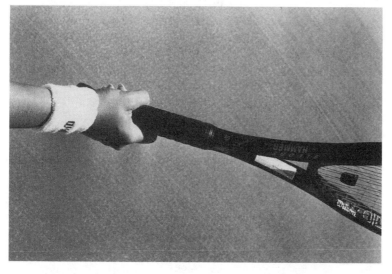

The Eastern forehand grip.
Photo Credit: June Harrison

When you grip the racquet, you should hold it firmly but not too tightly. Your first finger should be separated slightly from the others and your thumb should rest on your second finger. The top photo on the next page shows the Eastern grip from the backside.

The Eastern grip is the one you will use to hit your basic *forehand*.

If you are left-handed, you will do the same thing as the right-hander, only your left hand will slide down the side of the racquet. Your hand will be slightly on the left side of the center of the racquet as you look at the top. Check out the bottom photo on the next page if you are a leftie.

Tennis Talk

Forehand refers to the stroke hit from the right side by a right-hander or from the left side for a left-handed player.

Backside of Eastern forehand grip.

Photo Credit: June Harrison

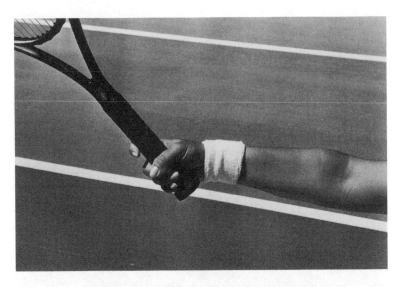

Left-handed Eastern forehand grip.

Photo Credit: June Harrison

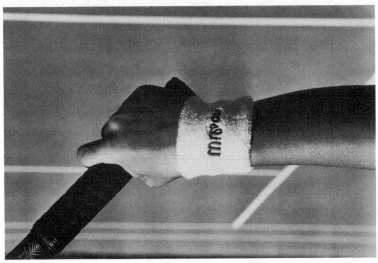

The Eastern grip should be used only for a topspin forehand. If you try to use it for any other shots, it may hurt your wrist or your elbow.

There is another grip you can use for a forehand that will give you a lot more topspin. This modified grip is called a "Western" grip. Many top players use this grip so that they can hit the ball hard and still keep it in with spin. I don't recommend this grip for a beginner, but you might want to try it, even in a modified way, if you are capable of hitting a very hard ball. This would be called a semi-Western grip.

For the Western grip, take your right hand as if you are going to use the Eastern and then turn your hand another half inch to the right. You can either keep your fingers close together or separate your first finger.

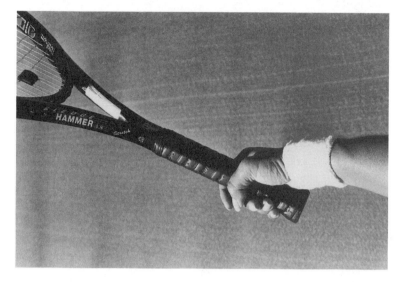

Western grip for a right-hander.

Photo Credit: June Harrison

For left-handed players, slide the left hand down the grip as if you are going to use the Eastern. At the bottom of the grip, turn the hand another half inch to the left.

Left-handed Western grip.

Photo Credit: June Harrison

Both of these grips will work for you when you learn to hit the forehand. Your professional will want you to try both, and then you will decide together which one is best for you. If you are trying to make a decision by yourself, I would suggest that you not go for the Western. When you first start to play and make contact with the ball, the least amount of grip changing you have to do will make the game easier.

Trish Says

Conchita Martinez hits her forehand with a Western grip. One day, I went out to hit with her coach and I told him I wanted to try a Western forehand. He laughed and fed me about 20 balls. I couldn't get one over with that grip. If I kept trying I might have succeeded, but I decided the Western was not for me. I'll leave it to Conchita and the others.

Tennis Talk

The **butt** is the very end of the racquet handle.

Double Faults

Remember to bring your non-racquet hand back to the racquet throat after each stroke. This way you can use your hitting hand to change your grip and your other hand to steady the racquet.

I now want to talk about the backhand grips. You have some choices, so let me explain.

To find the Eastern backhand grip, hold the racquet by the throat with your left hand and slide your right hand down the racquet. When you come to the *butt* of the racquet, turn your right hand so that it is half an inch to the left of center as you look down at the grip from the top. Look closely at the top photo on the next page showing the Eastern backhand grip so that you can tell the difference between it and the Eastern forehand.

Now for a Western backhand grip. Stand on your head...not really, but I sometimes feel that this grip makes you turn your hand inside out. Just like you did with the Western forehand, slide your right hand down the grip, but when you reach the bottom of the handle, turn your right hand an inch to the left. You will literally be around the back side of the grip, so the back of your hand is away from you. See the bottom photo on the next page for an example of the grip.

The grip that is still used by many players, certainly those who were taught prior to 1970, is the continental grip. This grip can be used for all shots. It is not necessarily the best grip for every shot, but it is certainly an easy way to play. You can hit slice forehands, volleys, slice backhands, serves, and overheads, all with a continental grip. It is not the best grip for a topspin forehand or backhand. It is an easy grip for a beginner to use because he or she won't have to worry about changing grips all the time. As you play more, you may want to experiment with other grips. To form the continental grip, take your right hand and slide it down the racquet handle so that you feel like you are gripping a hammer. Your thumb and first finger should form a "v" on the top of the racquet handle. The photo on the next page will show you how to find the continental grip on your racquet.

Eastern backhand grip.

Photo Credit: June Harrison

Western backhand grip.

Photo Credit: June Harrison

The continental grip.

Photo Credit: June Harrison

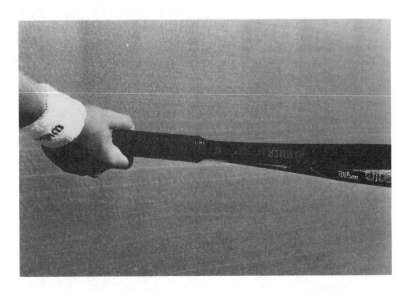

Whichever grip you decide you want to use, you will need to practice. Any grip will work if you use it often enough. I want to help you use the right grips for the right shots.

It Takes Two

Ever since Chris Evert used her double-handed backhand to win her way into the record books, players have been using this stroke. Chris's double-hander was not the first, but it is probably the most famous. To hit a backhand with two hands you will need to use the following grip. For a right-hander, you will use the Eastern forehand grip with your right hand. Then add your left hand directly on top of the right hand in a matching Eastern forehand grip as if you are left-handed. Some players modify the grips so that the hands are further around to help get better topspin. Look at the top photo on the next page to find the double-handed grip for you.

A grip with two hands gives you more power, but it does restrict your reach. Some players, like Monica Seles, use two hands on both sides. She generates incredible power, and when you have a superstar using a shot like this, you will have other players who want to copy her. For a two-handed forehand, you need to have fast reflexes. Some players switch hands so that the left hand is on the bottom. Others keep the right hand on the bottom and just add the other hand. Look at the bottom photo on the next page and at the photo at the top of page 128 to see examples of a two-handed forehand. The first one shows the right hand on the bottom. The second shows the switch so that the left hand moves to the bottom of the grip.

Double-handed backhand grip. (Right-handed)

Photo Credit: June Harrison

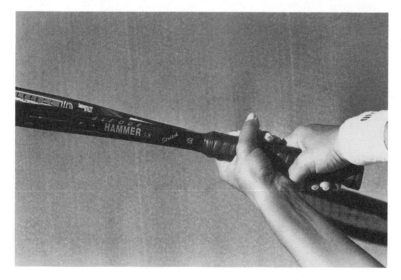

Double-handed forehand grip with right hand on the bottom.

Photo Credit: June Harrison

When you start to play, you will want to experiment with one and two hands. I think a two-handed forehand is tough to execute, but I would certainly recommend you try a two-handed backhand. Many beginners have a hard time hitting a backhand with one hand, so it is best to try all different ways.

Grips are very important, but you should try a few different ones to make certain you are using the right one. Depending on your strength and flexibility, you will find the one you need.

Double-handed forehand grip with left hand on the bottom. (Right-handed)

Photo Credit: June Harrison

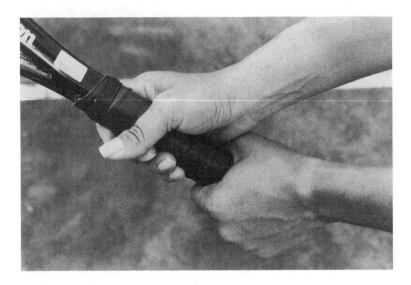

Left or Right, Which Is Better

Most adults know whether they are right- or left-handed. It is very difficult to tell which hand a very young child should use because children tend to be ambidextrous. I will ask a child to throw me a ball and then catch a ball. Sometimes the child will throw with one hand and try to catch with another, so it does take a few games of catch before you figure out which hand is dominant.

Trish Says

Marie Pinterova from Hungary uses both hands when she plays. She serves with her left hand, then switches the racquet to her right hand to play ground strokes. When it comes to hitting overheads, she uses either hand. I played her in the finals of the ITF World Championships. We had a very, very close match. I was forever trying to remember which was her forehand side. Although she lacked power off both sides, she confuses her opponents. It worked on me!

If you are completely ambidextrous, then I would recommend you try to play left-handed. Why, you ask? I firmly believe that, in tennis, lefties have a distinct advantage. First, I hate playing them. Second, they have a spin on their serve that is very difficult to return.

If you look through the record books, many of the more famous names have been left-handers—Tilden, Laver, McEnroe, and Navratilova, to name a few of the greats. Lefties can serve more easily into a right–hander's backhand on both sides. As most players are right-handed, we all tend to practice our passing shots and approach shots for righties. I know that when I play a leftie, I have to think every time I am going to play the ball so that I hit it to their weakness, which is usually the backhand, and not to their strength. Any time you have to think about your stroke in a match instead of hitting the ball instinctively, you risk making an error.

Trish Says

At one tournament, Martina Navratilova and I were staying in the same complex. After practice one day we decided to have a friendly set of doubles. My partner, who was a good A-club player, absolutely could not return Martina's serve. Martina was trying to be nice and not serve too hard, but in doing so she put so much spin on her serve that when it hit the court it spun wildly and jumped away from my partner. We all laughed, but it gave us a healthy respect for Martina's tour opponents.

Choke Up

If you are having trouble contacting the ball, particularly at the net on your volleys, many professionals will tell you to move your hand higher on the grip. This is called "choking up" on the grip.

I will often start a beginner with this grip because it really helps the new player gain confidence. By choking up on the grip, the beginner is likely to make contact with the ball more easily.

As you can see from the photo on the next page, whether you are right- or left-handed, your hand needs to move up to the middle of the leather-wrapped grip so that you are about two inches from the butt of the racquet.

Choke up for control.

Photo Credit: June
Harrison

I advise this only for young children with racquets that are too big for them or adults who have trouble connecting with the ball. I allow my students to use this grip only on volleys and basic ground strokes. It should not be used on the serve or the overhead where you need extension.

Double Faults

The worst mistake new players can make is to hold the grip too tightly. This causes loss in racquet head speed and possible injury to the wrist, elbow, or shoulder. So no death grips allowed.

I do not let my students use it for too long because it gives them a false sense of control. It is a good learning tool but should not be continued as you progress. Once you do it for too long at the net, it is very easy to slip into the choke grip when you play because it does give you more of the punch feeling you need on volleys.

With the advent of extender racquets, it does not make much sense to buy an extra-long racquet, balanced very carefully by the manufacturer for the specific weight and length, and then have you chop off the extra inch by gripping it higher up the shaft.

My advice then, choke up if you are having trouble connecting on volleys or ground strokes. Use it as a learning device, then try to move your hand back down into the correct position which is with the edge of your hand resting on the raised end of the racquet grip. Check the photo on the next page to make certain you know the correct hand position whether you are using Eastern, Western, or continental.

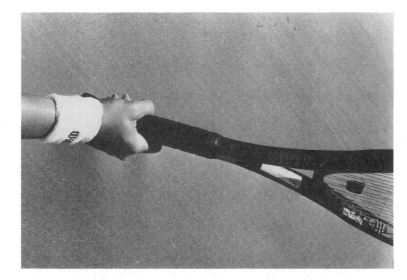

The correct hand position.

Photo Credit: June Harrison

Grips are the very basis of your game. Work on them early and I promise you will not have problems later on. Wrong grips mean inability to get more power, more mistakes due to not enough spin, and, of course, injuries due to strain on the arms, shoulders, and wrists. Did I scare you enough? Good, now listen to me so that you play with the right grips!

The Least You Need to Know

➤ You have a choice of grips; do not be forced into one that doesn't feel comfortable.

➤ Left-handers have a slight advantage in tennis.

➤ Choke up on the grip if you cannot connect with the ball.

➤ Do not hold the racquet too tightly.

➤ Double-handed grips give you less reach but more power.

Chapter 9

Something in the Way She Moves: Footwork

> ## In This Chapter
>
> ➤ Ready, set, go; how to get started
>
> ➤ Keep your balance; smoothest moves on the court
>
> ➤ Dancing feet; great footwork makes a champion
>
> ➤ How to react faster

There are only a few players that have gone down in the history books as being truly graceful tennis players. The first one that comes to mind is Suzanne Lenglen. In every photo of Lenglen, you see that her feet are off the ground as she is flying to hit the ball at full stretch. By today's standards she may not have been graceful, but I wouldn't be either with all those clothes on. Second to her is the Brazilian beauty Maria Bueno whose flowing strokes and Tinling outfits dazzled the crowds. The earlier men players showed class and style: Tilden, Budge, Australian star Norman Brookes, and in later years, Pancho Gonzales.

During the last 20 years, no one has been more graceful than Evonne Goolagong Cawley from Australia. Learning to play tennis barefoot in the outback, she glided around a tennis court as if she were on ice. Always smiling, Goolagong exemplified an athlete that was in love with her sport.

But, you don't have to be graceful to have good footwork. The current stars rely more on strength than balletic grace, but there are still a few players who warrant a second

look. On the men's side, Stefan Edberg is always smooth. Pete Sampras has great footwork and incredible reach. In my opinion, the most athletic is Patrick Rafter from Australia. On the women's side, Martina Hingis uses as little energy as possible as she scurries around the court. Her anticipation is her greatest strength.

To reach any level of professional tennis, you must have good footwork. To be one of the best professionals, you must have *great* footwork. I would like to share with you some of the pros' secrets to great footwork.

Ready Position

This is stage one of learning tennis. It is a position that you will constantly resume throughout each point, so it is very important that you find a comfortable *ready position*.

Stand on the baseline with your feet about shoulder width apart, toes facing the net. Take the racquet and hold it by the throat with your non-hitting hand. Hold on to the grip with your grip of choice, let's say the Eastern forehand. Make certain the head of the racquet is cocked up above the wrist, which means you need to firm up the wrist and push down slightly on the butt of the racquet. Extend your arms slightly away from your body. Bend your knees and put the weight onto the balls of your feet. You are now READY. Take a look at this photo and practice this position over and over again. You will be in it many times during play.

Trish at the ready position.
Photo Credit: June Harrison

The ready position does not vary much with each player. Some have a slightly wider stance, but that usually relates to their height and longer leg length. You will need to keep looking at your stance like a dancer does in a mirror. Check the knees, back, and arms. They should all look like you are ready to pounce.

Check that stance.

Photo Credit: June Harrison

Depending on the shot that is coming towards you, you will push off from the ready position to either the right or the left side. Remember, the ready position, or the split-step position as it is sometimes called, is the stance you come back to between each shot so that you can push off again in any direction.

Trish Says

I remember playing against American Frank Froehling once in mixed doubles. Frank is very tall and thin and when he stands in his ready position he looks like a giant spider. I looked up when I was ready to serve and he seemed to be covering the entire backcourt. I am sure he managed to force a few double faults out of my partner and me, simply by looking like he could cover everything.

The ready position is aptly named, because you assume it when you are waiting to receive serve and during every pause of play as the ball crosses the net. Get ready!

A Balancing Act

Tennis is a game of movement and balance. As you progress, you will no longer be trying to hit the ball from a stationary position because your opponent will be running you all over the court. It is therefore very important that you work on your footwork so that you always maintain your balance.

In this photo you will see that I am stretching for a ball. Yet, because I am able to keep my feet moving and maintain my balance, I am still able to make a good shot.

Maintain your balance.

Photo Credit: June Harrison

Maintaining balance is not simple when you are moving from side to side, trying to watch your opponent and the ball at the same time. For a start, you must always come back to the ready position, so that you are always pushing off from a balance point. In tennis, using your feet is a must; however, to keep your balance you will also need to use your head, shoulders, arms, back, hips, and legs.

Most of the movement in tennis is done on the balls of your feet. I don't mean on your toes—I mean the balls of the feet. To quickly check what this means, take a look at the top photo on the next page. Notice that my heels are up off the ground, but I have flexed my arch and kept the whole part of the front of my shoe on the ground.

Learning balance is very difficult. It is something that must come naturally. I can give you some tricks for improving your balance, but, like good footwork, it will take work and constant practice.

Trish, stay ready.

Photo Credit: June Harrison

When you are moving around the court, the two areas of your body that will help you the most are your quads (upper, outside thigh muscles) and your non-hitting arm. If you keep your knees bent and you keep coming back to your ready position, your quads will always be working. If you watch any good player, you will notice that he or she is always using the other arm as a balance. If you keep your shoulders in line and don't jerk your hips around, you will stay balanced.

If you choose to have a double-handed backhand or forehand, you will need to have extraordinary balance. Your normal balancing arm is still on the racquet so you will have to depend more and more on your feet, legs, and shoulders. Take a look at this photo of Chris Evert and see how her bodyline keeps her balanced.

Chris Evert: What balance!

Photo Credit: June Harrison

Double Fault

Keep your non-hitting arm up above your waist so that it always acts like a tightrope walker's pole as you keep your balance.

I am going to suggest that you try some of the drills my students do to improve their footwork. Some of them can be done off the court, and others need some space, like a tennis court.

First, let's grab a jump rope. When you first start, take it easy and make sure you don't jump on a hard surface. Don't jump too high and remember that you are trying to use your feet and not your legs. If you have ever watched a boxer jump rope using fancy footwork, then you will have some idea of how you should be working your feet. Jumping rope is the best and simplest exercise there is. All you need is a rope and the desire.

Using the lines on a tennis court, do some crossovers and sidestepping. Alternate the exercises—do five crossovers, then five sidesteps. Try not to look down at your feet so that you can work on balance as well as staying on the balls of your feet. This is also a good way to warm up after you have stretched.

Here is one last simple exercise that really helps your balance as well as strengthens your ankles. It is called proprioception. Stand on one foot with your knee slightly bent and both arms out to the side at shoulder height. Bring your other leg back with the knee slightly bent. Try to hold this position for at least 15 seconds. You will wobble around at first but keep trying it, switching legs, and you will improve. I am trying my best to keep my balance in this photo.

A stork can do better.
Photo Credit: Vicki Fort

There are many other ways to work on your footwork and balance. Plain old dancing is the most enjoyable, and you don't even know you are working on your tennis.

Shall We Dance?

If you have seen a men's singles match on red clay at the French Open, you have seen a choreographer's dream. I love watching men's tennis on a slower surface. You see every strength and weakness and the longer games show up those players who are not fit.

If you were to retrace all those steps that the players took during a match, you would find that they had danced a marathon. Good opponents will make you cover the entire court area from the net to 10 feet behind the baseline and 6 feet either side of the sidelines.

You need to learn how to get from the baseline to the net as quickly as possible. Then, unfortunately, you need to learn how to get back to the baseline again, all in the same point. Part of the learning process is fitness but mostly it is knowing when to split-step, when to push off, and which foot to use.

When you need to chase down a wide ball to your right, you have two choices. Push off from your left foot so that you can take a step with your right, or pivot on your right foot and cross over with the left foot and start running. Look at these two photos on the next page and you will see the different ways to begin your movement.

Double Fault

The best way to get maximum movement on clay is to slide to the wide or short balls. You must be well balanced and stop running about 3 feet short of the ball so that you can slide into the shot.

As you improve, your movements will become more natural and more fluid. Keep jumping rope and doing your drills. If you practice your footwork even half as much as you practice your strokes, you are well on the way to moving like a pro.

If you want to practice into the wee hours—go ahead. John Travolta plays a pretty mean game of tennis.

Trish, pushing off from her left foot.

Photo Credit: June Harrison

Pivoting on her right foot.

Photo Credit: June Harrison

Best Foot Forward

Once you have done all the drills and practiced your ready position, you will now have to make some decisions out on the court.

Tennis is a game of split-second decisions. When you see the ball coming off your opponent's racquet you have to decide—forehand or backhand, right foot moves first or left foot?

When you move to the ball, you will have to decide what you are going to do with the ball and where you are going to hit it. Too much to think about—you're right. This is why you are taught the basics first.

Tennis Talk

Weight transfer is the motion of stepping into the stroke and putting the balanced body weight onto that foot just prior to striking the ball.

Each time you hit the ball, one foot or the other must take the weight. When I first teach you the ground strokes, I will ask you to put your weight into the ball. Just before you hit the ball, you need to step and transfer the weight. Moving your balance from one foot to the other is called *weight transfer*. For the forehand, if you are right-handed, you will transfer the weight and step with the left foot. See the photo for the forehand.

Step with the left.

Photo Credit: June Harrison

When you prepare to hit a backhand, make certain you do not step straight across to the side. You always need to step forward, towards the net. If you are right-handed, you will step with your right foot towards the net just before you make contact with the ball. Check out the footwork in the photo on the next page.

The more weight you can transfer into the shot, the more pace (speed) you will get on the ball.

Step into the shot.

Photo Credit: June Harrison

Double Fault

When using an open stance to hit ground strokes or volleys, make certain that your shoulders have turned towards the side just like a regular ground stroke, where you step into the ball. An open foot position does not mean an open shoulder position.

Open or Closed

When you run to hit the ball, you will have to make all those split-second decisions. You will find that some of those decisions become instinctive as you play more.

When you play singles, you must cover more court than when you play in a doubles match. If you have to run very wide for a forehand or a backhand, you will need to cover as much court as possible and still be able to get back into position. There are two schools of thought on chasing these wide shots. The conservatives teach the old-fashioned way—try reaching the shot by crossing the leg closest to the net over to the ball. See this movement in this photo.

Crossover to reach the wide ones.

Photo Credit: Vicki Fort

The pros today, particularly those with Western or semi-Western grips, move to hit those wide balls with an open stance. This means that you do not cross your front foot in front of your body to reach the ball. You rotate your shoulders but you put the weight on the near-side foot (the foot nearest the ball). To hit a forehand you will lean on the right foot (if you're a right-hander) or left foot (if you are a leftie). Take a look at the difference in footwork in this photo compared to the previous one.

Rotate the shoulders and reach.

Photo Credit: June Harrison

As you can see, footwork is very important when you play, whether you are a beginner or a pro. It takes off-court work, on-court reactions, and some fancy moves to beat your opponents.

Now that you have bought all the equipment, found a court and a pro, stretched, studied the grips and the footwork, wouldn't you like to hit some balls?

The Least You Need to Know

➤ The ready position is used frequently during each point.

➤ Jumping rope is the best and easiest footwork exercise there is.

➤ Use your legs and arms to help keep your balance.

➤ You get more power if you transfer your weight before you hit the ball.

➤ On wide balls, using an open stance is now considered a better method to reach the shot.

Chapter 10

Time to Swing— Basic Tennis Shots

In This Chapter

➤ Catch me if you can; play catch to help your coordination

➤ Stroke the ball; don't use muscle

➤ Swing low, swing high; pick your shots

➤ A slice a day; your bread-and-butter shot

Now is the time for all well-read people to hit the courts. You have probably read more about tennis than I ever knew even when I was playing at Wimbledon.

When I first started to play, it was because I loved hitting the ball with the racquet. I enjoyed the feeling I got when I saw the ball go where I aimed it. It really didn't have a lot to do with beating my opponent or winning trophies. I just wanted to play. As I got older, winning mattered more, but I still played because I loved the sport. When I played the international circuit, there was no prize money. We received some expenses and hospitality, but when we won the tournament, all we were handed was a silver plate.

Trish Says

In 1971, I reached the round of 16 at the U.S. Open. I won $1,750 and this was really the first time I had won more than a few hundred dollars at any tournament. I thought that this was great. If I got that far today, I would take home about $45,000. In tennis years, I was born too soon.

Even before big purses, the tournaments were just as prestigious. Except for a few years when some of the players were banned from playing, all the best players competed. So, why did we do it? Not for fortune, certainly—maybe fame was a reason for some. It certainly wasn't for me. I believe it was for personal accomplishment and pride. And the best reason, because we loved the game.

I still play competitive tennis at an international level. Am I winning large amounts of money? No. Am I still improving my game? Yes. Do I still love to play? Of course I do. You cannot do the same thing for 50 years and not love it.

I love the challenge of trying to hit the ball perfectly every time it comes over the net. Some days, I cannot find that perfect stroke. The court seems too small and the net too high. On those days, I go back to basics. I go over in my mind how to hit the strokes. The same strokes I am going to teach you right now. Pay attention; you are going to hit the ball.

Play Catch

My father tells me that from the age of two all I ever wanted to do was play "bat and ball." Lucky for me, he was a good daddy. He would take me out into the backyard, throw me the ball, and let me hit it with an old, sawn-off racquet. If your father did that for you with any sort of a ball, you will be steps ahead of someone who has never played catch.

If you start tennis when you are very young, one of the first things a pro will do is throw you a ball and ask you to catch it and throw it back a few times. This will tell the pro which is your dominant hand, and it will also give some clues as to your hand-eye coordination.

As you get better, your pro will devise some ball games without a racquet that will continue to help you with your visualization techniques, concentration, and coordination. Even basic juggling is helpful, because you need to concentrate on your hands, the balls, and your timing.

As a beginner, try to find a friend or a wall to help you judge the bounce of the ball. Ask your friend to throw the ball towards you. Catch the ball after it bounces once. If you are friendless, and the wall is your date, so be it. Throw the ball underhand or overhand against the wall and then run and catch it after it bounces. Do this continuously for three minutes and you will be working on your footwork, as well as learning how to react to a moving ball. This is also a good rainy day activity if the courts are too wet.

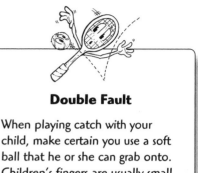

Double Fault

When playing catch with your child, make certain you use a soft ball that he or she can grab onto. Children's fingers are usually small, so it's hard for a child to hold a hard ball. Make it a fun, pleasurable, and satisfying experience.

If you have young children, take the time to play catch with them. It is fun. It is family time, and it is a healthy activity which will serve your child well as he or she grows up to play sports. It will also help you keep your eye on the ball.

How to Hit a Groundie

What is a groundie? If you listen to the professionals, you will realize they are talking about *ground strokes*.

Some professionals will teach you how to volley first, as this tends to be an easier shot to hit over the net. Certainly with young children, it gives them instant success.

So that you can get out on the court and rally with a friend, we will start with the ground strokes.

Tennis Talk

A **ground stroke** is a tennis shot you hit in the backcourt after the ball has bounced. A **volley** is a shot hit before the ball bounces. A **rally** is a series of shots making up a point.

Our first shot is the forehand. Refer to Chapter 8 if you need to refresh your memory on the grips. You will need to use the Eastern forehand grip. This is where your hand is slightly to the right of center if you are right-handed, or just to the left of center if you are left-handed.

Remember the most-used position in tennis? The ready position. I want you to start in this position, facing the net, feet apart, and both hands on the racquet, so that you are ready to move to the ball.

Ready to move.

Photo Credit: June
Harrison

A good professional will have you move to the ball and swing four or five times before you actually try to hit the ball. You will have a lot to think about as the ball travels towards you, so the more your stroke comes naturally to you, the easier it will be. I always demonstrate very slowly, two or three times, the exact swing I want just before I start to feed balls to my students. This way I hope they can picture the shot just before they go to start the motion.

The traditional forehand stroke is very simple, and I am going to keep it that way. You want to get the racquet lower than the ball, make contact out in front of your body, and swing out towards your target. Tennis is a game of variables, so you take your simple forehand and adjust to the pace of the ball, the height, and the direction.

The hardest thing to learn in tennis is timing. Each ball comes at you differently, so no two strokes are the same. I am teaching you the basic stroke and you will need to adapt to the ball.

Now let's prepare your body for the shot. You are going to turn your body to the side as the ball is traveling over the net. Keep the racquet in the same ready position as you turn to the side, then release your hand from the throat of the racquet. Take the racquet back so the head of the racquet is slightly below your hand and below the ball as you prepare to hit it. The shoulder turn and the racquet going back should happen simultaneously. As the ball is coming off your opponent's racquet and crossing the net you need to make some decisions—forehand or backhand, short or long. Your feet will need to react as much as your hands and shoulders.

Rotate your shoulders and hips.

Photo Credit: June Harrison

Now you have the racquet back, the other hand should be just above your hips pointing towards your target on the other side. As the ball comes over the net, move your feet to a position about 5 feet behind where you expect the ball to bounce. With your shoulder pointing at the net, and the ball coming to the side of your body, start to step with your left foot (if you are right-handed), towards the ball. If you are left-handed, you will be using your right foot. Start your swing from below the ball, make your contact point just in front of your front foot. The *racquet face* should be parallel with the net.

Making contact.

Photo Credit: June Harrison

As you are making contact with the ball, you begin to open up the shoulders so that they end up facing the target by the time you finish your follow-through. After you have hit the ball, continue your swing so that your hand extends out towards the far end of the court. Then finish with your arm and racquet continuing around in front of your face until the racquet comes over the left shoulder (for a right-hander).

A nice, long follow-through.

Photo Credit: June Harrison

I want you to remember the main points of the forehand swing:

➤ You need to turn to the side.

➤ You should have the racquet head below the ball before you make contact.

➤ You must follow through after you make contact.

➤ And the #1 rule in tennis—you must watch the ball!

Back to Backhands

When you first start to learn the backhand, pros will tell you, "don't worry, it is a very natural swing." Well, they are right. What they forget to mention, however, is how weak your wrist and arm are when placed in the position for a *backhand* hit.

When I was learning the backhand, I was given two choices, flat or slice. When you are eight years old, this is one too many, so I tended to always hit slice. A slice gives you control because you hit underspin, which causes the ball to stay on the open racquet face longer, while the flat shot is hit with the racquet face level and the swing is usually low and hard. I went a long way with a limited backhand. I can place the ball on a dime, but it is difficult for me to generate a lot of pace. Today, most beginners, particularly young players, are taught to hit with *topspin* and then the slice comes later. I will not even let my students hit a flat backhand anymore. So, here are your choices, which will be too many even if you are 80 years old!

Tennis Talk

Backhand is the stroke you hit by taking the racquet back across your body and making contact by leading with the back of your hand on the racquet.

To hit a basic one-handed backhand with topspin from the ready position you will need to remember a short checklist as you prepare to hit the ball. First, you must turn to the side. If you are right-handed, you will rotate to your left. Left-handers will rotate to their right. Even if you are going to hit the ball with one hand, you will take the racquet back across your body with both hands still on the racquet. You will hold the throat of the racquet lightly with the non-playing hand so that you can move your playing hand around to the Eastern backhand grip. This grip, if you recall, is to the left of center if you are right-handed and to the right of center if you are left-handed. As you can see from the bottom photo on the next page, both hands are on the racquet as I change the grip and turn my shoulders to hit a right-handed, topspin backhand with an Eastern grip.

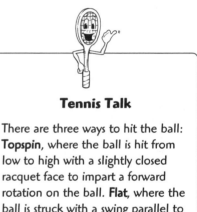

Tennis Talk

There are three ways to hit the ball: **Topspin**, where the ball is hit from low to high with a slightly closed racquet face to impart a forward rotation on the ball. **Flat**, where the ball is struck with a swing parallel to the ground and a level racquet face. **Slice** where the swing starts above the ball and the racquet face is open while it chops down on the back of the ball.

As the ball is traveling over the net and you are starting to get ready to hit a backhand, don't forget to move your feet also. Many players turn and step all at the same time. This gets you into the sideways position that you want, but now you have committed to a hitting position before you know where the ball is. You must move to the ball by staying behind it and to the side as you determine where the ball is going to bounce. While you are moving into position, take your racquet back to a point that is about one foot below the ball with the racquet face slightly closed (meaning that the strings are facing the ground just a little bit).

Rotate to prepare for the backhand.

Photo Credit: June Harrison

Good preparation for the backhand.

Photo Credit: June Harrison

As you are about to swing forward to make contact, transfer the weight to your front foot. This will be the right foot for a right-hander and the left foot for a leftie. Start your swing from low to high and attempt to make contact with the ball at about waist height. Your grip should be firm and your knuckles should be pointing towards the top of the net as you make contact. See how my weight is forward in this next photo.

Put your weight forward.

Photo Credit: June Harrison

After you make contact, continue your swing outwards and upwards while you begin to open your shoulders so that you will face the target when you have finished your swing. Notice the big follow-through on the topspin in the following photo.

Big finish.

Photo Credit: June Harrison

Check your backhand grip one more time for a good topspin on the ball.

153

Passing Shots

Billie Jean King was one of the first women players to have a truly good one-handed, topspin backhand. She would bend her knees and get that racquet down low, and then she would accelerate and swing her left arm back as she was hitting the ball with her right hand.

Now to my favorite backhand—the slice (as if you didn't already know). The really great players use both slice and topspin, but many of them use the slice backhand as their regular bread-and-butter shot. Steffi Graf had a great slice backhand even though she would run around it to hit her forehand whenever she could. But her detractors always said that she lost some of her matches on faster surfaces because she did not have a topspin backhand. She does have one—she just doesn't feel as comfortable using the topspin. So in a tight point, she always uses her slice. Martina Navratilova did the same. Very rarely did Martina roll over a backhand to give it any decent amount of topspin.

To hit the slice, your shoulder preparation is the same. Rotate your shoulders and bring both hands back on the racquet. Instead of dropping the racquet head down below the ball, position the racquet head up above your shoulders. Your grip moves to a continental grip, which is the grip right in the middle of the handle. Your hand makes a "v" straight down the throat to the base of the grip. Look at the difference in preparation for the slice in this photo.

Racquet starts up high.

Photo Credit: June Harrison

Shoulder rotation is very pronounced in the slice backswing. Your wrist is very firm and the racquet face is now open (facing the sky) at least 30 percent to help create the underspin and backspin. Closed face means the face is pointing toward the ground. As you move your feet to hit the ball, remember, you never want to catch up to the ball prior to contact. You must stay back behind the bounce and to the side. The one problem with a slice is the high ball. It is very difficult to get good power off a high slice ball. As you swing down and forward to hit the ball, continue to keep your wrist very, very firm. You do not want to drop the racquet head and lose control over the wrist. Keep your body sideways, step forward into the ball, and begin to give the ball a stroke similar to a kind of karate chop. Look at my position in the following photo.

Chop, chop.
Photo Credit: Vicki Fort

The hardest part of the slice is keeping control after the contact. Most players let their wrists go and fail to execute a full follow-through. The slice finish is more like a volley—short and sweet, with a very firm wrist, even at the end. Your shoulders don't open as much and your body stays down and forward for as long as possible. You want to imagine you are looking down the sight of a gun as you watch the ball, keeping your head and eyes on it for the follow-through. See how controlled my body and racquet are in this photo.

Slice finish.
Photo Credit: Vicki Fort

The difference between these two shots from the hitter's standpoint is the grip, the backswing, and the follow through. From the receiver's view, the ball comes towards you with either topspin or underspin. Either way, you will need to react quickly and keep your wrist firm to counteract the spin.

Thirty years ago when I was teaching, I started off my pupils with flat ground strokes and then progressed them to spins. With all the new equipment, players now can hit with so much more power, even as beginners, that I now try to make my students hit with spin right from the beginning.

Short or Deep

One of the choices you have to make when you are hitting the ground stroke is how deep you need to return the ball. If you already have your opponent way back out of position, then you do not want to hit the next ball deep again. The same applies if your opponent is up close to the net; you will not necessarily want to hit another short shot.

How do you change the depth of your ground stroke? There are a couple of ways. First, if you get under the ball more by dropping the racquet head lower, you will lift the ball higher over the net. This will make the ball travel deeper. Second, if you hit the basic ground stroke harder by accelerating the racquet head just before impact, the ball will go deeper.

However, altering the follow-through is the most often-used technique to make the ball travel deep. The longer and higher the follow-through, the deeper the ball will go. By using the follow-through, you also gain control of the ball. If you accelerate and add speed, the ball moves faster, but you will also lose some control. If you simply lift the ball and float it back, you run the risk of your opponent being able to attack the higher ball. So, I advise you to use the follow-through to help guide the ball deeper with control.

When you wish to hit the ball shorter, you will need to vary these same things. A slow ball will not go deep, but it may still float up high and short so that the opponent can pounce on the ball. The same will apply when you get under the ball too much. Again, you will need to vary the follow-through. Shorten it, the ball will go shorter. Obviously, the more compact the swing, that is, the less back swing and less follow through, the more control you have.

When you have your opponent deep, you should hit the next ball short. When you have your opponent close to the net, you may wish to

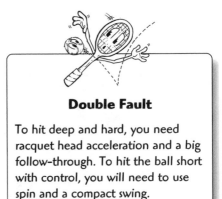

Double Fault

To hit deep and hard, you need racquet head acceleration and a big follow–through. To hit the ball short with control, you will need to use spin and a compact swing.

lob the ball over your opponent's head. The advantage of the lob is that it forces your opponent back to the baseline, and puts him or her on the defensive. I would not suggest that you attempt to drive the ball straight at your opponent, but that is an alternative.

To hit the ball short with control, you will need to use spin and a compact swing.

The Least You Need to Know

➤ Juggling or playing catch really helps your hand-eye coordination.

➤ Do not hit your ground strokes flat.

➤ Always bend your knees when you are hitting your ground strokes.

➤ The longer and faster your swing, the less control you will have over your shot.

➤ If you have your opponent deep, don't hit your next shot deep, also.

Chapter 11

Serve It Up

On rainy days in the locker room on the women's pro tour, the players would imitate different players' service motions and the other players would have to guess who they were. Not brain surgery, but these players were trying to stay calm and not think about their upcoming matches. It was amazing how many different service routines there were. You, too, can design your own.

The serve is the one part of the game where you are in charge. Your opponent has not forced you back. You are not off-balance or stretching. You can take as much time as you want. You do not have to hit the bad tosses. You are in control. How do you want to start? Do you want to bounce the ball two or three times? Would you like to stare down your opponent prior to starting your action? Some players flex their knees. Some rock back and forth. It is called the routine. You need to find one that is yours and only yours.

I am a serve and volley player so this is my favorite chapter, because I will teach you both strokes. If you are an aggressive player you will get lobbed a lot, so we have included the lob and the overhead as two other shots you will need to master if you are going to play the net.

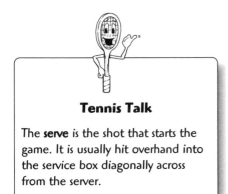

Tennis Talk

The **serve** is the shot that starts the game. It is usually hit overhand into the service box diagonally across from the server.

It's Your Serve

For all of its importance in the game, the serve is the easiest to teach. Most people know how to throw a ball. If you have never thrown one, shame on you; it will just take you a little longer to learn how to *serve*.

The hardest part of the serve is getting the proper grip, because your inclination will be to hold your racquet as you would a frying pan. You can get the ball over this way, but in the long run, you will not have a reliable serve. Use the continental grip for the serve. As a reminder, the continental grip is like a hammer hold. The "v" of the thumb and first finger is straight down the middle of the grip as you look at the top of the racquet.

Continental grip for the serve.

Photo Credit: June Harrison

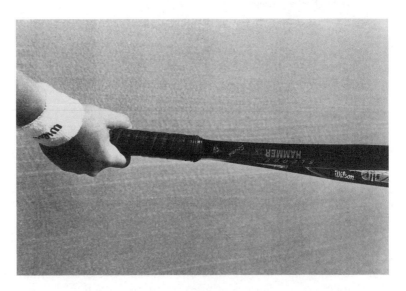

I am going to break the service motion down into three parts: the preparation, the toss, and hitting the ball. The serve we are discussing here is just a flat serve. I will walk you through the slice and twist serves later.

The first part is the stance. If you are right-handed, your left foot will be 2 inches behind the baseline at a 45-degree angle and your right foot will be the width of your shoulders apart parallel to the baseline. If you are playing singles, you will stand very close to the center hash mark on the baseline. If you are serving for doubles, you will need to stand closer to where the inner sideline meets the baseline.

Getting ready to serve.

Photo Credit: June Harrison

Point the racquet into the service box diagonally across from you. Take one or two balls, depending on whether you use a double-handed backhand—you cannot hold two balls when you hit with two hands. Rest the balls on the throat of the racquet in your non-hitting hand. Hold the racquet with the grip just above your waist and the racquet head up near your shoulders with your arms slightly extended. Everyone has a different personalized stance, so you can find your own way to start your service motion. Most players bounce the ball a few times before they start their service motion. Again, you need to find your own routine before starting your swing. Let your weight rest slightly forward.

Passing Shots

Among the men, Johannson, Sampras, Ivanisevic, and Philopousis all have serves over 130 miles an hour. In women's tennis, Venus and Serena Williams, Lindsay Davenport, and Brenda Shultz all have serves clocked at over 120 miles an hour.

Let both arms relax and drop them down until your ball tossing arm hits your thigh. Keep the ball facing your target so that your knuckles touch the leg. Keep the racquet arm swinging loosely back over your toes with the racquet head pointing at the ground. Transfer your weight slightly back to the back foot. Once your arm hits your leg, start to bring both arms up above your head. Stretch your tossing arm out to the court and then up to the sky with your arm straight, but not too stiff. Swing your racquet arm back towards the back fence, then up over your head. Your arm is straight but not stiff. Your grip is loose.

Now for the second part; once both arms are above your head, release one ball so that it goes straight up about an arm's length away from your head. A good, constant toss is the most important aspect of the serve. Bend your racquet arm at the elbow and the racquet will drop down across your back.

Lift those arms.

Photo Credit: June Harrison

Drop the racquet down.
Photo Credit: June Harrison

For the third part, the racquet head now needs to gather speed as it comes back up over your shoulder to make contact with the ball. Your racquet arm should be fully extended upwards slightly in front of your body. Your wrist will now go from being laid back to snapping up and over the ball. Your front foot will take all the weight and you should go up onto your front toes. If you were trying to hit the ball as if it were a clock, you would be making contact between twelve o'clock and two o'clock. Take your weight off the back foot, and in most cases your back foot will lift up and start to go over the baseline after you hit the ball.

Stretch up to hit the serve.

Photo Credit: June Harrison

After making contact, keep swinging the racquet up and out towards your service box. The head of the racquet should first point at the service box and then back down towards the ground as it continues across your body. Bring your back foot around and step over the baseline after your racquet comes down across your body. Make sure you do not drop your head as you are hitting the ball and continuing your swing.

Head up, finish the swing.

Photo Credit: June Harrison

Passing Shots

A server may hit as many lets as occur on his serve. It is unusual, but sometimes a server will get three let serves in a row. The Aussies always say the server needs to buy everyone on the court a beer if that happens.

The service motion is exactly the same whether you are right- or left-handed. Your feet will change, but the overall swing is still a basic throwing motion.

If you do not get the first ball into the service box, this is called a "fault" and you are allowed another serve. This second serve is usually hit more carefully than the first and with a little less pace. When you get better, you will be able to hit one or both serves with some spin.

If you do not get either of the two serves into the correct service box, you have served a double fault and you now lose the point.

During the serve, if the ball hits the top of the net and then drops into the service box, it is called a "let."

Under current rules, a let stops play and the point starts again. If the let occurs on the first serve, then the server gets two balls again. If it happens on the second serve after the server has served one fault, then the server gets only one more ball to serve over again. To speed up play, there is now some talk about ignoring the lets and allowing the play to continue if the ball hits the top of the net and drops into the service box. If the ball hits the top of the net during the point and drops into the court, play continues and the player may hit the ball in the air or it can bounce just like a regular ball.

Once the serve lands in the box, the receiver now must return the serve. The ball must bounce in the correct box, and then the receiver starts to move to the ball. The receiver must quickly decide whether the ball should be hit with a forehand or a backhand. The basic return of serve is just a regular ground stroke with a shorter backswing. The major concern as the serve approaches is how to move your feet so that you quickly get into position to return the serve.

First, you must always start in your ready position. Here it is again, just to remind you.

Ready to receive the serve.

Photo Credit: June Harrison

Your position will depend on the power of the serve. Your general stance should be on or just inside the baseline, about 6 to 18 inches inside the inner sideline. Often you will be able to move closer to the service line to receive a second serve. Many players dance around as the server is about to serve. This is partially to distract the server, but it also gets your feet moving as the ball is being struck.

When you play singles, you will generally try to aim the return to your opponent's weakness. In doubles, you will usually try to hit the ball crosscourt away from the net player.

To hit the return, split-step as the server is about to strike the ball. Keep looking at the ball once the server throws it up in the air. In Chapter 12, I will tell you about all the different serves and how to spot them. Pick either forehand or backhand, and move to the side of the ball and keep the ball well in front of you. Remember, the ball is traveling towards you, so you will need to be at least 6 feet behind the bounce of the ball. You must quickly get into your basic ground stroke position and make your contact.

Returning the serve.

Photo Credit: June Harrison

Push your racquet face out towards the far baseline and finish your follow-through out and up over the top of the net. If the serve is coming very fast, you will need to make your swing even shorter, both on the backswing and sometimes even on the follow-through.

After hitting the ball, you must get ready for the next shot. In singles, you will need to move very quickly towards the center hash mark on the baseline so that you are covering both sides of the court—forehand and backhand. In doubles, you do not have far to go but there are many more variables, so you need to react quickly. Recover with both your racquet and your feet back into the ready position.

Let's Volley

My favorite stroke in tennis is the *volley*. It is the easiest shot to learn and yet it is the hardest to perfect.

Most volleys are hit within the service box area. Some can be hit from behind the service line, but these are not winning volleys, just repositioning shots to get you up to the net.

Particularly in doubles, most of your points are won at the net. In singles, playing will depend on the surface and players' mobility. Playing the net in singles takes a lot of mobility and quick reaction time.

Again, take your ready position. This time I want you about halfway back from the net and the service line, straddling the center service line. This is your volley position for singles. For doubles, you will stand in the middle of one of the service boxes.

For a volley, I want you to feel like you are ready to pounce. Your racquet is very extended. Your knees are bent and your weight is on the balls of your feet. When the ball comes towards you, you will again have to make some decisions—forehand or backhand, forwards or sideways? You will not often have to move backwards for a volley. Once you make your decision, turn your shoulders slightly and keep your hands out in front of your body. You will need to transfer your weight to the outside foot. For a forehand volley, release your hand on the throat of the racquet after you turn. Your grip should be either a continental or an Eastern forehand. Keep the racquet head up above your wrist and keep your wrist very, very firm. Take a look at this next photo.

Ready to pounce.

Photo Credit: Vicki Fort

Lay the racquet head back a little so that your hand is more in front of the racquet shaft. Open the racquet face slightly. Now, if you have time, step into the ball by moving your opposite foot. Try not to step sideways across the court so that your weight goes backwards. You want to feel that you are going to get the ball—not that the ball is dictating to you. Begin your swing, which is more like a punch, by accelerating your racquet and arm so that you quickly hit the shot and get the ball off your strings as quickly as possible. I always tell my students to pretend that they have a hot potato on their racquet and they need to punch it off quickly. Your swing will be short and from the top of the ball down to the back, bottom part of the ball. After you finish, you should not have your racquet hand below the top of the net.

You can direct the ball by turning your shoulders more or by hitting the ball out in front or further back, level with your body. You need fast reaction time and good reflexes.

Trish Says

When I was playing competitive tennis, I was also playing world-class squash. Squash is a very strenuous sport so it helped me get fit. But more than anything, squash helped me tremendously with my tennis volleys, because squash is a very fast game. Playing squash is almost like practicing tennis against the backboard or the wall. The ball comes back fast. You have to make split-second decisions.

For a backhand volley, you can use two hands if you don't feel like you have enough power with only one. For a one-handed backhand, you must use an Eastern backhand or a continental grip. You cannot use a forehand grip because your wrist is in the wrong place. I don't recommend a two-handed grip for the volley because it really restricts your reach, particularly on low balls. If I can get you to hit the volleys with just one grip—the continental—you will have great reflexes and be able to move from serving to volleying very easily. If you have the right grips, you should be able to hit with one hand.

Punch that ball.

Photo Credit: June Harrison

The biggest problem on the volley is too much backswing. This will make you hit late and you will lose control over the shot. Keep the racquet up high, your grip firm, and your feet wide apart, and you will be able to block almost any shot that comes at you.

Somewhere over the Lob

The most underrated shot in tennis is the lob. Used offensively, it can change a point around immediately. As a defensive weapon, the high lob can put you back into the game by slowing down the point and keeping the ball in play.

To hit a forehand or a backhand lob, you use the basic ground stroke grip, which is the Eastern.

A defensive lob is hit when you are forced out of position. Most of the time you will hit it when you are outside the court area. A good opponent will come into the net after he or she has you on the ropes. If this happens, you will need to hit your lob high over the opponent. To achieve this, as the ball is coming towards you, prepare for the shot just as if you were going to hit a regular ground stroke. Just before making contact, make certain the racquet head is well below the ball and the racquet face is now open.

Preparing to lob.

Photo Credit: June Harrison

Swing from way under the ball and make contact a little later than for the normal ground stroke. After you make contact, continue with an upward swing so that the racquet face finishes pointing up to the sky at shoulder height.

Lob it high.

Photo Credit: June Harrison

As always, the lob has many variables. If you are way out of court, deep in the backcourt, you will need to hit it hard and high. If you are inside the baseline and you see the need to hit a lob, you should use a more compact swing so you don't hit the ball as high, because the ball does not need to travel as far. If your opponent hits you a slow looping ball, your stroke should be slow and loopy. If the ball coming towards you is fast, hard, and low, you should use a very short and compact swing, and you simply make contact with the racquet face open.

The shot that you will need to learn to return the lob is called the overhead. This shot is really a service motion with someone else throwing up the ball. The overhead needs to be practiced, because there are so many variables on this shot. The height of the lob, the depth of the lob, and the spin on the ball will all contribute to your positioning for the stroke.

The secret to a good overhead is timing and great footwork. When your opponent lobs over you, you will generally be in the service box. A good lob will force you to go back to hit the overhead. To do this without falling over, you need to turn sideways and quickly side-step your way back past the service line. See the correct footwork in this photo.

Double Faults

Never run backwards facing the net when trying to run down a lob or trying to hit an overhead. You must turn sideways and keep watching the ball.

Overhead preparation.

Photo Credit: June Harrison

As you are moving your feet, take the non-hitting arm, point it up to the ball, and use this arm like radar to track the ball. Take the racquet back over your shoulder and relax the racquet head down your back. Try to keep moving your feet until you are sure you are in the right position to hit the ball.

Trish Says

During the 1960s, there was a women's doubles team from Italy called Lazzarino and Pericoli. They reduced their opponents to tears because they lobbed everything. The predominately male Italian fans, who were not that interested in women's tennis, flocked to the court whenever these two played. As a player, you knew if you were drawn to play "P & L" (as they were known), you were going to have a stiff neck and a gallery of leering, vocal Italians.

Your swing to return a lob should be the same as your serve. As the ball starts to drop towards your hitting area, accelerate your racquet, turn your shoulders forward, and swing up and over your shoulder, making contact with the ball slightly in front of your body at arm's length. See how much you have to stretch for the overhead in this photo.

Pinpoint the hitting zone.
Photo Credit: June Harrison

Finish the overhead swing just like the serve. Bring the racquet across your body and wrap it around your hips. It is very important that you finish your swing, otherwise you will jar your shoulder.

If you have a good serve, you will generally have a good overhead. Do not be afraid of running backwards. When you are learning an overhead, ask the pro to clear away all the balls so that you are not concerned about tripping over a stray ball. The most important things to remember are great footwork and good timing. If you have both of these, you will not have to hit the ball hard to have a good overhead.

The Least You Need to Know

➤ The toss is the most important aspect of the serve.

➤ Keep the racquet head moving on the service motion.

➤ Punch your volleys. Don't take a big swing.

➤ The split-step, or the ready position, is the most-used body position in tennis.

➤ If you have good footwork and timing, you can hit any shot well.

Chapter 12

Spin to Win: How to Develop Spin

In This Chapter

➤ Over the rainbow; many different shots

➤ Open or closed; which stance works for you

➤ Watch that spin; understanding topspin

➤ Slice it up; how to have a perfect slice

➤ Decisions, decisions—now you have a choice

When the Australians first came on the tennis scene in the early 1900s, they brought with them a new grip. It was called the continental grip, and it allowed them to employ quick reflexes, particularly at the net. For many years, the continental grip was the grip that was taught. It was easy, because you need to find only one grip on the handle. Forehands and backhands, serves, too, were all hit flat with the same grip.

As the industry developed stronger frames, the ball was coming off the face of the racquet too hard. Some sort of control needed to be added to the ground strokes to keep the ball in play. Players like Bill Tilden, the powerful left-hander, started to hit with spin, usually slice, for both backhands and forehands. This enabled him to control the pace and still outmaneuver the opponents.

As more spin came to be used, the grips started to change to accommodate the change of racquet face needed to hit the spins. The 1950s saw an American domination of the sport and with it some major changes in style and shot making.

As the players got stronger, the spins got more pronounced. Players like the great Rod Laver, who had every shot in the book, caused tennis professionals to reevaluate how they were teaching the strokes.

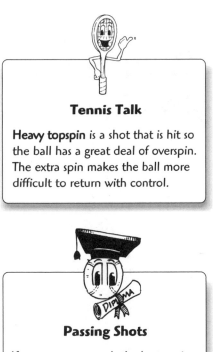

Tennis Talk

Heavy topspin is a shot that is hit so the ball has a great deal of overspin. The extra spin makes the ball more difficult to return with control.

Passing Shots

If you were to watch the best senior players in the world play their international tournaments today, you would not see one double-handed backhand and very, very few topspin backhands. We just weren't taught those shots in the 1950s. Everything was hit flat or with slice.

The double-handed shot makers came on the scene. Players like Bjorn Borg, with his heavy topspin off both sides, hit many a mishit into the stands on his way to winning five consecutive Wimbledons. The only way to beat a player with a lot of spin is with a lot of patience and a lot of spin.

When I get to this point with my students, they often jokingly accuse me of teaching them how to play tennis the wrong way just so I can continue teaching them and collecting my fees. We have a good laugh and keep working. Learning heavy topspin first would be like trying to ride a racing bike as your very first bike. You need to learn the basics before you can understand the more advanced techniques.

Now that you have mastered the basics, grab your racquet; let's go for a spin.

Top It Off

In Chapter 10, I showed you how to hit your ground strokes with some topspin. Remember that I told you I wanted you to hit with a little spin, not flat. So, you are halfway there in learning how to hit with heavy topspin.

Topspin makes the ball go over the net with overspin. The lower you get your racquet, the more you will be able to brush up from the bottom of the backside of the ball. Heavy topspin can be hit off both sides—forehand and backhand. As usual, the grips make a big difference when it comes to how the racquet face makes contact with the ball.

Let Me Show You the Forehand First

First, to be able to hit with all that topspin, the ball must be at least at knee level or higher. You are going to have to get under the ball more than before, so the racquet needs to have enough space to come from about 2 feet below the ball. It is also easier to hit with a lot of spin when you are back behind the baseline. As a beginner, you will find it difficult to think of all of this when you are trying to remember how to hit the ball. So, I will try to give you some examples of when you might think heavy topspin as opposed to regular spin. High, deep balls in singles should always be hit with heavy spin providing the opponent is not at the net. Heavy topspin forces the ball to go at least 4 feet over the net. If it does not go at least that high, then the ball will land too close to the net on the other side. You do not want this to happen because a short and high shot gives your opponent an easy put-away shot.

Trish hitting a big topspin.

Photo Credit: June Harrision

I want you to move your hand further around to the right on the grip if you are right-handed, and to the left if you are left-handed. This will give you a modified or semi-Western grip, which will allow you to drop that racquet head and get more under the ball. As I said in Chapter 8, I do not advise a full Western grip, because you have to change back and forth too much to hit other strokes. Plus, the Western grip gives you excessive topspin. If you are playing only recreational tennis or doubles, you do not need this much spin. See how the hand has moved slightly in this photo to give you the right semi-Western grip.

Get a grip.

Photo Credit: June Harrision

Double Fault

When you want to hit the ball hard, you must accelerate the racquet head through the shot. What this means is you must swing the racquet faster just before impact. To do this, you must be loose, relaxed, and willing to take a chance.

The topspin swing can be changed to adjust to your court position. If you are behind the baseline, your follow-through will be up very high after a very long sweeping swing. If you are hitting from the service line and the ball is high, you will have the same preparation but a much lower finish on the follow-through to help bring the ball down into the court. A ball that bounces short and high should be an automatic winner. The spin will help you control the shot as you hit it hard. The ball stays on the strings longer, thereby giving you spin as well as more control. Take a look at the big topspin forehand by Agassi.

Topspin is great, but if you are only a doubles player, you need to use it very carefully. Good topspin travels high over the net, which allows the net player in doubles to read the flight of the ball and attack. You may need to lower the path of the ball by modifying the topspin. This can be done by not using too much of a Western grip and by finishing lower on the follow-through.

Take the high backhand ball and use the topspin again to stroke the ball back deep to the opponent. This is where a double-handed backhand is the best shot. It is so much easier to hit a two-handed backhand when the ball is high. You must still get way under the ball and brush up just like the basic backhand. The extra spin will be achieved by moving your hands around on the grip so that they are more to the left of center than the basic Eastern backhand, or even the regular two-handed grip. This will close the racquet face slightly and force you to brush up more on the ball. Take a look at this photo of Bjorn Borg, who had one of the best two-handed topspin backhands.

Borg, one of the greatest topspin backhands.

Photo Credit: June Harrison

I find it difficult to hit a one-handed, topspin backhand off a high ball. I prefer the hitting zone to be more around my hips or waist so that I can get my racquet way down below the ball. I had to teach myself a topspin backhand because I was not taught this stroke when I was first introduced to tennis. To strike the ball with the right amount of spin, you must move your grip around to the Eastern or semi-Western grips. When you first do this, you are certain the ball is not going to go over the net. Your racquet is facing down so why would the ball go up. You are right. For the most part, the first few topspin backhands end up in the bottom of the net. Have faith. Change that grip and drop that racquet head, then swing up and out on the shot. You need to feel like you are brushing right up from underneath the backside of the ball again.

When you hit with topspin, you often hit from way back behind the baseline. Many times your weight will not be forward because you have been forced so far back. Whenever you can, hit every shot with your weight forward.

Your shoulders play a big part on the follow-through. On the forehand and backhand, your shoulders need to open up to face the net to complete the full brushing-up motion.

We now come to your footwork for the topspin. In the last few years, there has been a great deal of conversation about using an open or closed stance to hit ground strokes. Let's find out which position is right for your stroke.

Passing Shots

The pros often end up off the ground when they hit with a lot of topspin. The racquet head speed, the weight transference, and the big follow-through cause them to use their entire body. This makes them lift up and rotate as they finish. This is not recommended for beginners.

Preparation and Stance

The difference between a good player and a great player is often only the footwork the player uses to prepare for the shot. The better the position, the more likely you are to hit a good shot. Most topspins are hit with a big swing, so it is important that you be in the right spot to make contact.

Another good reason to incorporate spin into your game is the fact that the spin can control the ball even when you are out of control and off-balance.

The regular hitting position as seen here in this photo is with the weight on the front foot, shoulders well to the side, and the body down with bent knees.

Great position.

Photo Credit: June Harrison

Double Fault

Hitting with spin controls the ball. Slice slows it down and gives you more time for the ball to hang onto the racquet face. Topspin imparts speed and overspin, which allows you to clear the net easily and still force your opponent back deep.

Now the pros seem to hit most of their balls on the run and way back behind the baseline. It is almost impossible for them to get set before they hit the ball. The strokes that you see them hit are a far cry from the strokes I was teaching you in Chapter 10.

For this reason, I want to show you how to hit the ball with an open stance. It is difficult to teach this after telling students to step into the ball. It actually is easier if you let your feet do their own thinking. Instead of trying to make your feet do something they don't want to do, just let it happen. Take a look at this shot of me hitting the ball with an open stance.

Good footwork is key to hitting a great shot.

Photo Credit: June Harrision

To use the open stance, still pivot on the outside foot and then keep the weight on that foot as you continue to turn your shoulders and then swing back in to hit the ball. You will then need to transfer your weight back to the other foot if you have used a big topspin swing. You can also keep your weight on the outside foot if you can maintain your balance. Your balance is your key here. If you have good balance and controlled weight transference, then you can hit any shot you want from anywhere on the court.

The secret to maintaining your balance is in your knees, your thighs, and the width of your stance. I mentioned this in our footwork chapter, but it bears mentioning again. You can never bend too much in tennis, so always keep both knees flexed as you split-step and move in to hit the stroke. Keep your feet a good 18 inches or more apart. This will vary a little, depending on your height. The lower you need to get, the wider your feet will be so you can bend and transfer weight.

Double Faults

To keep good balance, lower your center of gravity by keeping your feet wider apart and your knees bent as much as possible.

I find it easier to hit an open-stance forehand than to hit an open-stance backhand. However, Monica Seles hits two-handed off both her forehand and backhand and often has an open stance for both sides. Her opponents will tell you it is very difficult to antici-pate where she is going to hit the ball. Because she is so open, it is hard to get any advance clues as to where she wants to place her shot.

As you hit more balls and get comfortable hitting from the regulation closed-stance position, I would then recommend you stop worrying about your feet. Hopefully, your brain will send a message to your feet to move, and then your feet should take over naturally from there. If you start off hitting with an open stance, don't let your pro correct you. As long as you have your shoulders rotated to the side where the ball is coming to, and your weight is balanced, it doesn't matter where your front foot is located. If you can strike the ball with good topspin, then you are doing something right!

Spin for Control—the Slice

The slice: The shot of champions from prior years is still one of the best shots in tennis. The slice, where the racquet face is open upon contact, or slightly facing up to the sky, allows you to hit hard with control.

Partly because of the grip, which was primarily the continental, the slice was the shot of choice for over 50 years. Until the big serve-and-volleyers forced players to hit more passing shots, there was no need for the topspin.

The slice is a hard shot to teach, and most players fight me all the way when I try to get them to open the racquet face. It does require some faith in the professional and a little patience on the part of the student. Don't be surprised when the first few slices go 20 feet in the air. It is hard to lock your wrist, lay your head back, open the racquet face, and still control the point of contact on this shot.

Let's look at the forehand slice first. This shot you will find yourself using more and more. It is a perfect approach shot when you want to go down the line in singles off a short low ball. You can also change direction and send it crosscourt at the last minute. The slice will not be a commanding shot, but you can turn it into a low driving ball that can be very well disguised.

Trish Says

Stefan Edberg had one of the best slice approach shots of any player and always tried to get into the net at his earliest opportunity. His slice had depth, speed, and stayed very low. This shot allowed him to get to the net. His opponents had trouble keeping the return low, so he was in position to take the high volley and put it away for a winner.

To execute the forehand slice, you need to react to the ball just like any other forehand. You will move your feet so that you pivot and turn, and then prepare yourself to move your body to the ball. As in all tennis shots, your shoulder rotation is very important and so is your backswing.

For the slice, your backswing should be high and in the continental grip. Your shoulders must turn and your weight must not be leaning backwards. You will generally hit a slice off low balls. Keep the racquet head above the ball, then bring the open-faced racquet down to the back underside of the ball. Keep your wrist very firm as you begin to make contact.

Check the preparation for the slice in the photo on the next page.

Remember you need to use the continental grip. A forehand grip or a semi-Western backhand will not work. A modified Eastern backhand would work, but the continental is better.

Turn for the slice.

Photo Credit: June Harrison

Now, the slice. The really great players use both slice and topspin, but many of them use the slice backhand as their regular bread-and-butter shot.

To hit the slice, your shoulder preparation is the same. Rotate your shoulders and bring both hands back on the racquet. Instead of dropping the racquet head down below the ball, raise the racquet head up above your shoulders. Your grip moves to a continental grip, which is the grip right in the middle of the handle. Your hand makes a "v" straight down the throat to the base of the grip. Look at the difference in preparation for the slice in the top photo on the next page.

Double Fault

You cannot hit a good slice if you do not lean your body into the shot. Pretend you are pushing against a stuck door and lean the whole side of your body into the slice.

183

Racquet starts up high.

Photo Credit: June Harrison

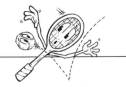

Double Faults

Many players forget their non-racquet hand. This hand is just as important as the one with the racquet. You will use it for support on the backswing, balance as you hit, and for additional length on your shot. Don't let the hand get below your waist.

Your shoulder rotation is very pronounced in the slice backswing. Your wrist is very firm and the racquet face is now open at least 30 percent to help create the underspin and backspin. As you move your feet to hit the ball, remember that you never want to find yourself level with the ball prior to contact. Stay back behind the bounce and to the side. The one problem with a slice is the high ball. It is very difficult to get good power off a high slice ball. As you swing down and forward to hit the ball, continue to keep your wrist very, very firm. You do not want to drop the racquet head and lose control over the wrist. Turn to the side, step into the ball, not sideways, and begin to give the ball a stroke similar to a kind of karate chop. Look at my body weight and position as I hit the slice in this photo.

Body weight is on the front leg.

Photo Credit: June Harrison

The hardest part of the slice is keeping control after the contact. Most players want to let their wrists go and fail to execute a full follow-through. The slice finish is more like a volley—short and sweet, with a very *firm wrist,* even at the end. Your shoulders don't open as much and your body stays down and forward for as long as possible. You want to imagine you are looking down the sights of a gun as you watch the ball, keeping your head and eyes on it for the follow-through. See how controlled my body and racquet is in this photo.

Slice finish.

Photo Credit: June Harrison

From the hitter's standpoint, the difference between these two shots is the grip, the backswing, and the follow-through. From the receivers view, the ball comes toward you with overspin or underspin. Either way, you will need to react quickly and keep the wrist firm to counteract the swing.

Flight of the Ball

When you first start to play tennis, you will be told to watch the flight of the ball, because it will help you decide on your next move. What does this mean?

When the ball comes off the opponent's racquet, you will need to react. How will you do this?

Tennis Talk

Firm wrist means the wrist and grip are under enough control so that the racquet head remains above the hand. Don't hold the racquet in a death grip—that is not what a firm wrist means.

First, how high and hard is the ball coming over the net? Can you see the seams on the ball? Will you have to move back and retreat and play defensively? Or, can you attack the ball and go for a winner?

The flight of the ball will tell you everything. It will show you whether you will be able to attack or retreat. When the ball is high and spinning it means the ball has topspin. This will send the ball deeper and you must anticipate what the ball is going to do. If the ball has backspin, it will not bounce as much towards you so you need better footwork.

You can also use the flight of the ball to help as you visualize it when you are hitting your shots. Remember that topspin must go higher over the net to get any depth. A slice should stay low so that the ball doesn't float and allow the opponent to attack.

Less than 2 feet over the net with topspin means the ball will bounce short. This is good for doubles but not such a great shot for singles because it gives the opponent an attack opportunity. A slice, when hit well, should stay low whether it is hit short or long. This makes it a very safe shot, but it is still not forceful unless you learn how to generate power as well as a lot of slice.

There was a player on the circuit in the 1980s named Caroline Stoll, from New Jersey. Caroline was a spunky player, very fast and competitive. Her biggest weapon was a huge topspin forehand. At an indoor tournament in Nashville, Caroline was playing a rather short opponent who also had a pretty fair topspin. The balls were going 20 feet over the net with incredible spin until one player made a mistake or came into the net and hit a volley. On one point, after five or six consecutive topspins, Caroline hit a very high, heavily spun ball, which bounced just inside the baseline. Her opponent went back to try to get the shot. She had to keep going back and back until she ran out of court and her racquet hit the curtain that divided the courts. She must have made contact with the curtain right where it opens to let players into the court, because she went straight through, disappearing off the court completely. She ended up in the next court where they were playing another match. These players were very surprised and stopped play. Caroline and the spectators on her court were a little stunned as her opponent completely disappeared. The chair umpire called to the opponent, because he could not see her either. She came back through the curtain after a slight delay, looking very angry. She took one look at the whole situation and at Caroline and then burst out laughing. We all started to laugh then because it had looked very funny. Just goes to show you how effective those big loopy topspins are.

So the bottom line is, watch the ball coming over the net and begin your reactions based on the height, spin, and pace of the ball, and watch out for the very deep ones.

The Least You Need to Know

➤ Topspin allows you to make fewer errors because the ball travels higher over the net.

➤ Good footwork is the solution to almost every mistake.

➤ A good slice will keep you in the point when you are under pressure.

➤ Learn how to hit with spin as early as you can.

➤ The higher the ball over the net, the deeper you need to be.

➤ Spinning balls are heavy balls, so get ready early.

Chapter 13

Service with a Smile

In This Chapter

➤ Hard, harder, hardest; how to get pace on your serve

➤ Go wide; slice it wide

➤ Into the body; use your opponent as a target

➤ Anything will do; just get the serve in

➤ Reach for the sky; you need to stretch

I have always felt that the serve is both the easiest and the hardest shot in tennis. It is the most natural motion and yet, when the match gets tight, the serve sometimes lets you down.

To have a good serve, you must stay very loose so that the racquet can accelerate into the contact point. The hand holding the racquet needs to be loose, the knees can't be locked, and the tossing arm needs to be flexible, not stiff.

I have always impressed upon my students the need to constantly practice the toss motion. Even if you don't have the space to swing the racquet, try to practice using both arms as you start the service motion. As you will see from this chapter, the toss is your key to every serve. It will give you spin, direction, control, and reach. Each player starts the motion differently, but by the time the ball is ready to be tossed, the tossing arm is almost always in the same position for every player.

In this chapter, I am going to show you all the different legitimate ways to get the serve into the service box. You may not be able to execute all of them. Others, you may be too embarrassed to use. Believe me, if you start to play competitive matches, there will come a time when your serve lets you down. You are going to have to go through my mental checklist to get your confidence and your serve back. If you have a reliable spin serve you will be able to serve your way out of any tight situation. So practice that toss and read on.

Cannonball Run

The first serve that most players learn is the flat serve. It is the most simple to teach and the easiest to understand. As I explained in Chapter 11, I am a stickler for the right grip on the serve. You must have at least a continental grip to be able to deliver a half-way decent serve. The stronger your wrist and the more action you want on the ball, the more you will need to move your grip around to an Eastern backhand grip.

Trish Says

It is usually much easier to teach a man how to serve than it is to teach a woman. Many women have never thrown a ball, so when it comes time to teach them how to serve, they have no basis for comparison. To help my students find a motion that they can relate to, I have tried having them imagine throwing a vase at a loved one when they are mad. Not a nice image, but it works.

It is always fun to hit the ball as hard as you possibly can and still get it in the box. It takes a good toss out in front of your body, perfect timing, and good height as you make contact with a very fast swing. Many beginners, particularly men, have the capacity to hit the serve hard; but they are afraid to really hit it because they feel it will go way out. Often it will, if you don't have the right combination of all the elements.

Learning to serve is like learning a language. If you start studying a language when you are young, you have no hangups about making mistakes, and you just keep doing it, you eventually master it. If you start when you are older with preconceived notions of how you should sound, you will be afraid to experiment. It is the same with tennis; if you start when you are older, you lack the natural fluidity and basic instincts of the young. So, when you are learning to serve, I want you to hit it hard. I don't want you to baby the serve. I can help you get it in if you will just learn to hit it.

Once you have mastered the basic serve, you will want to see how hard and fast you can deliver it. This very hard, flat serve is called a cannonball. The service toss will go directly in line with the shoulder of the hitting arm, a little higher than you can reach and at arm's length. If you were hitting the ball on the face of a clock, then the toss would be at twelve or slightly towards one o'clock. For a leftie, the toss can be at twelve or eleven o'clock.

Twelve o'clock high.

Photo Credit: June Harrison

In order to get the maximum power out of your shot, you don't want to toss the ball too high. It is very difficult to judge the ball, and you will lose power if you hit the ball when it is dropping.

To hit the hardest cannonball, get behind the back of the ball, then start to swing the racquet as hard as you can up and over the top of the ball. You must snap your wrist as you are making contact and come over the ball. Try to swing through towards your target in a straight line.

Remember, when you are hitting cannonball serves you have very little margin for error. Your toss must be in front and high enough to make you go into a full stretch as you hit the ball. Hit it—you cannot baby this serve.

Passing Shots

Steffi Graf has an unusually high toss for a player of her caliber. She hits her serve mainly hard and flat. When she is under stress, she does tend to hit her serve long because she gets under it too much when she tries to control the flight of the ball.

I think my favorite cannonball server is Mark Philoppousis from Australia. He averages 120 miles an hour on his first serves. He has great extension and control on his toss, and good knee bend prior to getting up and over the ball. Watch and learn the next time you see him play.

Slice by Slice

By far the safest and most widely used serve is the slice. Again, the grip must be more of an Eastern backhand grip to be able to slice effectively. This serve has a variety of uses. Because the ball stays on the racquet longer with this service motion, it is most commonly used as a second serve when control and reliability are required.

To slice the serve, you must first toss the ball more to the side. If you are a right-hander, as you are beginning the toss motion, rotate more to the right and have your tossing arm almost parallel to the baseline. The left arm goes up at about two o'clock to release the ball.

More to the right for a slice.

Photo Credit: June Harrison

The height of the toss is the same or it can be a little lower than the flat or cannonball toss, which is more at twelve o'clock.

If you are left-handed, you will need to rotate more to the left and place the ball towards ten o'clock to achieve the slice ball toss.

The racquet will swing back in the same path as for a regular serve. The racquet is still relatively loose in your hand, and the head of the racquet must always drop down your back. As you start your swing to the ball, you must bring the racquet up and slightly to the side. You should be planning on hitting the ball on the outside upper edge. For right-handers, this would be at two o'clock and for left-handers, ten o'clock. The face of the racquet will be more sideways, and the feeling you will have is of coming around the ball, rather than up and over it.

The finish of the swing is more around the body than the finish of a flat serve. You still need to keep your head up and get as much height as possible at the point of impact.

I try to teach the slice to my students almost as soon as they understand the service motion. I don't wait for them to master the flat serve before I introduce the slice. I try to make them use a slice serve as their second serve immediately. I feel that a slice, even a little bit, is better than a very slow second serve. When you get into a tight situation, you will need to slice that ball into the box rather than try to slow down your normal action.

Passing Shots

Seles and Navratilova, among the women, and almost any left-handed male player with a good serve will give a right-hander trouble.

Come around the ball.

Photo Credit: June Harrison

Left-handers always have very difficult slices to return, particularly off the backhand or ad court. Because a left-hander's ball normally curves off the side to your backhand, it is not an easy backhand shot if you are a right-hander. Add a lot of slice to the leftie's shot and it is almost impossible to return. The only way to counteract the curve of the ball is to stand wider than usual to receive the serve. However, most of the time when you do this, your opponent redirects the serve down the middle and you are caught out of position. The secret is to move just as your opponent is hitting the serve and hope you have guessed right. We righties always say the lefties have an advantage.

The slice serve is good for singles or doubles. You can use it to swing the ball into the opponent's body, or to pull the opponent wide. When you pull them wide in doubles, it is a good idea to tell your partner you are going to try this serve. Your partner needs to change his or her position depending on your service placement. If you go wide, the alley opens up more, so it should be protected.

In my mind, the slice is the best serve of all. Use it in all close situations. If you have the right grip, even if the toss is not perfect, the slice will occur simply because of the grip on the racquet. Don't be afraid—hit it and the slice will control it.

Kick It to Me

The kick, or twist, serve is the serve used by most of the pros, certainly the men pros. It is the hardest serve to teach because most students don't believe the ball is going to go into the box when you show them how to hit it.

Start with a pronounced Eastern backhand grip and a body position that is more parallel to the baseline than facing into the court. Bring the racquet back over your toes at a more pronounced angle to your body, rather than straight back to the fence.

A more pronounced stance.

Photo Credit: June Harrison

Toss the ball over your left shoulder and slightly behind your body. Make certain you bend your knees and arch your back toward the direction of your toss. After the racquet drops down your back, start to swing up from beneath the ball, hitting the ball at seven o'clock.

Continue to bring the racquet up across the back of the ball, swinging up to two o'clock on the upper right-hand backside of the ball. The idea is to start at the bottom and kick the ball from underneath and then brush up across the topside. This will impart a reverse spin that gives the ball a lot of control and kick when it hits the court.

Double Faults

When hitting a kick serve, you must arch your back and bend your knees; so, if you have a bad back or sore knees, leave this serve to the pros.

Brush up the back of the ball.

Photo Credit: June Harrison

To finish the swing after making contact, let the racquet continue out toward the court and then swing back down across your body. In some cases, with a severe twist motion, the racquet will finish on the same side of the body as the contact. This puts a lot of strain on the arm and shoulders, but it does add extra spin to the ball.

When a kick serve hits the court, it will bounce to the opposite side from the slice serve. This means that a right-handed kick serve will jump to the backhand of another right-hander. Hit correctly, the ball will bounce up high and away from the receiver, making a difficult backhand return of serve.

Passing Shots

Michael Chang made very effective use of the underhand serve against Ivan Lendl in Paris at the 1989 French Open. At a crucial time in the match, and with very little hope of winning, Michael delivered an underhand serve and caught Lendl way back behind the baseline. Lendl missed the ball and that was the turning point of the match. Michael just kept on plugging away until he won.

The kick or twist serve is a great serve, but it is hard on the back and knees, so you need to be flexible. You also cannot be afraid to hit the ball. You cannot half-hit a twist serve. Just grab that racquet even though it doesn't feel right and go for it.

The Underhander

This is not a serve you will see very often in the pro ranks, although there are a few memorable occasions when a player has decided to serve underhanded.

To execute the underhanded serve, you need to understand that it is done more for surprise than anything else. Some players use it as a safe serve but I personally don't feel that it is all that safe. The ball is hit like a slice ground stroke.

Step up to the baseline. Keep your feet apart with your front foot pointing at the net post and your back foot parallel to the baseline. Place the ball or balls in your tossing hand. Take the racquet back below the ball on your forehand side and then drop the ball from waist height.

The underhander.

Photo Credit: June Harrison

You must make contact before the ball hits the ground, otherwise it is a fault. You must serve it into the service box just like any other serve.

Be careful when you return this serve because there is very little pace on the shot and you will tend to overhit. If the ball is low, it is best to return it with a slice. If it is high, you can gather more pace with topspin.

Even among the pros, it is considered bad manners to serve underhand. It is certainly legal, and it does cause the receiver to stop and think. Any time you serve under-handed, you will probably win the point. So, pick your spot and be prepared for some dirty looks if you give your opponent the underhander.

Taking a Run at It

Most professionals will teach you how to serve by placing your front foot up about two inches from the baseline. This works fine if you have a consistent toss and good reach. Some players need to chase their toss a little, so they tend to stand about a foot behind the baseline. This gives them a running motion that can accommodate a bad toss. However, this does create a problem because the body is moving so much that the motion needs very good timing, otherwise the ball will be carried out of the service box.

If this motion seems right for you, make certain you stand far enough behind the baseline so that you don't *foot fault*. Remember, a foot fault occurs when one or both feet come over the baseline, or touch any part of the baseline, before you hit the ball.

All other motions on this serve are the same as a regular service swing—flat, slice, or twist. When running at a serve, you will also need to remind yourself to stretch up high to hit the ball because your basic body momentum is forward and not up. You will need to force your body up.

Tennis Talk

A **foot fault** occurs when any part of your foot crosses the center-line hash mark or the baseline before you serve.

Jump for Joy

Many of the really good players jump when they go to make contact with the ball on the serve. Again, this is for timing, as well as trying to get more height out of your body.

Most players who jump bring both feet together behind the baseline, bend the knees, and then jump with both feet over the baseline. Normally, when you serve you will land on the back foot which swings over the line and into the court as you reach up to hit the ball. When you jump, the front foot tends to come back down over the baseline first, followed by the back foot.

I teach a junior player who likes to jump on her serve, but is having trouble with her foot position. If she jumps and lands on her outside foot, in this case her right foot, she loses court coverage because she has to reposition her feet to move either back-wards or forwards. If she jumps and extends over the baseline and comes down on her left foot, she often comes down too soon. We have time to correct this, because she is only twelve years old. My feeling is that the serve has to be natural, because it is not a shot you should keep worrying about. It should be automatic. You must have complete confidence in your service motion, and it must be the same repetitive motion.

Jumping on the serve.

Photo Credit: June Harrison

Shorter players like to jump to get more reach. Again, whenever you add extras to the basic service motion, you allow more room for error. Yes, jumping gets more height but it also makes you collapse early, drop your head, and often foot fault.

As you can see, there are numerous ways to serve the ball. Just like your routine—whatever works for you is what is best for you. If you like a player's serve and want to copy it, go ahead. It may be the right swing for you and, then again, it may not be. Try all of these methods and, with the help of your friendly tennis pro, find the right service motion to suit you and your body type.

The Least You Need to Know

➤ Try to learn at least two different serves.

➤ Always keep your head up regardless of the motion.

➤ The slice serve is the easiest to learn.

➤ Learn how to vary your service placement.

➤ Depth on your serve is better than pace.

➤ Spin serves are good in doubles or when you want to get to the net.

Part 4
Your Advantage

You have now progressed to a better level and you need some new weapons. This is where you will learn how to hit all those special shots that you have only seen on television.

Tennis is like playing the piano. Once you have mastered scales and chopsticks, you move on to more difficult pieces until you can pick up any sheet of music and play it well.

With tennis, you practice all the basic shots until you can do them with your eyes shut, and you are beating all your regular partners, practice buddies, and teammates.

Your pro has entered you into some tournaments. You then discover there is another whole tennis world out there. A world where players don't all play as you do. Some spin everything and run all day. Some play with two hands on both sides. You now realize you need to be fitter and have more variety in your shot selection. You got tired in some of those matches and if you had been in better shape and had a kill shot, you might have won those third-set tiebreakers.

You notice that your nose is peeling from being out in the sun, your back is a little tight, and your shoulder feels tender.

In this part, I have answers for all of these problems.

Grab an All-Sport, slather on the sun screen, and let's go back to the practice wall so that I can be certain you have retained all the basics before I let you in on the secrets for all my favorite shots. Don't forget the ice packs.

Chapter 14

These Are a Few of My Favorite Things: Advanced Shot Selection

This chapter deals with all those shots you see on television in the professional matches—the shots that don't seem to work when you try them.

I feel that the difference between a good player and a great player is two things—the drop shot and the overhead. If you have these two shots and you can execute them confidently and with variety, you have two deadly weapons.

A drop shot keeps your opponent always guessing, particularly if you can play it from anywhere on the court and with both your forehand and your backhand. If you can disguise the shot, then you are going to win even more points. If you are over 50, then you should definitely learn a drop shot. It is the shot that wins most of the points in veterans' singles competitions worldwide. The older the age groups, the more drop shots you will see.

The overhead can be hit in a variety of ways. When you are in trouble, you will often lob. The answer to a good lob from your opponent is a great overhead return. If you are confident and able to generate pace and vary the placement of your overheads, you will never worry about your opponent's lob. Players with good overheads put so much pressure on their opponents. Usually, if you have a good serve, you will have a good overhead, and vice versa.

In this chapter, I will show you how to improve your overheads and hit those special trick shots. As with all of your other shots, these shots take practice. It is difficult to practice drop shots unless you have a very understanding practice buddy, but practicing all the different overheads is fun. Place something on the court for a target (preferably not your buddy) and aim for it. Let's get to work.

Drop Deadly

The drop shot is one of the last actual shots you will learn. It is also one of the most difficult to execute correctly. Learning this shot presents you with two problems:

1. It is a delicate touch shot that is delivered with a lot of feel of the ball on the racquet.

2. It is very difficult to know when to hit the shot.

To hit a drop shot, you will use two types of spin—underspin and backspin. A drop shot will usually be hit off a mid-court or short ball that is around waist height. When you first execute a drop shot, you will probably telegraph your intentions well in advance to your opponent and he or she will start running towards the net long before you finish the shot. However, as you become more proficient, you will be able to disguise the shot.

Take up the racquet as if you are going to hit a forehand volley. Your grip should be a continental because you are going to always slice on your drop shots. Providing the ball is above net level, bring the racquet down the backside of the ball and then lightly cup the racquet face under the backside of the ball. In the next photo, see how the racquet starts high but with a very compact backswing.

Drop shot time.

Photo Credit: June Harrison

A good drop shot should have enough spin to stop the ball from bouncing back towards your opponent. If a drop shot bounces three times in the service box, then it is a winning drop shot. The backspin will keep the ball low, and the underspin will make the ball spin backwards so that it stays short and close to the net. Drop shots should not be hit when you are off balance or way out of position. Most of the time you will execute the shot after you have run your opponent way back out of court. You want to make your opponent run as far as possible to hit the next ball and that means hit it short.

Passing Shots

Chris Evert had the best drop shot from the back of the court because she could disguise the shot.

Occasionally, you may be able to hit a drop shot off a short serve. This is more an element of surprise and should be used sparingly.

The backhand drop shot is also hit with slice. Most players find this easier than the forehand because the backhand slice is a more natural shot. It is executed the same way as the forehand drop shot, with a short high backswing and a chopping motion that then turns into a cupping feeling as you try to impart spin and yet slow down the ball. Here is the finish of a backhand drop shot. Notice how the racquet face is almost completely open but not extended too far away from the body in this photo.

Backhand drop shot finish.
Photo Credit: June Harrison

In singles, most drop shots are hit during a long rally and most often are straight down the court as opposed to crosscourt. In doubles, drop shots are not hit that often, because there is usually at least one player at the net. Many times during a doubles match you will hit angles. Short angles are actually drop shots and are executed with a slice and touch just like any other drop shot.

Trish Says

Once during a doubles match, I had to run back for the deep lob and found myself pushing off the fence to hit the ball. I hit the lob back, but my foot slipped under the fence and my shoe got caught. My lob was very short and I knew my opponent's next shot would be a short ball. My partner ran crosscourt to cover the short drop shot, while I pulled my foot up, leaving my shoe under the fence. I ran back to cover the open court my partner had left and the opponents were so surprised I recovered my position that they netted the next shot and we won the game.

When you are playing someone who has a good drop shot, you will need to be very aware of that person's *backswing* and court position. These are the only two things that will give you any indication of a drop shot. If a player can disguise the shot by taking a bigger swing and then really chopping the ball, then it will be very difficult to read the shot early. The rule of thumb is always drop a drop shot. This is actually the easiest shot to try because you will be close to the net. The problem is you will be at a full run and you will not have a lot of control. After you execute a good drop shot, move in so you are at least 4 feet inside the baseline. This allows you to be ready for the drop shot reply and yet still cover the ball if it is hit deep.

To practice your drop shots, take a basket of balls and stand about 2 feet behind the service line. Drop the ball around waist height and then try to execute your drop shots off both forehand and backhand. Once you feel that you can make the ball bounce three times in the opposite service box before it crosses the line, then start to think about disguising the backswing so that the opponent cannot read your stroke.

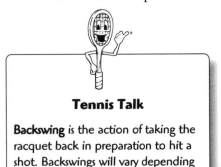

Tennis Talk

Backswing is the action of taking the racquet back in preparation to hit a shot. Backswings will vary depending on the shot selected. They can be high, low, long, or short.

If you hit a bad drop shot, there is not much you can do about it. Hustle back to the middle, just inside the baseline, and then move your feet and commit to one side and try to anticipate your opponent's shot. Your opponent will probably win the point anyway, so you may as well try to distract her and guess to which side she is going to hit the ball.

A good drop shot is usually a winner. A bad drop shot, one that bounces high or is hit too deep, will get you into trouble; but don't let that stop you from trying the shot again in the right situation. The hardest drop shot to hit in a match is the first one. Try it—you might be surprised at the result.

Topspin Lobbyist

Topspin lobs are the hold-your-breath type of shots that you always pray will fall back into the court. The forehand topspin lob is a lot easier to learn and to hit than the backhand shot.

Both shots are hit in either an offensive or defensive position, and when executed correctly, they are very difficult to read. The preparation is similar to that of a regular heavy, topspin ground stroke:

➤ Use a big, loopy backswing so that you can get way under the ball.

➤ Use the same grips as you use for a topspin ground stroke—but more spin is achieved if a slight Western is used.

The shot is used when the opponent is close to the net. Most topspin lobs are not very high over the net, but because they are hit with so much spin, it is very difficult to judge them and hit a regular overhead. From the moment the ball leaves the racquet, it is spinning very quickly. Initially, the ball rises slowly and looks like it is going to bounce high for an easy high shot, but due to the quick flick of the wrist at the end of the swing, which brings the ball back down, the flight of the ball is very deceptive.

To execute a topspin lob, use a modified Western grip, get way under the ball, and brush up as if you are going to hit the heavy, topspin ground stroke. As you are finishing the brushing motion, accelerate the head of the racquet and swing it quickly across and over the top part of the ball. The racquet motion for the forehand will go from four o'clock to ten o'clock for a right-hander, eight to two for a left-hander.

I believe the backhand lob is very hard for most people to execute because they need very strong wrists to flick the racquet head up and over the top of the ball. As you can see from the photo on the next page, the finish of this shot gives it away, but by the time your opponent realizes what you have hit, it is too late to do anything other than stretch up and try to make contact with the ball.

Double Faults

When returning a topspin lob you need simply to meet the ball, because all the topspin on the ball makes it difficult to hit a regular overhead.

With a flick of the wrist.
Photo Credit: Vicki Fort

There are many top-ranking pros who do not have topspin lobs, but the really effective players are the ones with all the shots. Many clay-court specialists have this shot, because, on clay, it is a great defense against an attacking opponent. Even when watching the pros, you will see many of them hit forehand topspin lobs, but only a few players have the deadly backhand topspin lob.

Angling for Winners

It is very simple in tennis to keep the ball going back and forth down the middle when you play singles. In doubles, the middle is your bread-and-butter shot and one that keeps you out of trouble.

In singles, the opportunities to hit angles are few and far between. You will need to get your opponent way back behind the baseline before the opportunity for an angle shot opens up. When the court does open it will be obvious, and the next shot will also be one that will not require a lot of forethought.

The further back you are from the net, the harder it is to hit a sharp angle. To create a sharp angle in singles you need to hit with spin—either topspin or slice. Because I don't have a great topspin backhand, I tend to hit most of my backhand angles with slice. To hit an angle, it is helpful if your opponent has given you an angle to work with. You need to come under the ball and then around the outside so that you create topspin and sidespin. This will allow the ball to clear the higher part of the net and then spin off to the side. This shot is most often hit with an open stance. Most of the drag or pull that creates the angle is done at the last few moments of the follow-through. You can also create a basic short angle by hitting the ball out in front, but this often results in your hitting the ball wide. As I have said before, you need the spin for control and, in this case, for disguise. As you can see from this photo, I could have been hitting almost any forehand because my stance is open; but the final pull across the body is the only indication of the short angle.

Check the finish.

Photo Credit: June Harrison

Players with two-handed backhands are able to get good angles, because it is easier for them to pull the follow-through across their body to make the ball go crosscourt and short and wide. It is a more natural follow-through than with one hand. A one-handed topspin backhand with a sharp short angle is tough to hit. You need a strong wrist and the correct modified Western grip to get the rolling motion required to hit a high, backhand volley.

All of the topspin shots I've discussed are very effective because they pull the opponent way off court. So, even if your angle is not a clean winner, the next shot should be. The topspin angles are used more often in singles, while the slice is used in doubles.

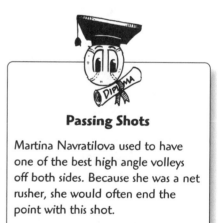

Passing Shots

Martina Navratilova used to have one of the best high angle volleys off both sides. Because she was a net rusher, she would often end the point with this shot.

Using a slice for a short, sharp angle is also effective because the ball stays low and skids away from your opponent. The forehand slice is more difficult to hit than the backhand because it is more difficult to lock the wrist on the forehand, which gives the slice the control you need to keep it low, with heavy spin.

I feel that the slice is almost like a drop shot, but with more pace. In doubles, the slice is used in almost every point by one team or the other. If your opponent plays back, it is a great way to pull the team wide and make them hit a high ball while you are waiting at the net. If your opponents are already at the net, then it is the most effective shot you could play next to a lob. If you play too far back from the net, you will be very susceptible to this short-angle slice.

To execute the shot, use the continental grip with a firm wrist and make certain you bend your knees. This is really my mantra for hitting any slice. This shot must have a firm wrist, because it is a touch shot, just like the drop shot. The only difference is the follow-through, which is longer and more across the body to give it the acute angle.

Practice this shot a lot with your hitting buddy. Both of you can stand in the corner of the service box and try to hit short angles back and forth to one another. The idea is to keep the ball low and wide so that you pull the opponent out of position and open up the middle for the put-away.

Double Faults

Hitting a wide angle to your opponent opens up the possibility of your opponent returning an angle, so cover your court accordingly.

Don't forget your wide serves, which will also do the same thing. As a beginner, you will not be able to create a lot of angles because of the need for spin. Spin is the mark of an advanced player. If you have played other ball sports and you can quickly understand spin, you will be way ahead of your beginner friends. Don't be afraid to learn the slice. Once you understand the basics, it is a very easy shot to execute and it will get you out of many troublesome situations.

Once you master the spins, hitting angles becomes much easier and you will raise your game at least two levels.

Skyhooks, Scissors, and Spikes

The shots discussed here are the ones you hit when nothing else will do the job. Let's take the skyhook first. This shot belongs to Jimmy Connors. He actually preferred hitting a skyhook to a regular overhead. He could place it anywhere on the court with pace.

The skyhook is hit off a high ball when you are up at the net. The ball is coming at you high, but not high enough to be hit with a normal overhead. It has some pace and you realize quickly it is going to stay in and you cannot reach it with a volley. You will not even have time to turn sideways, so don't worry too much about form on this shot.

Passing Shots

The skyhook is one of Jimmy Connors' favorite shots. He lets the ball get so far behind him you don't think he is going to be able to reach it. But reach it he does, and he puts it away more often than not.

For a regular overhead, you take the racquet behind your head and down your back so that you can get ready to come up and over and snap the wrist. Not so with the skyhook—take the racquet back almost like throwing a javalin or like a baseball player running back with the arm extended and raised back behind the head. The arm and the racquet are acting almost as one.

Most players will play a skyhook off a good lob from their opponents, so it will be more of a placement shot, played so that they can maintain the net position. Not everyone can do a "Jimmy" and hit it with power and accuracy.

Contact is made above your head and slightly behind the normal overhead contact point so that you are reaching back and up. The follow-through is more like a serve but with no wrist snap. Your arm continues to arc, and your racquet and arm come up and over the ball almost like topspin in the air. Try to control the ball and bring it down into the court between the baseline and the service line. If your opponents are aggressive, they may attack this shot, because it is very difficult to hit the ball down at their feet if they rush the net. Being at the net gives them the advantage.

Now let's discuss the scissors. This refers to the footwork required to be able to get back and hit a very difficult overhead off a very deep lob.

When I teach this shot, the students either get the footwork immediately, or they never do. It is a natural movement if you are well-coordinated, but it can be very scary going backwards, trying to jump at the same time. If you have to think about which foot to take off from and which one to land on, you will never be able to do it. Here goes.

If you are right-handed, turn as if you are going to hit a regular overhead. This means kick back with your right foot and turn your shoulders to face the side. Take the racquet down your back in the continental grip and make certain your grip is not too tight.

At this point, you will have to decide how to attack the overhead. Have you back-pedaled enough to be able to hit the ball in front with a powerful wrist snap? Or is the ball still behind you and still going back even further? If it is going back further, you may have to go back further, too, but usually you have run out of time and you have to execute your shot. The best way to still hit a good overhead is to jump. It is not a good idea to jump straight up because you can hyperextend your knees or come down on your feet the wrong way. As you are reaching back, push up off the back foot, which will be the right foot if you are hitting a right-handed overhead. Now is the time to do the scissors kick with your toes going towards the net. Make certain you don't lock your knees, because you must remain loose and balanced. Once you have done the scissors kick, you will want to land back down on the opposite foot from your pushing off foot.

The scissors overhead is necessary when the ball is going behind you and you have no other way to reach it. As I said, if you have to think about which foot to jump with and which foot to land on, you are going to miss the ball. This has to be a natural reaction to the shot. If you are not very tall, you may wish to try this shot, because it will certainly make you a better doubles player. You can practice hitting scissors overheads off deep lobs, but to hit them in a match, you must feel the right footwork and just go for it.

Most good players can execute a scissors kick overhead. The player that used it the most and hit it most successfully was Rosie Casals. Rosie was just over 5 feet tall but she liked to serve and volley. She was a great doubles player and often partnered with Billie Jean King. When they were both at the net, obviously their opponents would lob over Rosie because she was shorter. They were always rather surprised by the reply. Rosie would run back, do a scissors kick, and jump higher than most other players could reach to slam back the overhead.

And now for the spike. This is a fun shot and when you get to do it, you feel great. You need to be very close to the net and the ball cannot be traveling too fast. The ball is usually mishit by the opponents, as this is not a ball you would want to give to someone waiting at the net.

To hit the spike, you will almost want to do a little scissors kick so that you can get over the top of the ball. You need to take the racquet back like you do for a regular overhead, and quickly get the racquet cocked back so that you can snap the racquet over the ball. In order to get the spike effect, you must accelerate the wrist snap and quickly hit the ball almost completely on the top. The follow-through is much faster and closer to your body, and will often not be a full motion because the swing is so fast.

The basic idea is to hit or spike the ball down into the service box as hard as you can so that it bounces back up very high and goes over the head of your opponent. Don't try a spike if one, or in the case of doubles, both opponents are back deep. This shot works best when the opponents are a little too close to the net, which often happens after a rally. It is a great feeling seeing the ball bounce over your opponent's head.

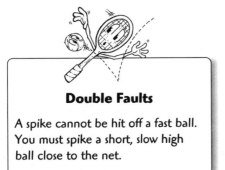

Double Faults

A spike cannot be hit off a fast ball. You must spike a short, slow high ball close to the net.

Sidearms, Round Arms, Any Arm Will Do

I love this shot! Maybe it comes from my days of playing squash, but I can hit sidearms from anywhere on the court off both forehands and backhands. It is very useful because it gets you out of trouble and it can even be a winner if it is hit correctly and in the right spot.

The sidearm is most often hit from just behind the service line. When your opponent tries a lob or mishits a ground stroke, the ball will often come about 6 to 8 feet over the net. This is not high enough for you to hit an overhead, but it is too high for a volley. Your preparation should be similar to a ground stroke, but with a high backswing. You can almost take a full backswing unless you are close to the net and the ball is coming too fast. The contact point for this shot should be above your shoulders and slightly in front of the body. The stroke can be topspin or slice depending on your balance and court position. The sidearm should not be viewed as a winning hit, but rather as a placement shot to get you back into an attacking net position.

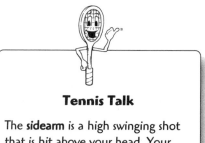

Tennis Talk

The **sidearm** is a high swinging shot that is hit above your head. Your body is turned to the side for either forehand or backhand. Your swing is almost the length of a groundstroke. It is generally played from around or behind the service line.

Once you have made contact, swing through like a short ground stroke. For a slice, you will finish out in front at net level. For a topspin, you will finish with the racquet out towards the far baseline. At the end of the swing, the slice will have an open racquet face, and the topspin will have a closed racquet face. Court position will determine how much spin you can or will need to impart on the shot. Always have a firm wrist on a sidearm. It is not an overhead.

Turn for the sidearm.

Photo credit: June Harrison

On the sidearm, it is very important to turn your shoulders because you will get all of your power and control from that motion. Note the shoulder position in the picture of the sidearm.

Double Faults

The biggest mistake players make on the sidearm is letting the ball get too low. This shot must be hit above the shoulders for you to be able to swing and generate the pace you need.

Because this is a placement shot, your target should be deep and crosscourt. Your opponent may try to come to the net because she might think you cannot hurt her with your sidearm. If this happens, your target may be at the feet of your opponent, which means you will hit the ball shorter and the swing will finish lower.

Always use your other hand to help hit a sidearm. This will help keep your shoulders turned and it will give you extra strength. Release the second hand just before impact. Those with double-handed backhands will have extra strength on this shot due to the two hands on the high ball.

Can You Do This?

Now we come to the behind-the-back and between-the-legs shots that make the crowd go wild.

For many years, the-behind-the back volley was the "ooh and aah" shot from the gallery's standpoint. In doubles, this shot most often happens at the net when there has been a fast exchange of volleys between all four players. One player may be covering the alley and the opposition hits down the middle. The forehand player will stick his racquet across his waist behind his back in a forehand grip and volley the ball back over the net. It is not advisable to do this instead of a regular backhand volley, because you don't have much control. It is strictly a reflex action and it all happens very quickly. You will not have much choice of direction, but it is a way to get that fast volley back over the net. You may even win the point because opponents are often taken off-guard and are not ready for the next shot.

The basic between-the-legs shot is again hit off a quick volley. Usually the net player is on the service line and the opponent has a high volley or overhead, which he hits right at the net player's feet. A good doubles player will be expecting this shot and will be ready for anything. When the ball comes at your feet, you keep your feet apart and place the racquet behind your back with the head of the racquet pointing down at the ground. You won't have much time to think about a grip, but a continental should be used in all of these trick shots.

Sometimes the ball will bounce right in front of you, but most of the time the ball will be coming fast at your feet. The pace of the ball rebounding off your racquet face (which will be slightly open as it is between your legs) will make the ball go up and over the net. I wouldn't expect any miracles, and you will probably lose the next shot, but, again, the element of surprise always helps in this situation.

The next shot belongs to Maria Bueno, the fiery Wimbledon Champion from Sao Paulo, Brazil. This shot is the over-the-shoulder sidearm hit off a lob that you have let bounce. Maria had a great overhead, but sometimes I think she let the lob go over her head just so she could run back and hit this shot because it looked so pretty and she could direct it almost anywhere.

She would run back for the lob and instead of moving slightly to the side of the ball so that she could hit another lob off her forehand or backhand side, she would run almost in a straight line with the ball. Just after the ball bounced, she would keep it more on her backhand side, but the ball was still in front of her as she was running back to the baseline. Taking her racquet in the continental grip, she would hit a forehand over her left shoulder without looking into the court. The racquet came up from her waist and she almost flicked the ball, which she would keep about 1 foot over her left shoulder. If her opponent came in, Maria would often lob, but usually she would hit a flat hard drive deep to the baseline. This allowed Maria to keep her opponent deep and she recovered her position. Not only that, the crowd was definitely on her side.

The last spectacular shot belongs to two players who made it look so easy they had their opponents convinced they could do it any time they wanted. Gabriela Sabatini and Yannick Noah, two attractive and popular players during their time on the tour, developed a shot that became known as a "Sabatweenie."

I warn you not to try this shot without watching it carefully first, because you can do serious damage to your personal body parts if you don't swing at the right time.

Again, this shot is hit off a very deep lob that has gone over your head. Obviously, the safe reply is another lob so you can recover your court position and your balance. However, at the pro level, unless your lob is perfect, you are going to be faced with trying to return another good overhead.

Trish Says

I can remember the first time Yannick Noah hit a Sabatweenie in a match. He was playing a very close match at the French Open and of course, he was a crowd favorite. The French are very vocal when their countrymen are playing. In the third set Noah went back for a deep lob, letting the ball stay in front of him all the way to behind the baseline. The crowd thought he had lost the point, but just as the ball was about to bounce for the second time, Noah flicked his wrist and hit the ball at full swing between his legs. The ball sailed back past his surprised opponent who had come to the net after his lob. The crowd went crazy and his opponent had no chance after that because every time Noah hit the ball, they shouted "Yannick, Yannick."

Noah's fans wanted him to try the shot every time he got a deep lob. Sometimes I think he hit the shot more often than he should have simply because he loved to hit it.

Sabatini loved the shot, too. Many of the men pro tour players can now hit the "tweenie," but not too many of the women tour players try it.

To execute the Sabatweenie, you need a lob that forces you to run back deep. It cannot be done off a good topspin lob, because the ball will bounce too far away from you. As you run back, position the ball directly in front of you as you are facing the back fence. You need to be relatively close to the ball, and you must be prepared to let the ball get very close to bouncing a second time. If you have ever played squash or racquetball, you will understand how to hit this shot. You need to take the racquet up above your right shoulder if you are right-handed because it is a forehand. Hold your racquet with a loose, continental grip. As the ball drops down in front of you, let it get just below your knees and then snap the wrist quickly so that the racquet head meets the ball and then the head of the racquet will go through your legs. Make certain your legs are wide apart; you may need to lift one leg slightly to complete the swing. When you do this, you will pull the ball to one side, so try not to move the body too much as you are hitting the ball. Take a look at this photo as I try to do my "tweenie."

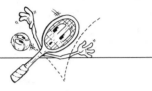

Double Faults

You must let the ball get very low when you try the between-the-legs reverse shot. Remember, the ball needs to go between your legs, so it can be only about 6 inches off the ground when you hit it.

Be careful!

Photo credit: June Harrison

You can try these shots when you are playing singles or doubles for fun. You may find that they come easily to you and that you can transfer them into your competitive games. Good luck and have fun with them. Remember that you will not have a lot of control—so be careful.

The Least You Need to Know

➤ The drop shot is the most important shot in your tennis arsenal.

➤ The second most important shot, which will keep the ball in play and you out of trouble, is the lob.

➤ Spin will make you a better player, so learn it.

➤ You have lots of choices when it comes to returning lobs.

➤ Keep the ball in play any way you can.

➤ An angle shot is usually returned with another angle.

➤ You don't have to be facing your opponent to hit a winner.

Chapter 15

Let's Get Physical—
Fit to Play

In This Chapter

➤ Daily workout—home, gym, and court

➤ Cross-training—sports that will help

➤ Recognizing the signs that you are tired

➤ Most common tennis injuries

➤ Time off

➤ Care of injuries

Tennis is a competitive game that you can play throughout your life. The only requirement is that you stay reasonably fit by doing other exercises, and that you protect your bones and muscles by doing stretches. In this chapter, I will explain some of the different workout routines and cross-training that will complement your tennis game, and help to prevent tennis injuries.

I have a five-step routine that will help you play better tennis. These five steps are:

1. Warmup
2. Stretch
3. Strengthen and cross-train
4. Cool down
5. Stretch again

If you do all of these five steps, it will also be like buying a life insurance policy. Sometimes, even with the best intentions, you may find that you have moved differently, slipped on something on the court, or perhaps you have overexerted yourself because of fatigue. This routine will help you guard against injuries.

In addition to the cross-training routine, I have included two very important sections in this chapter. One is recognizing the signs that tell you to stop playing before you are injured; and the second is what to do if you are injured. There are some common tennis injuries and certain prescribed ways to care for them.

Two years ago, I was defending my national title. The tournament was being held at my club, so I was the *tournament director* for the event and playing in it, too. This was no small undertaking. There were problems to take care of, courts to schedule, and I had to squeeze in some practice time as well. I was a little preoccupied. I wasn't eating properly. I wasn't sleeping enough, and managing the event was taking away from my workout time.

I remember walking on the court to play the final round. The competition was tough and my mind was on scheduling the afternoon matches before it rained. I rushed through the warmup as well. We started to play the set and I kept losing my concentration. I lost the first set 6–4. I won the second set in a close game. In the third set, my opponent was leading 5 games to 4 and I started to feel rather tired. I moved for a wide backhand and, all of a sudden, my ankle rolled over and I fell. I was taken to the hospital and discovered I had a grade-three sprain. Most people would have gone home and rested, but that afternoon I was scheduled to play with my doubles partner in the finals. She had flown in from California, and I just couldn't let her default. I took some painkillers and had the doctor wrap up my ankle. I played and she moved a lot around the court to cover for me. Despite all of this, we won. Now this might sound great, but by not stopping, I was unable to play for two months longer than I expected, and I had to go through additional hours of physical therapy and pain. The moral of this sad story is: Take time off to let your body heal. Moreover, do not play when you are distracted. I learned this the hard way.

Let me now share with you some of my workout routine tips and all the other things I have learned about how to care for my muscles.

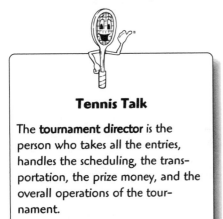

Tennis Talk

The **tournament director** is the person who takes all the entries, handles the scheduling, the transportation, the prize money, and the overall operations of the tournament.

Daily Workout

Like you have to do with anything else in life, you have to approach your workout schedule with a plan. This is very important because there are certain muscle-building exercises that shouldn't be done on consecutive days because you may end up injuring yourself.

Most important in the beginning is to get a complete physical to make sure that you are in the shape required to commence a vigorous exercise program. You want to make sure that the exercise program you are about to embark on is not too strenuous for you.

Next, begin looking at local gyms. The primary requirement for the gym is that it should be close to your home or office. If it is too far, you will not discipline yourself to go. Walk around to make sure it is clean, well lit, has good ventilation, new equipment, and at any given time, is not too crowded. You should probably talk to some of the clients to find out how they feel about the hours that the gym is open, the classes that are offered, and how good the trainers are. The trainers should be pleasant, knowledgeable, helpful, and fit.

After you choose a gym, get in touch with one of the trainers who will tailor an exercise program for you. You should explain to the trainer that you have decided to take up tennis and you want an exercise routine that will build muscle strength, stamina, speed, and flexibility. Some of the exercises will be done on the court, in the gym, and at home. Let me run through my weekly routine for you. I have found that over the years, when I stick to my exercise routine, I perform well.

> **Double Faults**
>
> Travel with two Velcro-wrap ice packs in case you injure yourself. You don't even need to find ice because the wraps come with a Thermo ice pack that I just put in a freezer.

At Home

My daily, and I mean *daily*, routine at home is mostly to insure that I loosen up my muscles to avoid injury and maintain my flexibility. I stretch at home in the morning. I hear the excuse already, "I barely have time to get where I am going to, let alone exercise for an hour." Well, the beauty of this plan is that it takes less than 15 minutes.

I start out with the abdominal area. This is an important area because most movements in tennis start from the stomach, groin, or hip area. Strength and control in this area are vital to every phase of the game. So I strengthen these muscles with sit-ups, then go right elbow to left knee, and vice versa (see the top photo on the next page). I have gotten so I can do about 50; but you can start with 10 and build up.

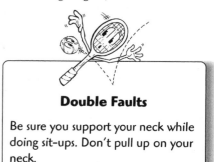

> **Double Faults**
>
> Be sure you support your neck while doing sit-ups. Don't pull up on your neck.

Tighten those muscles.
Photo Credit: Vicki Fort

After my sit-ups, I usually do leg lifts (two reps of ten on each leg). This improves the strength of my muscles in my legs. See the next picture for how to do these properly.

Get a leg up on your opponent.
Photo Credit: Vicki Fort

Next, I do a back exercise to strengthen my muscles in my back. Lie on your stomach and press your stomach and thighs against the floor. Keeping your knees on the ground, lift yourself up with your arms. Hold then relax. Do two reps of ten (see the top photo on the next page).

Back up those shots with strong muscles.

Photo Credit: Vicki Fort

I finish with stretching out my calves. I stand about 3 feet from a wall, lean forward slowly, and hold this position for about 20 seconds. I repeat this five times (see photo below).

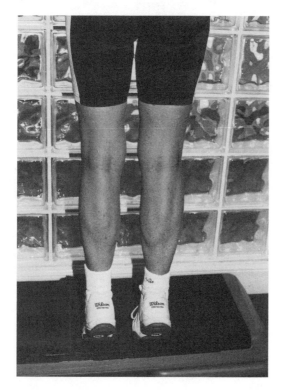

Stretch out those calves.

Photo Credit: Vicki Fort

Now I can get dressed and face the world, which for me means off to the courts.

In the Gym

I am very lucky because at BallenIsles Country Club, where I am the director, there is a fitness area that has all the modern equipment. Certified instructors teach aerobic classes that I try to make whenever I have time. I would like to go every day but my schedule does not always permit that. If I cannot join the classes, I use a stationary bike, treadmill, or a cross-trainer (which uses the arms and the legs simultaneously).

Aerobic exercise is very important to my tennis game. It builds my confidence, it increases my stamina, and it gives me the mental edge I need because I know I can outlast my opponent. I usually spend about 45 minutes on aerobics three times a week—sometimes more, depending on the week. See the following pictures for the different aerobic equipment I use.

Good, solid aerobic exercise.

Photo Credit: Vicki Fort

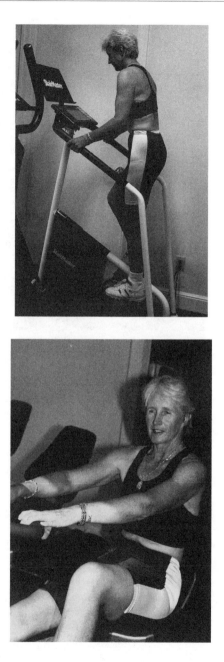

A little strenuous, but good aerobic activity.

Photo Credit: Vicki Fort

It may not be the Tour de France, but it is great aerobic exercise.

Photo Credit: Vicki Fort

After the aerobic exercise, I use light weights two days a week, but never on consecutive days. I usually do some muscle building with some of the equipment in the gym. I like to build up my shoulders and pecs with the Gravitron. It really helps with my serve (see the top picture on the next page).

Build up those shoulder muscles.

Photo Credit: Vicki Fort

I then like to work the arm muscles with this piece of equipment shown in the next picture.

Armed and ready.

Photo Credit: Vicki Fort

I also do some leg lifts with the leg-lift equipment shown in the next picture.

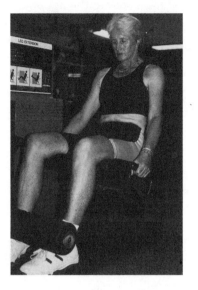

Get a leg up on your opponent.

Photo Credit: Vicki Fort

Just a quick note here: Be sure you do not set the weights on these machines too high. You should really work with a trainer in the beginning so that you learn the equipment and what weight levels are good for you.

I use my weight training program to help develop my muscular endurance. It also improves my range of motion, and reduces my risk of injury because it strengthens my muscles. To compete at a high level of tennis, you must reach your potential in muscle development because tennis is a sport that requires strength, endurance, flexibility, and a full range of motion.

On the Court

Besides the pre-tennis stretching discussed in Chapter 7, I also work on my agility and balance on the court. In tennis, there are a lot of stop-and-go movements, so you must have good footwork and be well-balanced to be able to move and hit correctly without hurting yourself.

Many drills for footwork and agility can be done on the court without a racquet. One of my favorites is to stay low to the ground and run quickly and touch the singles line, the doubles line, and then back to the centerline. Move quickly but keep your balance.

Double Faults

Don't work out with weights and then go out and play tennis—you will risk injuring yourself because your muscles will be tired.

Another drill that I do is the up and back drill. This one helps me cover the court when someone is firing lobs and drop shots at me. I start at the net on the side where the post is. I back-pedal to the baseline then I shuffle to the service line in the middle, then back-pedal to the baseline on the other side and then sprint to the other net post. This is a fast-paced drill and you really have to be balanced. Make certain you stay on the balls of your feet so you don't trip.

There are many other on-court drills you can do. You should discuss your weakness in terms of court coverage with your pro. Find a drill that will improve your weaker areas.

Cross-Training

Many other sports complement tennis by keeping the tennis player physically fit and conditioned. The following are my three favorites.

Swimming

Swimming is a wonderful form of exercise. It offers no stress on your bones and joints. It strengthens your upper and lower body. It also is a very calming exercise since you are alone with your thoughts, no loud music, no screaming, just swimming at your own pace. I find that swimming after a tennis game is ideal, especially if I am hot and a little sore. Swimming also cools my muscles and the motion stretches out my limbs. In fact, before I became interested in tennis I swam competitively in Australia.

Trish Says

I used to swim with my father and uncle in a salt-water tidal pool that was cut from rock next to the ocean. It was often cold and we would all quickly dive in and start swimming on those cold mornings. One morning, all three of us dove in and started a leisurely crawl to loosen up. As we swam to the far side to turn, we all stopped because a 3-foot baby octopus had been stranded by the tide in the pool and was calmly waiting on the far wall. You have never seen three people swim so fast back to the other wall. Training was cut short that day.

To this day, I swim five to six times a week, if weather permits.

Everyone in the pool.

Photo Credit: June Harrison

Running

Running allows me to improve my stamina on the court. I try to do some short sprints every few days so that I can simulate the stop and go motion on the court. Sometimes when I travel and have access to a gym, I do a short run to maintain my aerobic exercise.

The extra benefit of running outdoors is that you get to enjoy the beauty of nature. That's what I am doing in this picture.

Taking in the sights.

Photo Credit: June Harrison

Basketball

I have always loved basketball. This was one of the sports I played at school in Australia. Basketball is a great complement to my tennis game. It helps develop hand-eye coordination, quickness, and the ability to stop and go. It definitely helps develop multiple vision, which is the ability to see the ball, where you are on the court, and where your opponent is all at the same time. I find this is very important in tennis.

Anyone for a pick-up game?

Photo Credit: June Harrison

Cross-training minimizes the risk of over training any particular muscle group. If you want to excel in tennis, it is very important for you to build all your muscle groups, improve your agility, and increase your stamina. This will help you take your tennis game to the next level.

Courtside Quotes

"Spend more time preparing and less time regretting."
—Virginia Wade

Recognizing When You're Tired

Cross-training helps you minimize the risk of injury, but you can take cross-training too far. You must be able to recognize when your body is fatigued. I watch for a few telltale signs to indicate to me that I am overtired (I will discuss these further in Chapter 19). It is very important that you recognize the signs and just back off from all exercise before you injure yourself. A few signs that I watch for indicate I am overtired:

➤ I don't want to get out of bed in the morning.

➤ My whole body aches and cries out for rest.

➤ I pray for rain so I don't have to teach my students.

➤ My tennis game seems stale.

➤ I am a little more irritable.

➤ I have trouble concentrating.

When I find that I have any of these signs of fatigue, I take some time off. A couple of days is usually enough. When I come back, I find that my game has improved substantially. I concentrate better and I move better.

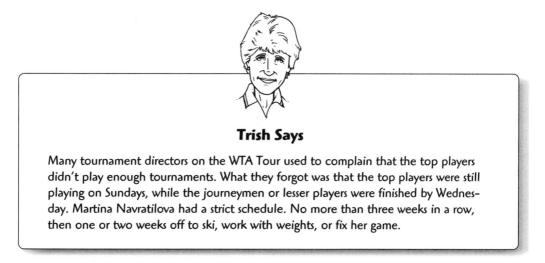

Trish Says

Many tournament directors on the WTA Tour used to complain that the top players didn't play enough tournaments. What they forgot was that the top players were still playing on Sundays, while the journeymen or lesser players were finished by Wednesday. Martina Navratilova had a strict schedule. No more than three weeks in a row, then one or two weeks off to ski, work with weights, or fix her game.

I can't stress enough how important it is to know your own body and its limitations. Don't be afraid to take time off. Your game and your body won't suffer.

We have all heard the old adage: No pain, no gain. Those words have sent many an athlete to the emergency room with unnecessary injuries. Pushing yourself is not going to help you perform better. Pushing yourself beyond your limit will result in fatigue and injuries. When you reduce the level of your tennis workout, you will actually improve the level of your game and you will be less likely to injure yourself. Your muscles need time to recover. Over training will cause you to burn out mentally, and you will not be able to reach your goals.

I am all for trying to reach your potential as the best tennis player you can be, but not when your body is fatigued. I guarantee that the only thing you will be feeling is boredom and restlessness. You will not be enjoying your tennis.

Over the years, I have witnessed new players who take up tennis with a passion. They are out there six to seven days a week, five to six hours a day playing tennis. They just can't seem to get enough. They start to advance and they work harder to reach new levels. However, somewhere along the way, they stop advancing and, in some cases, they even take a step back. The player who once came to the court with a smile now looks angry and irritable. His or her frustration level is increased and you can tell that tennis is no longer fun for that person. Many players abuse their bodies to the point where they sustain injuries. Others just burn out mentally and stop playing altogether. I try to tell them to take it easy and not overdo it. Rome was not built in a day, and your tennis game cannot improve that quickly either. Enjoy the process of learning and advancing to each new level. As they say, slow and steady wins the race.

The Most Common Tennis Injuries and How to Deal with Them

Sometimes when you overdo it, you will develop some new aches and pains. Occasionally, you will injure an arm or a shoulder because you did not warm up correctly. If you hit the ball correctly and you have the right equipment, you should not sustain any injuries. However, few of us are equal to Wonder Woman or Superman.

Here follows a description of common injuries and how to take care of them.

Tennis Elbow

This is the most talked-about tennis injury because it results from incorrect swings rather than from overuse. The muscles and tendons in the elbow become inflamed from bending your wrist backward and turning your palm face up. Hitting a backhand late causes it, as does trying to put more spin on a serve, thus turning your wrist. You will experience pain on the outside of your elbow. Lifting objects, holding on to your racquet, or turning your hand in a clockwise direction will be not only painful, but hard to do.

There are certain things you can do to treat tennis elbow, depending on how far along it is. If it is not bad, and you are just noticing beginning signs, talk to your pro about fixing your backhand stroke so you don't hit the ball late. You can wear any number of elbow supports. These supports actually help absorb the shock on your tendon. You can also do some specific exercises to strengthen elbow muscles. You will also want to do some flexibility exercises to relieve the pain you are feeling by trying to strengthen your muscles. Talk to an exercise trainer so that he or she can advise you on the best thing to do.

I suggest that players ice their elbows for at least 15 minutes after playing. Once again, if it is bad, take time off from tennis to rest it.

Wrist Injuries

There are two types of wrist injuries common to tennis players. One is an overuse injury. This happens when you play too much and the injury gradually becomes worse over time. For this type of injury, you should take time off from tennis, take anti-inflammatory products, and do some strength training. Another type of wrist injury related to tennis is a sprain, caused by a wrong wrist movement. This should be iced and rested, and, again, you should do some strength training.

Double Faults

If you suffer from tennis elbow, try switching your racquet to composite, graphite, titanium, or hypercarbon because these materials transmit the least amount of shock to the elbow.

Rotator Cuff Problems

If you feel pain in the front of your shoulder or on the outside of your upper arm, you may be suffering from a strained rotator cuff muscle. Tennis players suffer this injury from their serve or their overheads. The best way to treat this is with a strength-training program. You will want to strengthen the muscle so that the shoulder is held firmly in place and the tendons do not become inflamed or irritated. Some good exercises for this are the arm curl, reverse arm curl, front lift, lateral lift, and bent-over lateral lift.

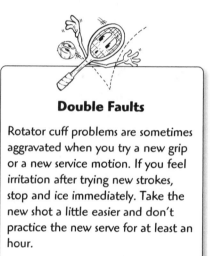

Double Faults

Rotator cuff problems are sometimes aggravated when you try a new grip or a new service motion. If you feel irritation after trying new strokes, stop and ice immediately. Take the new shot a little easier and don't practice the new serve for at least an hour.

Knee Injuries

Tennis requires many quick directional changes, twisting and turning, and stops and starts that will sometimes result in cartilage and ligament damage in the knee. You must treat these injuries with ice; then elevate the knee, add some compression to avoid swelling, and rest. You should see a doctor immediately. A knee injury is not something you want to neglect because it can become worse very quickly when ignored.

Hamstring Injuries

Your hamstring muscles are in the back of your thigh and help you run. They become pulled when you over-stretch, as you do when you run to get a ball. You will feel a sharp pain in the muscle and your thigh will probably swell. You will have to rest, ice, and use some compression. The length of your rest depends on how bad the pull is. When you are free of pain, you can start to stretch it out, as long as you don't pull it again. One stretch that I like to do is done on the side of the court. I place my leg on the net and bend over and reach for my feet.

Groin Pulls

A sudden lateral movement can cause a groin pull. Rest is important in a groin pull, followed by a stretching program. This is a tough area to stretch out correctly so ask a personal trainer to suggest some specific exercises. Yoga Stretch–99 is very good (yoga movements follow a standardized numbering system). This injury nags on so make certain you don't return too quickly to the courts.

Ankle Sprains

Because there are many side-to-side motions in tennis, ankle sprains are common. You should have an ankle sprain x-rayed and looked at immediately. Sprains are sometimes worse than breaks but usually in tennis you will just experience a slight sprain unless you take a bad fall.

RICE

What does rice have to do with tennis injuries? Isn't it something I eat with my Chinese food? Yes, you are right, it is a food, but when used as an acronym it means:

Rest

Ice

Compression

Elevation

When you do all of these together, you will reduce the swelling that takes place after an injury. Reducing the swelling is critical to your returning to the game. A swollen joint has very limited function. If you reduce the swelling, you will save days of recovery time.

The Least You Need to Know

➤ Workout daily to improve your tennis game.

➤ Mix different kinds of aerobic exercise to improve stamina and muscles.

➤ Weight train to improve muscle endurance and strength.

➤ Don't weight train right before you play tennis.

➤ Cross-train to vary your muscle workout.

➤ Listen to your body and know when to take some time off.

➤ If you injure yourself, take care of it immediately, rest, and don't play while you are injured.

➤ Stretching and muscle building will go a long way in preventing injury.

➤ RICE means rest, ice, compression, and elevation—very important to reduce swelling and hasten recovery.

Chapter 16

I've Got You Under My Skin

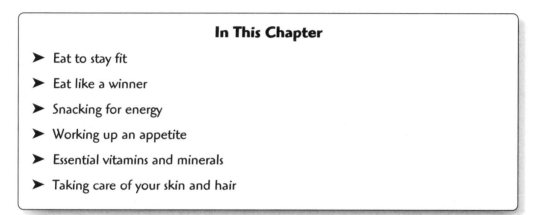

In This Chapter

➤ Eat to stay fit

➤ Eat like a winner

➤ Snacking for energy

➤ Working up an appetite

➤ Essential vitamins and minerals

➤ Taking care of your skin and hair

You have just spent the last hour practicing your forehand, but instead of getting better, you are actually getting worse. Your frustration level is rising and you just feel totally spent, and you ask yourself why. There is a simple answer: You have just run out of fuel. In simple terms, either you did not eat enough or you did not eat properly.

I remember I was playing Virginia Wade and Roger Taylor, both from Great Britain. It was my third match of the day and it was very late. We split sets and I could feel my energy level dropping as well as my concentration wavering. My partner, Bob Howe, said, "Take one of my butterscotch chews, it will give you a quick boost of energy." We won, and I have loved butterscotch ever since.

In this chapter, I will explain to you some of the basics of what your tennis diet and skin care should be. Your diet is as important a factor in becoming a good tennis player as your strokes. Remember, without fuel, neither your body nor your mind can function. Skin care is very important because of the risks of skin cancer from sun exposure.

Trish Says

I have a weakness for ice cream. If I don't keep it in the house, I can go for a week without missing a scoop. Otherwise, if I have it in the freezer, I act like a homing pigeon. I love it so much I make certain we have ice cream even if we are out of bananas, which is a very bad thing for an athlete.

Sensible Healthy Eating

Good eating habits should be routine throughout your life. It makes no difference if you are planning a career as a pro athlete or if you just want to be a social player, you must eat sensibly. If your eating regimen is poor and you drink or smoke in excess, you run the risk of injuring yourself or being more open to disease.

So what is a sensible diet anyway? I can sum it up in two words: moderation and variety. This translates to eating a balanced diet with all the things you enjoy, but not overdoing it. Most athletes know if they listen to their body, it will tell them what it needs to function in top form.

Let me go through some of the basics of good nutrition.

The five food groups must be included in your daily diet. All of one without the other will be of no help. It is like having a perfect forehand and no other stroke, making winning any match impossible. Here is a list of the five food groups and what's in each one:

1. *Carbohydrates*. This group is made up of breads, cereal, rice, and pasta. They allow your body to store fuel needed to exert energy over an extended period.

2. *Vegetables*. This group is important because it supplies your body with the vitamins and minerals that you need to stay healthy. They help produce the enzymes and hormones to protect your body against infection and disease.

3. *Fruits*. This group supplies your body with the vitamins and fibers that your body needs to help it function efficiently.

4. *Dairy products*. This group provides your body with protein, calcium, vitamins, and minerals. This group protects your bones and muscles.

5. *Proteins.* This group is made up of meats, poultry, fish, beans, eggs, and nuts. Protein sources contain some B vitamins, iron, and zinc, and are very important to help tissue grow and repair itself.

There are recommended guidelines as to how much of each group you should be eating a day; but again, everything in moderation and balanced.

Pre-Game Fueling

Before a big match, you might want to consider a few things. First, that the match may take a number of hours so you should eat plenty of carbohydrates that can be stored up and used as fuel during the match. Second, you are probably not going to want to eat just before a match, but rather, 2 to 4 hours before competition so that your food can be digested and stored in your body. Third, you will not want to drink a lot of caffeine since it is a diuretic. You will get a quick energy burst, then become dehydrated. It is very important to hydrate before a match so that your body will have a chance to absorb the fluid. Hydrating not only will stop you from suffering heat exhaustion, but also will help carry nutrients to your muscles so that they will function in their top form. During play, you need to drink 5 to 10 ounces of fluid every 20 minutes or so. After the match, drink at least 2 cups of fluid for every pound of water weight lost.

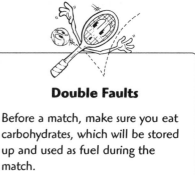

Double Faults

Before a match, make sure you eat carbohydrates, which will be stored up and used as fuel during the match.

On-Court Snacks

During the match, one of the most important things to do is to make sure you're drinking enough water. You must drink before you feel thirsty, because by the time you feel thirsty, you are dehydrated. Your body is made up of over 75 percent water, so when you lose even a small amount, it will negatively effect your performance. People that do not exercise need at least 8 glasses of water a day, so you can imagine if you are playing in the hot sun and really moving about, how much additional water you will need. A good rule of thumb is to drink 8 ounces of water for every half hour you are playing in the sun. Some might say this is too much, but to perform up to your potential, it is better to err with too much rather than too little water.

Trish Says

During one match on a particularly hot day, I looked over to my partner and she looked like she was going to faint. She felt very dizzy. I noticed she wasn't sweating much. She was suffering from heat exhaustion, which was turning into something serious: heat stroke. So please, make use of those changeovers and drink plenty of fluids regardless of whether you feel thirsty or not.

During the match you may also start feeling hungry and get a little lethargic. At this point, during the changeover, reach for something that will provide you with a quick energy boost.

Before 1986, some of the pros on the court used fruit and glucose tablets to replenish fluids and energy. Since the advent of sports bars and power drinks, people are relying on these for quick and easy absorbing and digestible foods that are converted to energy.

Energy bars are very popular with people who tend to exercise a lot. They can be purchased in most tennis shops or gyms. They are convenient and since they don't require any refrigeration, they can be kept in your tennis bag for a long time. (I wouldn't try this with a piece of fruit). Many of these energy bars are low in fat and have a good amount of vitamins and minerals. The down side is the taste and calorie content; although I have to admit these bars have come a long way in the taste department since they first hit the market more than a decade ago. They used to taste just like cardboard and they were very hard to swallow because of their consistency.

Another quick source of energy and a good fluid replacement are the power drinks that are now on the market. They contain carbohydrates and *electrolytes*. They have been on the market for more than 25 years, and many athletes reach for them during exercise. I drink them when the match seems to go longer than an hour. Fluids are very important and carbohydrates give you that energy lift that will enable you to play at your peak performance.

I also will have a banana with me during a match. I find it is easy to eat during the changeover. It is a good source of potassium, vitamin A, and fiber. A medium banana contains about 100 calories. I usually find a banana to be quite filling and easy to digest during a match. Also, you don't have to worry about washing it because of the peel.

Drink up!

Photo Credit: Vicki Fort

So, to sum up, on-court snacks should be easy to digest, not high in fat, and somewhat easy to eat. You should definitely be replacing fluids during your match, and you may want to consider a power drink to replace lost electrolytes.

Postgame Rewards

Again, at the risk of sounding like a broken record, I must advocate drinking to replace lost fluids. This is vitally important for your muscles. The fluids will carry nutrients to your muscles and will enable them to heal. Carbohydrates are needed to replace muscle glycogen, which helps with the recovery of your muscles. A small amount of protein is essential to repair any muscle damage.

After one of my long matches, I make sure I drink enough fluids and have a meal that contains some type of lean protein like turkey or fish, and a carbohydrate, like pasta or bread. I usually will treat myself to something that is a little sweet like frozen yogurt or a cookie. I tend not to be very hungry after I play, and I need a little bit of time to calm down; but usually within 45 minutes, I can sit down to a meal.

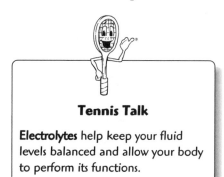

Tennis Talk

Electrolytes help keep your fluid levels balanced and allow your body to perform its functions.

Vitamins and Minerals

Vitamins are very important to help convert food to fuel, prevent diseases, and heal injuries you may have sustained. Most foods that you eat have vitamins in them. But to get the recommended dosage of different vitamins, you should take a good multivitamin. Because I have a balanced diet that contains many fruits and vegetables, one good multivitamin is really all I need.

Double Faults

Too many high dosages of the wrong vitamins can actually be more harmful than good for you. Check with a nutritionist.

Minerals do many things: They help produce energy and keep your bones in good shape; they regulate your metabolism; keep your blood pressure low; and help keep your body fluids balanced. You get most minerals you need from eating a balanced diet, but you can benefit from taking a supplement. If you are a woman, you should take a calcium pill to help prevent osteoporosis. I take one every day.

If you are an active person, you want to make sure your body can function in top form. Taking one multivitamin and a calcium pill helps me to perform to the best of my ability, but you should check with your physician or nutritionist to make certain you are taking the right vitamins.

Saving Face

One of the most difficult aspects of being a tennis player is dealing with the harsh effects the environment has on your skin. When I was younger, I relished the golden glow of my tanned skin. Today, I see freckles where there were none, and brown spots that I regularly have checked. My dermatologist has already removed a few suspicious moles and I am thankful that none have yet become cancerous.

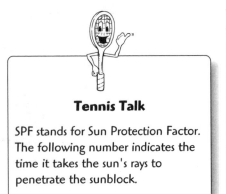

Tennis Talk

SPF stands for Sun Protection Factor. The following number indicates the time it takes the sun's rays to penetrate the sunblock.

We all know that sunscreen is a must. I've learned throughout the years that there are many things available to protect us externally as well as internally. I get facials and massages as often as my schedule allows, and the facialist I see has recommended a skin care routine for me to follow.

Every morning I use a gentle cleanser that contains vitamins, a light toner, and two sunscreen products. I like the Murad products because they were developed by a dermatologist and they actually work! I also like the fact that everything is lightweight so I can reapply sunscreen throughout the day if necessary.

Great skin care.

Photo Credit: Vicki Fort

This is my regimen:

1. Wash my face with Murad Environmental Shield Facial Cleanser
2. Tone with Murad Hydrating Toner (tightens and firms without drying the skin)
3. Moisturize with Murad Essential Day Moisture SPF 15
4. Apply Muraskin Sunblock SPF 30 (this is an oil-free sunblock that really lasts)

All of these products contain vitamins and antioxidants that protect my skin from sun damage.

Trish Says

It is so hard to force myself to get into a skin care routine. It is second nature for me to stretch and watch what I eat, but I find it hard to take the time to make certain my skin is clean, my sunscreen is applied, and remember to take my vitamins.

On days when I'm not playing, I use the Murasun Oil-Free Sunblock in SPF 15 that comes in a bronze shade. It gives my skin a radiant glow and seems to blend in the spots.

My hair really takes a beating, too, so I usually have a scalp treatment every time I color my hair. Since I've been doing this, my hair looks much shinier and seems stronger and the color seems to last longer. I also like the Murad hair products for chemically treated hair. I sometimes alternate with their thinning-hair products, which seem to give my hair lots of body.

I have many different hats and caps which help protect me from the sun. Here I am in one of my Ellesse hats.

Top it off.
Photo Credit: Vicki Fort

I also consider my vitamins part of my skin care routine. I take a multivitamin, calcium, and an antioxidant supplement called Environmental Shield on a daily basis. Vitamins can actually protect your skin from the inside, too.

What Should You Do?

Whether male or female, everyone needs to protect their skin. The following list of products was developed by my facialist who recommends them to help keep your skin safe and healthy. All of these products are created by Dr. Howard Murad and can be found across the country in beauty salons and skin care centers. For a location near you, call 800-33-MURAD or 800-336-6873.

If you have normal to dry sun-damaged skin, you should try:

➤ Environmental Shield Facial Cleanser

➤ Environmental Shield Toner

➤ Skin Renewal Complex

➤ Essential Day Moisture SPF 15

If your skin is on the oily side, try:

➤ Refreshing Skin Cleanser

➤ Clarifying Astringent

➤ Oily Prone Skin Formula

➤ Skin Perfecting Lotion

If you are prone to acne or breakouts, try:

➤ Clarifying Skin Cleaner

➤ Clarifying Astringent

➤ Acne Prone Skin Formula

➤ Skin Perfecting Lotion

➤ Purifying Clay Masque

Every skin type should use a sunblock with at least an SPF of 15 on a daily basis, and a water-proof SPF 30 when exercising. The following products protect you from the sun; plus they also have antioxidants and are oil-free:

➤ Muradun Oil-Free Sunblock SPF 15

➤ Murasun Waterproof Sunblock SPF 30

There are many different lines of sunglasses. Buy a good brand with plenty of wraparound protection. Make certain they don't slip off when you are sweaty. Comfort as well as protection is important. I have three or four pairs of sunglasses and I rotate them every week. See what you think.

Double Faults

As much as it gives me "hat hair," I always wear a cap to protect my hair and my face from the sun. It is part of my skin care routine. The hat goes on automatically at 7 A.M. and doesn't come off until I am at my desk inside.

Passing Shots

Most of the professionals do not play matches in sunglasses because they hamper peripheral vision. Those of us who teach use them all the time to protect our eyes from sun damage. There is a new lens on the market now that actually helps you see the ball on a sunny day.

Looking cool.

Photo Credit: Vicki Fort

More on Sun Care

One blistering sunburn before the age of 18 doubles your chances of developing skin cancer. Get a full-body skin cancer screening each year as part of your physical. Wear long sleeves whenever possible and a hat. Many dermatologists offer one free screening a year. Ask your local medical group, or you may contact the Skin Cancer Foundation at 212-725-5176.

A T-shirt offers SPF of only 8! This means sun-protective clothing is essential on the tennis court. Wearing a sunblock helps, but you must reapply it often to ensure its benefits. Sun-protective clothing is available today with either an SPF reading or an ultraviolet protection factor (UPF) coding.

Consider the following when purchasing clothing:

➤ *Weave.* Tightly woven fabrics offer more protection than loosely woven ones.

➤ *Color.* Darker colors let in less light than lighter ones.

➤ *Weight.* The heavier the fabric, the less ultraviolet light is let through. However, if the fabric is lightweight and closely woven, you will achieve the same protection.

➤ *Wetness*. Wet fabric will decrease ultraviolet protection by as much as 50 percent. Keep a dry shirt close at hand.

These companies offer clothing in sun protective fabrics for sports use:

Sun Precaution   800-882-7860
Sun Skins   800-610-0094

The clothing is actually quite cool as you can see.

It doesn't matter what age you are; you should protect yourself from sun exposure. Follow these tips and you will save your skin and enjoy a good game.

Double Faults

Make certain you carry lip-moisturizing sunscreen and regular sunblock in your tennis bag. Remember, if you are out in the sun you need to reapply them every few hours.

Cover up.
Photo Credit: Vicki Fort

The Least You Need to Know

➤ Choose your diet from the five basic food groups for a balanced diet.

➤ Before a game, be sure you drink enough fluids and eat some carbohydrates.

➤ During the game, drink during every changeover.

➤ After the game, replace your lost fluids and carbohydrates.

➤ Power bars and drinks can give you the extra edge you need to perform.

➤ Make your skin healthy by following both a daily routine of vitamins and skin care.

➤ Protect your hair from the sun as well as your skin.

Chapter 17

Practice Makes Perfect

In This Chapter

➤ Improving your game at home

➤ When you hit the wall

➤ Practice, practice, practice

➤ Raise the level of your match play

➤ Making drills interesting

We all know the saying, "Practice makes perfect." In tennis, practice may not make you perfect, but it will go a long way in making you a better player. Without practicing what you are learning, the hundreds of dollars you spend on lessons and the time you have devoted, are wasted. If you want to really improve your game, you must practice your strokes, your strategy, and your entire game.

In my years of teaching tennis, I have witnessed many things. I have seen players with natural abilities that walk on the court, play their game, and go home. They don't improve and they can't figure out why. Players they used to beat are now beating them. I try to tell them that it is not enough just to play matches, you must go out and practice. In many cases, practice will allow you to only maintain your level, not improve. However, if you practice properly, you will improve all facets of your game.

In this chapter, I explain the different ways you can practice and some of the drills my students like to do.

What You Can Do at Home

To help hand-eye coordination, try juggling. Take one ball in each hand and try to throw the ball from one hand to the other. If you can, try it with three balls (four or more balls and you can join the circus!).

Courtside Quotes

"In the years I have played tennis, I have looked for a born tennis player, but I have yet to find one."

—Bill Tilden, on the importance of practice

To practice your serve, grab two balls and go to your garage or outside. Place one ball in each hand and run your arms through the motion of the serve. After a few practice runs, release the ball from your tossing arm. Try to simulate the start of your serve. The main goal of this drill is to place your toss comfortably in the right spot. Holding a ball in your racquet hand is just a reminder that this hand does something, too. I would not recommend doing this under your chandelier.

Pros and amateurs alike know that jumping rope is the best overall exercise. It works your arms, and, if you do it the right way, it really helps your footwork. Take a look at this picture and you can see the simple exercise I do all the time.

Fancy footwork.
Photo Credit: Vicki Fort

Some people are very visual and by watching themselves in front of a mirror, they can actually see how the stroke should look. Just like dancers who workout in front of mirrors so they can see their positions, tennis players need to be able to see how they look, too. I tell some of my students to go home after a lesson and try to recreate the stroke they just learned in front of a full-length mirror. Many come back and say they are amazed at how seeing themselves in the mirror really helped reinforce what I had been telling them.

I also ask my students to focus on what we practiced during the lesson. I tell them to think about the stroke and try to master it in their minds. How do they want to look when they hit the ball? This little visualization really does work and, again, it reinforces what you learn in a lesson.

Double Faults

To get the most out of practice, work on one thing at a time. Try to concentrate on what the pro told you in your lesson. Constant repetition of the same thing will make you improve faster.

The Dreaded but Wondrous Wall

The wall is a wonderful place to go to practice your shots without being distracted by anyone. You can work on timing, watching the ball, footwork, and improving your reaction to shots.

Stay 39 feet away from the wall (this is the distance of the baseline to the net). You can let the ball bounce twice before you hit it so you can work on your rhythm, or you can work more on footwork and chase it after one bounce. Analyze your strokes. You are trying to work on how you are making contact with the ball, and the position of your body and feet. Are you finishing your stroke?

Practice your serve. Try to hit wide, in the middle, spin, and flat. When you practice your volleys, move in and don't let the ball bounce. This will be fast paced, so you must learn how to react quickly and anticipate where the ball is going.

Keep in mind that the wall does not replace the court for a warm-up before a match; but it can be used in an emergency. Use the wall in addition to all your other practice routines.

Trish Says

I use three different drills for a good workout at the wall. They are as follows:

1. Pick a side of the wall and hit crosscourt consistently. This works on directing the ball. Do both sides forehand and backhand.

2. Hit crosscourt, then hit down the line. Mixing it up will improve your lateral movement and your footwork.

3. Stand close enough so that you do not let the ball bounce. Practice hitting forehand and backhand volleys. To make it more advanced, hit with a little more pace. This works on your reflex volleys using a volley grip, and helps improve your footwork and eye-hand coordination.

Sometimes when I want to have a good workout and just be by myself, I will spend one hour on the these drills, and afterwards I feel like I played a very tough opponent.

Trish Says

When I was nine and ten years old I used to go hit on the wall next to my coach's court every morning before I went to school. I could amuse myself for an hour playing games and hitting targets which he had painted on the wall or on the ground. I played endless matches against myself and the wall. I believe this is one of the reasons I have such good volleys.

Ball Machines

Ball machines are used to help you get your stroke down through repetition. Muscle memory plays an important part in your stroke production. It is very important to feel how the shot should be executed, and then repeat that action many times. By removing any distractions and variables, the ball machine, like the wall, allows you to concentrate solely on what you are trying to do.

The unbeatable pro.

Photo Credit: Vicki Fort

By moving the ball machine to different sides of the court, changing the depth of the feed, the pace of the feed, and the interval of the ball feed, you can practice different shots. Some ball machines can be set to do all of this for you.

The three drills I tell my students to do with the ball machine are as follows:

1. Hit forehand and backhand ground strokes back and forth and work on not missing. Keep the ball deep. You will be known as the human ball machine around the club because you will be able to return groundstrokes without mistakes.

2. Hit a crosscourt forehand; then run in and hit a crosscourt forehand volley. Run back and do it again. Also, do this on the backhand. Change directions after doing crosscourt, then go down the lines. Soon you will see the improvement on your placement.

3. Hit forehand and backhand volleys, concentrating on getting depth. Start at the service line. This is where many people tend to try to put the ball away; but it can't be done because they are too far away. Instead, this is when you should hit your volley for depth. Try to get every ball past the service line. Your volleys will improve very quickly.

Double Faults

Have your pro check on you using the ball machine the first time you are practicing a new shot, just to make sure you are doing the shot correctly. You don't want to practice the wrong strokes.

I recommend that all my students work with a ball machine so their strokes become second nature. It definitely helps with consistency. One must be able to get the ball back into the court many times consecutively. The constant repetitive motion is very important in learning tennis.

Practice Buddy

I always try to pair my students with other students who are at their same level of play. Not only do they have other people to play with, but they also have what I call a "practice buddy." This is someone you can go out with between lessons to work on strokes, serves, and volleys. It is a very cost-effective and fun way to improve. Usually friendships are formed this way and both students improve more rapidly than if they were practicing by themselves. I think what usually happens is a friendly competition develops and both want to get better than the other, and this helps both players reach their goals.

Trish Says

Ten years ago, I had two new students who were around the same age and new to the game. I suggested that, to enhance their lessons, they should practice with each other during the week. It turns out they both were a little competitive. They started practicing more and more with each other. They became good friends and doubles partners and are now traveling across the nation playing tournaments together.

Here is a list of some of my favorite ways to use a practice buddy.

➤ *Serve and return.* These are two of the most important shots in your game, yet many people neglect to practice them—especially the return. Take turns serving and returning from both sides. You will be amazed at how the level of your game will improve.

➤ *Serve, return, then play out the point.* Here you should work on coming into the net on both the serve and return.

➤ *Passing shot.* One of you must stand at the net and one of you at the baseline. The one who is on the baseline should try to get a passing shot past the net player. Work on both sides. You can even practice your lob.

These are just a few of my favorite drills for buddies. Teaming up with a practice buddy is a great way to improve, have fun, and learn how to get to that next level.

On-the-Court Practice

For most tennis players this is their favorite practice. After you have taken your lessons, hit the wall, worked with a ball machine, drilled, drilled, and drilled some more, what's left? The game. You ask, how can a game be considered practice? In a game, you are practicing not only your strokes, but your mental concentration as well. You are practicing moving to the ball, moving back to the position, and what shot you should be hitting next. You are practicing your mental toughness, knowing what to do in tight situations, what shots to play when you are down, what shots to play when you are up. Also, depending on your opponents, you will be practicing playing against different styles of play—the lobber, the baseliner, and the serve-and-volleyer. All of this is great practice for you. One important note: When you do go out and "play practice," spend some time afterwards to review the game. Where were your strengths and weaknesses? You should then take that knowledge back to your pro and work on it.

I usually have my students try the following drills when they are playing practice matches:

1. Your opponent is up Love–30, you are serving. See if you can come back and win your serve.

2. You are now up 40–Love, and you have only one serve for the rest of the game. It has to be your first serve, not a second. See if you can go out with an ace.

3. Now you are returning and you are up 30–Love, but down 5–4 in the third set. Try to tie it up.

You would be surprised at how adjusting a score, even in a practice game, changes how you play. This is excellent practice to help you become match tough.

These drills are good ways for you to see your weaknesses. Are you a good returner or server? Can you finish off the match, or are you choking on your serve and return? This will make you work on improving what is not working for you and make you more competitive.

Courtside Quotes

"Most of us who aspire to be tops in our field don't really consider the amount of work required to stay tops."

—Althea Gibson

Drills, Drills, and More Drills

In this section, I just want to go through the different drills that I have found to be the most successful through the years. I will break down the drills for the different shots starting with the serve.

Serving

Priorities when serving are:

➤ Get the serve in the court.

➤ Vary the placement to the opponent's backhand, forehand, or at the body.

➤ Adjust the amount of spin—if your serves are long, add more spin. If your serves fall short, use less spin and aim higher over the net.

➤ After you can control the skills at placement, add speed and power to force a weak return.

Before each serve, perform a ritual prior to beginning the motion. Don't rush between serves. Rituals help relax and focus the server by slowing the process.

Passing Shots

When serving and volleying, it is helpful to hit the serve with spin so that it travels higher over the net and lands deep into the box. This will give you more time to get closer to the net, which will make it easier for you to hit a good first volley.

Pressure Serving

Create the scenario that you are up in the third set 6–5. You need four serves to win. You need to:

➤ Serve to the outside half of deuce court

➤ Serve to the inside half of deuce court

➤ Serve to the outside half of ad court

➤ Serve to the inside half of ad court

This helps you focus on where you are serving. You are not concentrating on the score but rather on getting the serve where you want it.

Serving Power

On clay courts, to help practice power and depth on your serves, I would recommend placing some tape or string across the service box about 12 inches inside the service line. Serve a basket of balls and then go and check the ball marks in the service box. Hopefully most of the marks will be behind the tape and inside the service line. This means your serves have good depth. If your marks are slightly oval instead of round like the ball, then this means you also had pace on the ball.

On hard courts, the best way to achieve the same results is to place six empty ball cans about 12 inches inside the service line. After practicing a basket, check the service box and see how many cans are left in the box. This will give you another easy test for power and depth on your serves.

Serve and First Volley

Hit a serve, move in, take a split-step position, and then concentrate on making good contact with your first volley shot, which should go crosscourt. Again, place targets on the court at which to aim your volley.

Remember that split-step position—it is the most important one in tennis. Here it is again being demonstrated in this photo.

Split every time.

Photo Credit: June Harrison

Returning Serve

This is a very important aspect of the game. If you miss a return of serve, you are giving your opponent a point. It is very important to practice all the different returns you will want to hit. As usual, repetition is the key to all tennis strokes. Do these drills and you will find you have a reliable and confident service return.

➤ Adjust your position on the court based on the speed and depths of your opponent's serve. Move inside the baseline and attack a weak second serve. Move behind the baseline to counter a hard first serve.

➤ Watch the ball as the server tosses the ball, split-step just before she contacts the serve, and begin your return with a quick shoulder turn.

➤ Shorten the length of your backswing from your normal ground strokes.

➤ Hit most of your returns crosscourt or deep down the middle to increase the margin for safety. If your opponent's serve is weak, attack it by going to your opponent's weakness.

➤ Aggressive service return by running around weaker stroke.

➤ Cutting off angle: Move forward on diagonal to defend against wide serves.

Return-of-Serve Drills

Return the serve, aiming your different shots at various targets. Remember, you have four basic returns of serve. You need to practice all four:

1. Crosscourt deep
2. Crosscourt short
3. Down the line
4. Lob/ground strokes

Your objective in your ground-stroke drills is to practice consistency, depth, and direction. Good footwork and early racquet preparation play a big part in perfecting your ground strokes.

To promote consistency, stand in one section of the baseline, have someone stand on the opposite side, and see how long you can keep a rally going while hitting behind the service line. For direction, try down the line and crosscourt; then rotate one down the line, one crosscourt. To improve depth, try to make the ball travel at least four feet over the top of the net.

Mid-Court Shots

Control and placement are the two most important things to get out of mid-court drills. You also want to avoid setting up your opponent for a winning shot.

Double Faults

You should slice mid-court low balls, and use them as an approach shot to get closer to the net to hit a volley.

There are two things you want to think about while practicing your mid-court shots. First, balance is critical to all mid-court shots; and second, the closer you are to the net, the shorter your back swing. Here are three mid-court drills:

1. *Approach from mid-court.* Practice taking your ground stroke early and attacking without over hitting.
2. *Air approach.* Don't let the ball drop too low. Place it deep crosscourt.
3. *Half-volley.* Bend low, shorten your backswing and keep the ball low over the net.

Net Play

The objective of net play is to end the point quickly with a winner, or to pull your opponent off court. You have less time to react so you must always have your racquet up in front of you. To practice net play, you and a friend should stand in the service box, diagonally across from one another. Hit volleys back and forth, trying each time to increase the number of volleys you both execute.

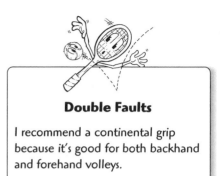

Double Faults

I recommend a continental grip because it's good for both backhand and forehand volleys.

Volleys

Most volleys are won by an angle shot and by keeping the ball low, or by adding pace to the shot. I find the following drills help my students improve their volley. In all of these drills, I feed balls to the students.

➤ Volley to a target. I set up cones on my side of the net in different positions and my student has to hit them.

➤ Aim down the line, then crosscourt.

➤ Close in to the net and try for short angles off both the forehand and the backhand side.

Tennis is a game of skill and a little luck. Since luck is out of most people's control, you have to work on your skill level to get better. The only way I have found to successfully do this is through practice.

The Least You Need to Know

➤ You will never achieve your highest level of tennis if you do not practice.

➤ Practice sessions should have an objective so that you know what you will be working on.

➤ The wall and the ball machine are both good ways to practice by yourself and work on things you are learning in your lessons.

➤ Practicing with a buddy will help you work on different shots while you both get better.

➤ Practice games are essential to the development of your game plan. Take notes after the game so you can further practice what you need to know.

➤ Drills reinforce certain shots and help commit to memory the way to execute them.

Part 5

The Competitive Edge—Putting It All Together

I am very proud of you. You are now stretching before every strenuous activity. You have taken care not to get any serious injuries by doing all the right exercises and eating all the right foods. You should be as fit as a fiddle and you are winning most of your matches. So, what's wrong?

You are playing the same players week after week and you feel stale. You think perhaps you will not get any better and this will be your tennis game forever. You are now expected to win your matches and you feel pressure.

Your friends invited you to a doubles round robin and you didn't know there was so much to learn about doubles. You always seemed to be in the wrong place.

Don't worry! I am getting to the mental part of tennis in this section. I will help you stay relaxed even on match point. I will even give away my secrets for playing in the wind. Best of all, I will unravel all the mysteries of doubles—the best game in the world. At least I think so and I want to share my doubles tips with you. I guarantee if you follow my advice you will be a savvy doubles partner. Are you ready to go poaching?

Chapter 18

Playing Tough

In This Chapter

➤ Picture this: using imagery to improve your game

➤ Give yourself a pep talk

➤ Rituals for maintaining your focus

➤ Self Motivation; how to get yourself going

You have practiced and practiced every conceivable shot in tennis. You've hit perfect forehands that were unreturnable. Your serves were aces; you could hit anywhere in the service box that you wanted. Your volleys were angled winners that sent your practice buddies against the fence in a useless effort at trying to retrieve them. I have not even mentioned your unbelievable backhand that can just as easily send a winner down the line or crosscourt. Yes, you have the ultimate tennis game—you hear people walking by your practice court saying they wished they had half your game. You feel you are more than ready to go out and win any match you play. Your pro thinks you should enter your annual club championship tournament. He convinces you there is no one at the club with better strokes and you will win easily. So, you enter. The first round you are matched up against someone you have seen hit. Her strokes are much weaker than yours. They tend to push the ball over the net. So, you think this is going to be over in 20 minutes and maybe you can even schedule your next round.

I am sure at this point, you can guess the scenario. The first serve comes. It's weak, you hit out. The second serve comes, you hit a return trying to adjust to the lack of pace and you hit the net. After a few more errors, you are down 3–0. You feel a little panic. Your muscles tighten; you start talking to yourself, saying things like:

➤ "What kind of idiot am I?"

➤ "I can't believe I hit that in the net."

➤ "All that practice time down the drain."

Courtside Quotes

"I just try to concentrate on concentrating."

—Martina Navratilova, on the key to her success

And so on. Then you start a downward spiral. Your mind starts wandering and you start playing tentatively, barely hitting the ball. Fear and anger take over; you even bang your racquet a few times. You lose and you can't believe it. You walk off the court shaking your head, vowing never to play tennis again.

All I can say is, "Been there, done that." As a matter of fact, every tennis player who has ever played has at one time or another been there. That is probably why there are volumes of books written on the mental aspect of tennis. According to Jimmy Connors, one of the all-time great pressure-point tennis players, tennis is 95 percent mental at the professional level. He feels that at that level, everyone has all the strokes and is in good physical shape. The only difference between the winners and losers is the mental toughness—the ability to concentrate during the match and not get distracted by bad line calls, people off the court, and your own mind drifting. Or, as one of my Australian friends calls it, taking a walkabout.

So let's see what we can do to make you mentally tough.

Imagery: 60-Second Photo

Have you ever sat daydreaming that you just did something like win the Nobel Prize? Well, most tennis players on any level sit and daydream that they just won the U.S. Open or Wimbledon. This is not all bad or a waste of time. If you see yourself doing something, then you will know how it feels to do it.

Imagery is the process by which you use the information that you receive from all your senses, from the environment, and from mental pictures of these activities, and then use those pictures as model for what you should be doing. Let me give you an example of the way this can help in your tennis game. I had one student who just could not get a service motion. Try as I did to explain the fundamentals to her, she just wasn't getting something. The rest of her game was progressing nicely except for the serve. A friend of mine, who was on the pro tour, visited me one day. My friend had one of the most consistent serves I had ever seen. Her serve motion was very fluid. I asked her to do me a favor and let me videotape her service motion. I taped a few different angles of her service motion. I then had my student view the tape. I told her to close her eyes and imagine it was her serving like the pro. We then went to the courts. I am not saying her serve was perfect, but it was the best she had ever done. I think the fact that she had a clear picture in her mind of what a serve should look like helped a great deal.

Imagery is a technique used by many different athletes. It helps program the mind for what the body should do. By watching athletes perform and storing in our memory banks what they do, we will be able to retrieve it later.

You can practice imagery. Before a match, visualize yourself hitting a perfect forehand, backhand, and so on. Then you can try to imagine how that would feel if you were able to achieve that. You can also play out the match in your mind, going through it point by point. Imagine how you will hit a wide service return. What will the stroke look like? How will you feel when you serve an ace? What will it look like? This will not only help you visualize what the strokes will look like, but it will also help with your anxiety during the match. Because in your mind, you saw yourself hitting winning shots.

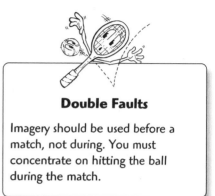

Double Faults

Imagery should be used before a match, not during. You must concentrate on hitting the ball during the match.

You know how to do them. You have done them in practice and you have done them in your mind. It is almost like you have played the match before and the real match is just a formality. You will be much more relaxed. It will be like watching a rerun; you will know what's coming next.

No-Fault Tennis: Self-Talk

Now that you have spent a little time daydreaming, how do you feel about talking to yourself? It is very important that you boost yourself up during a match. Let's face it, your opponent is not going to do it.

It is essential that during, and even before, a match, you build up your confidence. You can do this by clearing your head of all negative thoughts about the upcoming match and your ability to win.

You should fill your head with only positive thoughts such as, "I will win," "I love my backhand," and "I have practiced my serve over and over to the point that it is one of the best parts of my game." These positive thoughts will then enter your subconscious mind and help these ideas occur. If you have very positive thoughts, it will relax you and you will believe you can, and should, win.

I once had a student who had beautiful strokes. During her practices, she would hit winner after winner, but every time she got into a match, she lost to lesser players. After every match, she felt very dejected. She started going to these matches expecting to lose, and it became a self-fulfilling prophecy. She would walk on and say, "I am not going to win," "My backhand may not work today," and so on. Finally, I had to get her to stop playing matches. It was ruining her joy of tennis. After a month of building up her confidence, I set up some very easy matches so that she would believe in herself again. We practiced pep talks on and off the court. I made her repeat simple thoughts to herself like "I believe I can win the match" and "Even if I miss one forehand, I still have an awesome forehand." After she won a point during a match, I made her say things like "Boy that was a great shot." All negative thoughts were put aside. Slowly, without her knowing it, I started to set up matches with better players. She kept winning. Her positive talk had really helped her.

So remember, talking to yourself is alright in tennis, but only if it is positive.

Trish Says

Concentration is one of the hardest concepts to teach a new tennis student. In my frustration, I once criticized a student after she missed the sixth easy shot. I told her to just concentrate on hitting the ball. She said she was. So I asked her a couple of questions. Who just walked by the court? What was the score on the adjacent court? Which team was winning? She could answer all my questions and she could even tell me what the person who just walked by was wearing. This proved that she had not really been concentrating as much as she thought she was.

Hit the Ball: Improve Concentration

Concentration is the third step to improving your toughness for tennis. You must be able to train yourself to think of only one thing while you are playing, and that is hitting the ball.

By concentrating on just hitting the ball and nothing else, you take away all other distractions. While you are playing, your mind should not wander to what the score is, what is going on around you, and, even worse, what you will be doing after the match. If you would make it your total focus to watch the ball and just hit it, you will take away any distractions that might make you miss the ball.

Being able to concentrate on only one thing is something that takes practice. Most of our day is spent doing one task while thinking about two or three other projects that we have to do. Take driving for example. How often do you get behind the steering wheel, turn the car on, and drive to where you have to go while your mind wanders to the music on the radio and what you have to do for the day? Maybe you are even drinking a cup of coffee. It is amazing that we even get to where we are going.

We are so used to doing and thinking about so many things at one time, that when we really have to focus on one thing, it is not so easy. You must train yourself to do this. Look at the picture below. See how I am looking at the ball as I'm hitting it?

Total concentration.

Photo Credit: Vicki Fort

You can practice concentrating while on the court. Every time you get another thought in your head, tell yourself to just think about hitting the ball. After doing this over and over, you will train your mind to concentrate on just hitting the ball.

Once your mind is on that action alone, you will take away some of the nervousness you feel when you worry about winning or losing. Your thought process will be, hit the ball, get ready, then hit the ball again. You will just think of the action of hitting, not whether you will win or lose.

So, go out with that one-track mind and hit the ball. You will be surprised how much better you will do.

Double Faults

The more you work on your shots during practice, the more comfortable you will be with them. So, during the match it will be easy to concentrate on just hitting the ball.

Rituals

Did you ever stop to think just what a ritual is? A ritual is something that you do repeatedly in the same manner. There are many rituals that you do every day without even knowing it—washing your hands before you eat, checking your rearview mirror before pulling your car out, or even kissing your kids goodnight and tucking them into bed. Rituals make us feel good. They put order to our lives and give us a comfort factor.

In tennis, you can use rituals to your advantage. By doing certain things in between points, or before a serve, you allow yourself to calm down. For example, look at the next photo. Before every serve, I bounce the ball twice.

Service ritual.

Photo Credit: June Harrison

This ritual of bouncing the ball calms me down and allows me to concentrate on my serve.

I have another ritual I perform during a match between every point: I look at the strings on my racquet. This again allows me to clear my mind of any thoughts and just concentrate on hitting the ball. It also calms me down and gets my focus back onto the next point.

Whatever ritual works for you should be incorporated into your daily game.

Clearing my mind.

Photo Credit: June Harrison

Look Like a Winner, Be a Winner

This might sound like a very simplistic statement, but it isn't. If you believe you have the ability to win the match, you will walk on the court with your shoulders back, your head up high, and a smile on your face. You will look confident and feel confident.

Know that you are out there to have fun. Let's face it, tennis is a game and, except for the handful at the top, most people do not get paid to play. Your confident attitude will be transmitted to your opponent. He will feel a little intimidated by it. Be sure you are pleasant on the court, but not overly friendly. Don't be afraid to make your calls. Make sure you say it loud enough for him to hear. If you make a bad shot and miss a point, do not yell at yourself. Smile, walk back to the baseline and wait for the next point to begin. Believe me, this is more intimidating than showing your anger.

So remember, look like a winner even when you are not winning at that moment. The more you carry yourself off as a winner, the more you will win.

Courtside Quotes

"A ritual is a set pattern of deliberate steps you take between plays to keep your mind off negative thoughts."

—Jim Loehr, well-known sports psychologist

Trish Says

I was once playing a match and I hate to admit it, but my opponent was a better player. She won the first set, and the second set was close. I decided that I would not show her any sign of weakness or insecurity. She lost a long rally and started talking to herself negatively. By the third lost point on an unforced error, her shoulders were slumped over and I could tell she was getting tight. I ended up winning that set. By the third set, she was just going through the motions. I won it easily. She had stopped believing in herself and her body language was telling the story.

The Least You Need to Know

➤ Use imagery to visualize what your strokes should look like before a match.

➤ Before a match, give yourself a pep talk and fill your head with only positive thoughts about your tennis ability.

➤ During a match, if you hit a bad shot, shake it off and believe in the fact that it was just a mishit and your strokes are not falling apart.

➤ Concentrate on one thing during a match—hitting the ball.

➤ Tennis rituals are very important to help you focus and keep your mind on positive thoughts.

➤ If you carry yourself as if you are confident, you will win, and this positive attitude will transmit to winning.

Warming-Up

This is what you have been waiting for—match day. You have practiced all your strokes that you learned in Chapters 8 through 13. Your equipment is the newest and the greatest and, thanks to Chapters 3 and 4, you have everything you need. You learned all of the dos and don'ts of tennis and you picked out the best pro to help with your game, all thanks to Chapters 5 and 6. Your body is one lean fighting machine that you stretch out daily. You have changed your eating habits and now drink an adequate amount of water. And, let's not forget how mentally tough you are. You are ready, willing, and able for the task at hand, and the words that keep ringing in your head are: "Send me in, Coach!" Well, I am going to, with just a few more simple suggestions for match day.

Stress Reduction

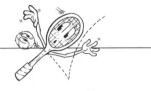

Double Faults

Practice all of your shots before a match so that you will feel less stress during the match.

Everyone handles match day differently, but there are still some common things that most of the pros and many of the top club players do.

The first thing all players do is try to reduce the stress they may be feeling right before a match. Each player does this differently. Some stress is OK, actually desirable, because it gets your adrenaline going and pumps you up. But too much stress will be counterproductive and will not allow you to perform your best.

There are a few basic things you can do to reduce your stress level before a match. First, you can make sure you are confident of your strokes. If you feel that your strokes work for you, you should be able to relax just a little bit. Don't worry about your opponent's strokes, because there is little you can do about them. Just keep telling yourself that your strokes are good. Concentrate on all of the positive things about your strokes. The more positive you are about your game, the less stress you will feel before the match.

Prescription for reducing stress: Take two buckets of balls and practice.

Photo Credit: Vicki Fort

The second way to reduce the amount of stress you may feel before a match is to make sure you are in the best physical shape that you can be. This means knowing that you got enough sleep the night before the match. There is nothing worse than trying to play a match after you were out partying until dawn the night before. If you know that you got enough sleep, you will be more relaxed before your match. You should also be confident that you have the stamina to play a long match. You can achieve this by exercising and eating well on a regular basis.

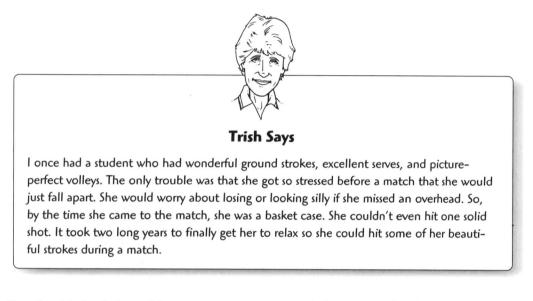

Trish Says

I once had a student who had wonderful ground strokes, excellent serves, and picture-perfect volleys. The only trouble was that she got so stressed before a match that she would just fall apart. She would worry about losing or looking silly if she missed an overhead. So, by the time she came to the match, she was a basket case. She couldn't even hit one solid shot. It took two long years to finally get her to relax so she could hit some of her beautiful strokes during a match.

You should also feel confidence in your equipment. As I mentioned earlier in the book, if you know that your equipment is right for you, and it is in excellent condition, you will not be stressed about this before the match. Notice in the following photo how I check my bag and my equipment before my match.

Check it out.
Photo Credit: Vicki Fort

Double Faults

Do not do strenuous exercises right before your match. You do not want to go to your match tired.

The rest of the ways you choose to reduce the stress you are feeling are purely individual. Some people find that tuning out the world and listening to their favorite CD helps. Others find that reading a couple of chapters in a great novel prior to their match works for them. Still others find going over notes that their coach has written about their own tennis game helps them feel more confident and reduces their stress. From the picture below, can you guess how I relax before a match?

Music to my ears.

Photo credit: Vicki Fort

Fuel for the Fire: What to Eat

Because I have already told you what to eat before, during, and after a match in Chapter 15, I will only highlight some of things to keep in mind:

➤ Do not eat many fatty foods before your match. Your stomach will be working overtime trying to digest it during the match.

➤ Eat carbohydrates because during the match they convert to energy.

➤ Drink a lot of fluids before the match to keep you hydrated.

➤ Try to eat 1 to 2 hours before your match.

Check Your Bags: The Importance of On-Time Delivery

If you are like me, you probably have a busy schedule. You try to fit more things in the day than is humanly possible. Thus, like me, you probably run a little late to appointments. Around the courts where I teach, there are two times: the real time, and Trish's time. But when it comes to match play, I am always on time or just a little early. There are reasons for this.

First, on match day, you are under a little stress as it is. You don't want to start getting anxious that you are going to be late for your match, and you won't have time to get ready and to stretch. Second, I believe it is rude to your opponent. If a time has been set, it is your responsibility to be there on time. And if these two reasons aren't enough, there is always the reason that if you arrive too late, you will be defaulted.

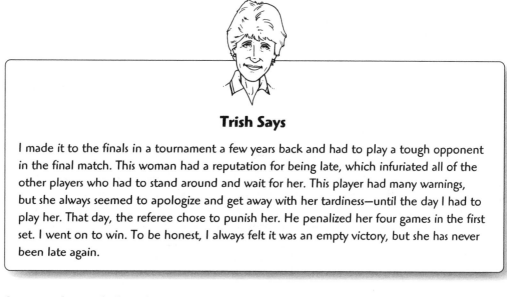

Trish Says

I made it to the finals in a tournament a few years back and had to play a tough opponent in the final match. This woman had a reputation for being late, which infuriated all of the other players who had to stand around and wait for her. This player had many warnings, but she always seemed to apologize and get away with her tardiness—until the day I had to play her. That day, the referee chose to punish her. He penalized her four games in the first set. I went on to win. To be honest, I always felt it was an empty victory, but she has never been late again.

So remember, to help reduce your anxiety, make sure you show up on time. The photo on the next page shows how you should arrive at a match.

Bring on my opponent.

Photo Credit: June Harrison

Double Faults

Before stretching, jog around the court three times to get your heart rate up and your muscles warm. Jog very slowly and deliberately. Do not make any swift moves or jerky actions. It is not good to start stretching completely cold.

Limber Up: Stretching

I have already given you a whole chapter on stretching; the purpose of this section is to review a few simple stretches that you should do right before a match.

Most people will be a little tighter than usual before a match. The anxiety they feel about the match will translate to muscle tightness. This is why you must be extra careful when you stretch. But you must be sure you stretch before the match, otherwise you may be even more likely to injure yourself.

Two or three court stretches can be very helpful right before a big match. The first stretch I do is for my Achilles tendons. As you can see in the top photo on the next page, I go to the net, put one foot in front of the other, and bend toward the net. I hold this for about 15 to 20 seconds on each side.

Achilles stretch.

Photo Credit: Vicki Fort

After I stretch out my Achilles tendons, I do my simple groin stretch that I showed you before. Bend to one side and stretch the inner thigh as I'm doing in this picture. Do both sides and hold for 15 to 20 seconds.

Stretch out those inner thighs.

Photo Credit: Vicki Fort

The third leg stretch that I usually do right before a match is for my hamstrings. I find a chair and put one leg up on it and gently bend over and touch my toes as in the top photo on the next page. Once again, remember to stretch both legs for 15 to 20 seconds.

Hamstring stretch.

Photo Credit: Vicki Fort

After I feel that my legs are warmed and stretched, I use my racquet to stretch my shoulders and arms. The first stretch I do with the racquet is to hold it behind my back and stretch and hold it for 15 to 30 seconds on both sides (see the next picture).

Racquet stretch.

Photo Credit: Vicki Fort

The next and last thing I do is move away from the court a little and just swing my racquet easily for about 30 seconds, as in the photo on the next page.

Swing that racquet.
Photo Credit: Vicki Fort

These stretching exercises should not take more than 5 minutes. I assume that you have already done your major stretching before taking the court. These few stretches limber you up a little and, in a way, reduce the stress you may be feeling in your body.

Friendly Fire: Warm-Up with the Coach

Before every match I play, I will find either my coach or my doubles partner, and do a nice, easy warm-up. This helps my strokes and reduces any anxiety I may have about my game. This warm-up usually takes place about an hour before the actual match and takes less than 30 minutes. I start out doing some easy ground strokes, then progress to volleys, overheads, and then serves. It gives me a chance to make sure all of my shots are working and are consistent. During my warm-up, I do not try to kill the ball. I just work on consistent shots and focusing on the ball.

These warm-ups with my coach are usually very positive and reassuring. No negative thoughts come into play here. We usually have a few laughs to reduce the stress I may be feeling. After the warm-up, I head for the showers and put on my lucky outfit. Yes, like most players, I do have a lucky tennis outfit. I may be a little superstitious. The outfit changes from year to year, or match to match, depending on how I played.

Friendly fire.

Photo Credit: Vicki Fort

Show Me What You've Got: Warm-Up with Your Opponent

This warm-up is very different from the pre-match warm-up. It is usually shorter and its purpose should be to see how your opponent plays and where her comfort zone is.

Watch her serve. Try to assess whether she has a flat serve or a slice serve. Is it hard and deep, or just soft and somewhere in the middle of the box? Warm-up your lobs. This will help you determine where the wind is. Make sure you warm-up your overheads, too. In a match, this could be a shot you get tight on. Try your volleys to see how your opponent steps in to return them. As a matter of fact, try moving your opponent around a little bit so you can see what her footwork looks like. Which way does she move better—right to left or back to front? Can she keep a consistent rally going, or does she try to hit a lot of winners? Does she seem to like it when you hit with a lot of topspin and pace or slice? Make mental notes of all of these things. Your observations will come in handy during the match. The more data you can accumulate during a warm-up, the better it will be for you during the match. Of course, your opponent is sizing you up as well.

Passing Shots

Most professionals keep books on their opponents. This is their play book, just like the ones football players keep. The pros review their opponents' playing patterns so they know what to expect.

Don't Get Overdone, Just Warm

I just want to touch on this briefly. There is a fine line between being sufficiently warmed-up and relaxed before a match, and being overtired. Only you know where that line is. Some people have a tremendous energy level and need to warm-up a little longer, while others can't focus for that long and their stamina waivers after only a short warm-up. So, be sure to pace yourself and don't do too much before a big match because you want to save all your energy for the match.

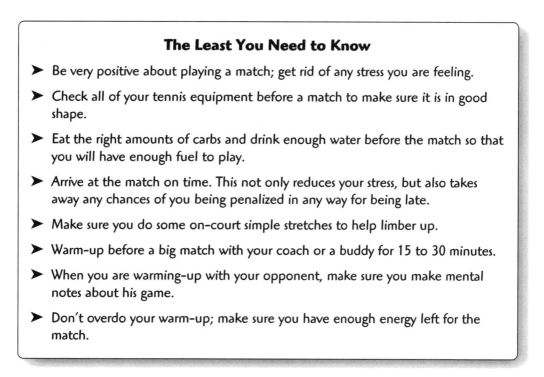

The Least You Need to Know

➤ Be very positive about playing a match; get rid of any stress you are feeling.

➤ Check all of your tennis equipment before a match to make sure it is in good shape.

➤ Eat the right amounts of carbs and drink enough water before the match so that you will have enough fuel to play.

➤ Arrive at the match on time. This not only reduces your stress, but also takes away any chances of you being penalized in any way for being late.

➤ Make sure you do some on-court simple stretches to help limber up.

➤ Warm-up before a big match with your coach or a buddy for 15 to 30 minutes.

➤ When you are warming-up with your opponent, make sure you make mental notes about his game.

➤ Don't overdo your warm-up; make sure you have enough energy left for the match.

Chapter 20

Game, Set, Match: Strategy That Works for You

In This Chapter

➤ How does your opponent play

➤ How to play in different conditions

➤ Playing on different surfaces

➤ It's all in your mind

➤ Controlling anxiety

➤ Learning from the match

In the previous chapter, I touched upon warming-up with your opponent and what you should try to get out of it. It is very important to try to accumulate as much knowledge as you can about the person you are playing, and under what conditions. These are all variables that will affect your match. Of course, whom you are playing will be the most important factor in determining the outcome of the match. Let's say you and your opponent are evenly matched. If this is the case, knowing and taking advantage of the different variables will make the difference between winning and losing a match. In this chapter, I will discuss some of these factors.

All tennis players have favorite surfaces, shots, sides, and weather and playing conditions. Likewise, they also have pet peeves. Some players hate the wind. Others dislike playing with a partner who won't communicate. Sometimes, matches are lost because a player lets her petty problem interfere with her concentration.

I am going to give you all the help I can so that this doesn't happen to you. Tennis is a great game but it is a tough game to master. You don't need any extra distractions. Pay attention and stay focused on your game plan.

Double Faults

Assess where your opponent's comfort zone is early in the game—whether it's the baseline or net—so that you can adjust your game accordingly.

Sizing Up the Competition

Every player has his or her own style of play. Some hit the ball with a lot of pace; others just push the ball around the court. Some players love to lob and drop shot their opponents to death, while others rush the net and volley every point. Part of your job on the court is to determine your opponent's style of play as early as possible, and modify your game to counteract his game. What you should try to do is take away his favorite shots and make him hit his second- or third-choice shot. Most club players do not have a consistent second or third shot that they can hit, so you can force your opponent to make errors.

Now I'll tell you about some of the typical types of players I have come across in my career and how I like to handle them.

The Human Backboard

All I can say here is patience, patience, and even more patience!!! This player is a human backboard. She stands on the baseline and gives back everything you give her. She loves to get into long rallies because she knows you will eventually tire or try to end the point. Usually her ground strokes are pretty good and she has the confidence to execute them over and over if necessary. This type of game is a little bit boring—not only to play, but also to watch. Points are not won off of winning strokes, but off errors. What I do here is play her game until I get an opening. Then I come to the net and hit a crisp volley. If I can't do this, I try some drop shots. This forces my opponent to the net and then I attempt a passing shot. This will often work because her comfort zone is the baseline and I am bringing her in to make a shot that she doesn't like from an uncomfortable position.

Passed again.
Photo Credit: Vicki Fort

The Pusher

This, to me, is the most frustrating opponent. The game is slow with very few tactics and it's just not fun. This player always gets the ball back over the net, never doing much with the shot. There is no pace on the ball, and you try either to kill the ball or push it back with poor results. If you try to kill it, the ball may go long or wide. If you push the ball back, it will probably go into the net. What I have to do is calm myself down and tell myself I am in for a long match. I need to move my feet and attack the ball as I hit my shots. This allows me to control the point. This strategy took years to implant into my tennis brain because it is so foreign to my style of play. I still find it hard to practice what I preach on this one.

Double Faults

Patience is a virtue you must have when you are playing a human backboard. Wait for an opportunity to make the winning shot instead of making an unforced error.

Trish Says

I was once in a doubles tournament early in my career when my partner and I were the number one seeds. As such, we were expected to win. Our first round was against two unknown players. Once we started to play, we realized that they were "pushers." We never did get our rhythm going, but finally won in a third set tiebreaker. I have since learned how to play pushers, but I avoid them in friendly matches.

The Lobbyist

A player who lobs most of the time is often small in stature or does not move well on the court. His lobs are executed for a variety of reasons. If you are playing a net rusher, the player described next, you may not be able to hit many successful passing shots so you resort to a lob.

More than likely, the player who lobs constantly does not have good ground strokes but can play mid-court shots well. So, his style is to keep you back deep, come into the middle of the court, and then start moving you around. You will find you do an awful lot of running against this style of player.

My advice is *not* to do as I indicated for the human backboard and the pusher, which was wait, bide your time, and work the point until you can play your shot. Playing against a lobber, you need to take charge early. Don't keep running back, letting the ball bounce deep, and trying to play your shot behind the baseline. You will get into long, long rallies and you will never be in a position to hit an attacking shot. You must attack right from the start by taking the lob shot in the air with what I call an air approach shot. This shot is discussed in Chapter 14.

An air approach is exactly what it sounds like. You take the lob in the air as a high volley, usually in the area of *no man's land.* You will need to take a fairly long stroke at the ball because of your position and the fact that the ball coming towards you has no pace. By doing this you will be able to keep your opponent deep and you will be on your way into the net. You are counter punching with an attacking shot rather than another lob. Still, be patient and work the point but don't stand back and wait if you can take the air approach.

Tennis Talk

No man's land is the area inside the baseline and just behind the service line where it is tough to execute any put-away shots.

Get out of there!

Photo Credit: June Harrison

Serve to Volley

This type of player loves the net, so you know right off the bat she loves to volley. If I had to classify myself, I would say I am a serve-and-volleyer. I love to hit a serve and rush to the net. To me, this is how tennis should be played, particularly on a fast surface. Maybe I feel this way because I've played a lot on grass courts where serving and volleying are essential to winning. There are many things you can do to take the upper hand away from this type of player—but I am not going to tell you because I don't want people to beat me!

Volley winner.

Photo Credit: June Harrison

Alright, but don't tell anyone else. Let's consider your options. First and foremost, stay relaxed. Often your initial reaction to someone who rushes the net is to watch him come in and then try to hit a shot very fast right at him. The problem here is twofold: First, while watching him, you are taking your eye off the ball; thus, you may miss the ball completely. Second, by rushing your shot, you will hit an inferior shot and maybe give him an easy opportunity to play a winner.

However, hitting the ball directly at the net rusher is not all bad. This will work well if your opponent does not have quick hands or if, as in most cases, he has not split-step and he cannot get his balance. If he gets the ball back, it may be a weak shot because he was not in position. Just a little note here—don't expect to make friends with this shot. Some opponents get a little upset when you take aim at them. I feel that if someone is at the net, then they have to be ready at all times and it is a fair shot.

If hitting the ball at your opponent does not thrill you, you could try a lob. A good lob will make your opponent run back to the baseline and hit a ground stroke or a lob off balance.

Run it down.

Photo Credit: June
Harrison

The most natural shot to play against a serve-and-volleyer is the *passing shot.* This can be either a down-the-line or crosscourt topspin or slice. You force your opponent to stretch and hit off-balance. Down-the-line is preferable because you actually have more court open; but it is more difficult because you are hitting over the high part of the net. The crosscourt is the easier shot but you are hitting the ball across your opponent, making it easier for your opponent to reach. A low, dipping crosscourt shot, rather than a hard, deep shot, is better. It will land more at his feet, which will cause him to hit up. Either way, a passing shot is a pressure shot hit into a smaller court area. This is why the net rusher is very effective.

The main idea with a net rusher is to keep him guessing. Don't always hit down the line; mix up the shots so that he cannot automatically move to one side and anticipate the ball. You can vary not only your shot, but also your pace. You can hit a hard return first, then a soft return and even a lob. This forces your opponent to wait until you have executed the shot before making his move, which gives you more open court space.

These are four types of players you may come across while playing different opponents. If you assess your competition early, you can adjust your game in the beginning of the match, so that you can jump to an early lead.

Double Faults

If you execute a good lob, follow it in and take the net. Your opponent's shot will most likely be weak and you should be able to hit a good volley or an overhead.

Tennis Talk

A **passing shot** is a drive or a chip that is executed in an attempt to deceive the net player so he or she is unable to play a shot.

What Are the Conditions of the Game? Playing in Different Conditions

Being cognizant of court conditions before your match is very important. There are a few simple things you should make note of during your warm-up. First, where is the sun and what direction is the wind coming from? Both of these are very important because they affect many of your shots and how you and your opponent will play them. You will have to make a decision immediately based on these two factors when you either win or lose the toss in a match. Remember, you have four choices if you win the toss, and only one if you lose the toss. The position of the sun and the direction of the wind affect these choices. If you are given the option, you should choose the bad side for the first game and then you will have the good side for the next two games. Some people disagree and choose the good side first so that they can feel confident in the first game and jump off to a 1–love lead. This is really a personal choice and it depends on a number of things. Are you comfortable with your serve? Do you rush the net and therefore have to hit a lot of overheads? Whatever you do, you need to take the time to consider all the conditions when first taking one end of the court over the other.

Once this selection is over and you get down to business you will need to be constantly reminding yourself which way the wind is blowing. Whether it is a north-to-south wind or a side wind, it will affect how you play every shot.

Passing Shots

Every correctly built tennis court runs north and south because of the position of the sun.

My first coach used to say, "With the wind get in, against the wind, hit out." This means that if you are hitting with the wind, attack the net. If you are hitting against the wind, be sure to finish your stroke. It is a saying that has stuck with me all of these years. Every windy match, I think of his little ditty and it works.

The final thing you should make note of is the temperature. If it is a very hot and humid day, remember to drink a lot of water. If it is a cold day, stretch longer and try wearing a vest over your shirt so that your back is kept warm until you have played a few games. If it is cold enough, I sometimes play the whole match in my vest.

Trish Says

At the ITF World Championships in Nottingham, it got so cold that we played all of our matches in our warm-up suits. One of the American players looked like he was going skiing because he wore long leggings under his warm-up, a shirt, a sweatshirt, another sweatshirt, a woolen hat, and gloves when he walked out on the court. His opponent from Germany was running around in tennis shorts and shirt. They looked like they were playing in two different countries.

What's on the Surface? Playing on Different Court Surfaces

I know I have said tennis is a game that is the same all over the world, because the rules and the etiquette do not change regardless of where you play. There are, however, different court surfaces. I talked about the different surfaces in Chapter 5. In this chapter, I want to stress the style of play you can expect on different surfaces and what game complements each surface.

Grass Is Always Greener

As you know, grass is my favorite surface. The ball stays low and moves fast, so I love to serve and volley. You have to take the ball early because there is no real bounce. I love to hit my slice on grass. I take the ball early, and keep myself and the racquet low. Remember that slice serves, slice approach shots, and slice volleys are all very effective on grass. You have to do a lot of bending. After a long match on grass, you need to stretch out the hamstrings, quads, and buttocks.

Clay Helps Mold You

If you have great, deep, consistent ground strokes, clay is your surface. The ball will move slowly, giving you a chance to set up and hit your ground strokes. You can work the point and get your opponent way out of position. Drop shots are good for a clay surface and volley players have a more difficult time because the baseliner has more time to set up and hit the passing shot. You must be patient. You will also need to learn how to slide when you play on clay. The secret to sliding on a clay court requires: first, the right clay-court shoes; second, good balance, using your knees and thighs; and third, stopping about three feet short of the ball and sliding the last few feet as you get ready to hit the ball. It takes practice, and the best way to practice is to go out on the court. Stand on the baseline with your racquet in hand, run towards the net, and, as you get halfway inside the service line, stop running and try to slide the rest of the way until you can touch the net with your racquet. Look back at your slide mark and if it is not at least 18 inches long, you will need more practice. Don't try this on a hard court!

It's Hard to Play on Hard Courts

Playing on a hard court can be fast-paced like grass, or it can be slow like clay. It all depends on the final surface placed on the court. Hard courts have a small amount of sand placed in the final green topping which will make them fast, less fast, slow, or slower (the more texture, the slower the court). It is really up to the clubs to decide how they want the courts to play. A newly resurfaced hard court will play slower than an older, slicker one.

Unlike on grass, the ball does not stay low on a fast hard court. You can serve and volley on the faster courts. You may need to be selective about coming to the net on the slower courts. On a very slow court, you may have to play more of a clay-court game. The one problem with hard courts is that they are hard on your knees and back. All that constant pounding on your legs can take its toll. Remember to bring wraps and ice packs when you play a lot on hard courts.

It's a Game Coping with Mind Games

Whether playing in a friendly match or in a tournament match, you will inevitably come across an opponent who will try to play mind games. You might even be doing the same thing and not even be aware of it. Many of these mind games, which people play during and even before a match, are legal; but some people might consider them bad sportsmanship. Let me give you an example of gamesmanship.

Double Faults

Avoid using mind games during a match. You will probably find them as distracting as your opponent does.

After a long rally where you've won the point to give you 40–15, your adrenaline is pumping and you're eager to play the next point. You are ready to serve and as you look up your opponent is toweling off in the back of the court. She is stalling for time. She is trying to get her composure back and slow down your momentum. As long as she does all of this within 25 seconds, she is not doing anything illegal.

Or, you are playing a person who quick serves you. He doesn't wait until you are ready to return serve before he starts his motion. You have tried holding up your hand before he serves but he doesn't notice it. When this happens, I bend down and tie my shoe. Often the serve goes sailing by because he didn't notice I wasn't ready. The server gets another serve and you get time to get set. All legal.

Another of the more flagrant disrespectful mind games is hitting the ball away from your opponent when sending the ball back to him to serve. This means he has to walk further to fetch it before starting play. This gives you time to catch your breath, but it is not good sportsmanship. Instead of doing this, just hang on to the ball a little longer before you slowly send it back to him. This allows you to control your frustration and anxiety without looking like a bad sport.

When playing a tiebreaker, you are not allowed to stop during the change of ends. Many players towel off and get a drink. They are doing this to aggravate you as well as to satisfy their needs. Don't let it bother you. Concentrate and win the tiebreaker.

Some players don't even know that they are playing these mind games. I know women who chatter all the time they are playing tennis. They talk between points, during the changeover, and sometimes even during play. It is their way of letting off steam when they are nervous. It is also their basic personality. It bothers some players, because they cannot concentrate. If it is a friendly game, you can ask her to keep the talk to a minimum until after you have finished a set. In a match you can ask her to not talk during play, and the best thing you can do is ignore all the comments and questions. The chatter will soon stop if you don't react.

We are all capable of playing these little mind games. I feel they don't belong on the tennis court. I let my racquet do the talking during a match. These games are for players who have bad reputations. I want you to be a fair, respected, and yet feared opponent both on and off the court.

Trish Says

My doubles partner Charlene told me about a match she played where her opponent was always going to the back fence and hanging on to it looking like she was going to pass out any second. Charlene wasn't sure whether her opponent was really sick or just stalling. She found out later there was nothing wrong with her opponent. She had a reputation for stalling and histrionics.

Keep Your Balance: Control Anxiety

Every tennis player has experienced anxiety before and during a match. It is only natural to be anxious about a match where you will be under pressure and unsure of the outcome. It's how you deal with the anxiety that will determine what kind of match player you are. Do you choke on crucial points?

People choke during a tennis match for different reasons. The two main reasons are: "I am afraid to win" and "I am afraid to lose."

Being afraid to win means that when you are way ahead, instead of playing your normal game—a game that has served you well and helped you get to this winning position—you back off and wait for your opponent to lose the match.

Being afraid to lose means that you are tight right from the start. You are not hitting your shots. You are playing a tentative, defensive game and that is not your style. Again, you want your opponent to lose the match; and you want to go out there and play your best tennis, win *or* lose.

Courtside Quotes

I don't care who you are, you are going to choke in certain match ups. You get to a point where your legs don't move and you can't take a breath."

—Arthur Ashe

You need to go out to your matches well prepared and confident. If you are neither, you stand a better chance of tightening up or choking. The solution is to practice your shots so that you can hit them consistently and under pressure.

When you play a match, it is natural to get tight when the score is close. You need to rely on your muscle memory to reproduce your usual strokes. You also need to concentrate on your mental state. In Chapter 18, we gave you some hints on how to be mentally tough. Talk positively to yourself during the tight situations. Stay focused on the ball and play one point at a time. Now is not the time to visualize yourself winning the match. You must concentrate on each point.

Stay calm.

Photo Credit:
June Harrison

In some cases, you may be up against a better player. Or you may be evenly matched but she has more experience, and when it comes to the key points, you cave in. In this situation, remind yourself you have nothing to lose. This puts pressure on her and takes it off you.

In all cases, you have to have positive thoughts. You have to calm yourself down, take deep breaths, and just concentrate on hitting your shots. Do not spend time thinking about what will happen if you lose the match. You must concentrate on the here and now and just hit the ball. Stay loose.

Trish Says

When I am in a tight match, I think about the ice skaters in the Olympics. They are out there on the ice, all alone. If they fall, they can't win, plus they look silly and they could even hurt themselves. They have only one chance every four years and they only get one shot. I can make a mistake and still come back and win. My pressure is nothing like their pressure.

What's the Net of It? What I Learned from the Match

Every time you step on the court you are facing a new challenge. No two players have the same strokes or the same mental approach. This is why tennis always makes you think, not just play.

On those rare occasions when you do lose a match, it is important to take away some thoughts that will help you improve and prevent you from making the same mistakes again.

If your serve let you down, practice with a basket of balls the next day and try to analyze your mistakes. If your forehand let you down, but you have been hitting well in practice and other matches, you were probably nervous, so your shot was not fluid and your follow-through was not nice and long. Maybe your opponent attacked your backhand because she saw that as your weakness. Maybe now is the time to practice those topspin passing shots. Your friends were watching and they said you missed too many returns of serve on crucial points. Play some practice matches with your friends where you are down 30–0 and see how many games you can win from that score.

Just maybe, you were beaten by a better player. In many cases, this is true and most people don't want to admit it. Just take a deep breath and understand that you have more work to do. Enjoy your current playing level and know that unless you are Pete Sampras, there are always players better than you out there. You know, Sampras doesn't win every tournament either.

The Least You Need to Know

➤ It is important that you recognize the style of your opponent's game and try to play to his or her weakness.

➤ Be cognizant of the different weather conditions. Adjust your game for sun, wind, and heat.

➤ Court surfaces play differently. If you have the option of choosing one that complements your game, take it.

➤ You may come up against an opponent who likes to play mind games. Be aware of what he is trying to do and just concentrate on your game.

➤ Sometime in your playing career, you may become anxious during a match. Recognize it and concentrate on staying focused but relaxed.

Chapter 21

People Who Need People—The Game of Doubles

In This Chapter

➤ Do you have what it takes to be a good doubles player?

➤ Why do people play doubles?

➤ The net game in doubles

➤ How to join a tennis ladder

➤ Join the leagues—form a team

➤ What's your rating?

I know I have said that I have favorite strokes and I am partial to certain players, but now I'm going to talk about my real passion—doubles, both ladies and mixed.

I liken good doubles to a high-action chess game. In both, you have to think while you are playing. Your object is to maneuver your opponent out of a winning position. And you need to have quick reflexes and nerves of steel. The only difference between playing doubles and playing chess is that, in doubles you are running around like a lunatic, while in chess, the player sits very quietly and doesn't use up as many calories.

Doubles players get fanatical about their matches. Winning and losing becomes a hot subject at the lunch table. Unfortunately, some friendships and even marriages are at risk when lifelong friends and spouses step onto the doubles court together. A good win can cement a relationship for another year. A bad loss where one partner blames the other can cause a rift that sometimes reaches huge proportions.

Detractors from doubles always say that they never get enough exercise when they play doubles. They obviously have never seen the Jensen brothers play. The Jensens never stop moving, poaching, changing sides, and running all over the court. Good doubles is just as strenuous as singles. As you get older, you won't want to run for those drop shots and lobs. It is a game that you can still play well even if you are not very mobile.

The game of doubles is one reason why the USTA's motto is "Tennis, a sport for a lifetime." You will never be bored when you play doubles. There is always a new challenge, a new partnership, or a new tactic to overcome.

Grab your partner and let's hustle.

What You Need to Do to Be a Good Doubles Player

I have been playing doubles almost as long as I have been playing tennis. I started playing on my backyard court in Australia. My father didn't want to listen to my brother and sister and me fight over whose turn it was to use the court. So, he figured if we all played doubles, no one could complain. The more I played doubles, the more I loved it.

I am currently the number-one doubles player in the women's 50s division. I believe that one of the reasons I am a good doubles player is because I started when I was very young. It was fun for me and I felt much less pressure when I played junior doubles. In Australia, they had junior events in singles, doubles, and mixed, so we all played a lot of doubles. I also believe that this is one of the reasons I like to serve and volley. When I played doubles as a junior, my coach made all of us come into the net. After a while I became very comfortable up there. I love to volley and it shows.

If you are just starting out in tennis, you'll discover that doubles is actually easier to play because you have some help out there. You have to cover only half the court. You have support from your partner and you have another person to bounce ideas off of. After you have done this, it seems awfully lonely out there when you play singles.

Doubles takes practice, just like singles. Although you are covering only part of the court, you need to know which part. Knowing which part will make you a good doubles player. The best way to learn is to watch and play a lot of doubles.

Love that volley.

Photo Credit: June Harrison

So, I am going to teach you how to be the best doubles partner you can be. There are some tricks and some basic rules to follow. For the most part, being a good doubles player is no different from being a good singles player. You must learn the basics, practice hard, play a lot, watch good players, and be patient. It doesn't all come together at once.

Why Doubles?

There are various reasons why you might decide to take up the game of doubles.

Often, it is because your friends play tennis and it is a way to spend time with them. For some players, singles is too strenuous. They want the exercise, but they don't want it to be so tiring that they can play for only 45 minutes. Most players like doubles for the challenge and the opportunity to play as a team with another person. There is the fun of winning a point together and figuring out strategically just how to do that. It can be a very social experience where you practice your shots together, drive to matches together, and either celebrate or commiserate after the match together. It is truly more fun for many people to be on the court with a partner playing a match.

Double Faults

Many players feel that they can play only one side in doubles. To be a good player—one that is sought after—you should be flexible and able to play both forehand and backhand.

I teach many doubles strategy lessons at my club. Women in particular, many of whom have never played doubles before, walk on the court not expecting much. By the time they have a few lessons, they realize how challenging doubles really is. You can be one of the best tennis players at the courts in singles, but unless you learn the simple basics of doubles, I assure you, you will not be up to that level in your doubles play.

I often watch my ladies teams and I enjoy seeing how many are really enjoying playing as a team. They talk, joke, give each other the occasional high five after a good point, or maybe a pat on the back after a lost point. You can see from their faces that they are having fun at what they are doing.

Many people find that tennis is a fun family activity, and doubles allows the entire family to participate.

I tell all my students that they should experiment with doubles. I tell them to give it a year, and if they don't like it, stop. I believe the game sells itself. I have never seen anyone give up the game of doubles because they didn't enjoy it. I have seen players get frustrated with a partner and want to change their combinations, but I have never experienced a player who got fed up with the game.

Trish Says

My doubles partner also plays national mother/daughter championships. She is much better than her daughters, but she does it to spend time with them and to share a sport they all love. One year she plays with her older daughter; then the next year she plays with the younger one. They have won a national title, but most years they play for fun. Her husband and son also play. They are a true tennis-playing family.

Playing doubles also allows you to cover less of the court than you would in singles (the doubles court is 36 feet wide versus 27 feet wide for singles play; but in doubles you are responsible for only half). This enables you to focus on your strategy, strokes, and the technical aspect of the game. Some people play doubles tennis because they live in a cold climate and have to play indoors. Court time is expensive, so they share the cost with three others instead of one other. Others play doubles because their club requires doubles during some prime hours to accommodate more members.

Whatever your reason is for wanting to play, you are going to have to learn certain basic doubles principles—so let's start.

The Ten Commandments of Doubles

First and foremost, play to have fun. You should feel like this is something you are enjoying. There is nothing worse you can do to your partner than walk on the court looking like you want to be somewhere else.

Talk to your partner all of the time. There is no such thing as a team that talks too much in doubles. Not only will you be communicating strategy, but you will also be relieving and sharing the stress.

Make sure you move as a team. You never want to find yourselves colliding for a ball and leaving the rest of the court open.

Whose ball is this?

Photo Credit: June Harrison

Be aggressive. Go after every ball on your side. You should try to hold up your side of the court playing as aggressively as you can.

Take over the net. The team that has both players at the net usually wins the point.

When returning shots, keep the ball away from the net person. If you give it to him or her, your opponent has a very good chance of putting it away.

Do not go to sleep while your partner is returning shots. Look alive, move around, anticipate the next shot, and make your opponents think of you as a threat.

Passing Shots

Australian star Roy Emerson always joked, "First to the net, first to the pub!" This was his basic doubles philosophy and with his Grand Slam record it obviously worked.

Courtside Quotes

"People enjoy doubles more than singles, because they have to do less work, have a partner to blame for defeat, and have someone to listen to their gripes as they play."

—Bill Tilden

Don't be a ball hog even if you feel you are a better player than your partner. Certain shots belong to your partner and certain shots belong to you. By taking your partner's shots, you put your team in jeopardy by being out of position.

Try to get your opponents to back off the net by using a lob. It is a very effective shot in doubles and allows you to get to the net.

Finally, be very supportive of your partner. Even if he or she hits a bad shot, don't make faces or utter sarcastic remarks. Remember, your objective is to have fun as a team, and if possible, win the game.

Now that I've given you some basic principles, let's talk strategy.

Court Position

As you may already have figured out, there are four people on the court in doubles. Each has a job at any given moment. The starting positions are shown in the following photo.

One up, one back.
Ready to play.
Photo Credit: June Harrison

The server should stand behind the baseline to serve the ball. In order for the server to be able to cover most returns, the server's position on the baseline should be at least halfway between the far sideline and the center hash mark.

The server's partner should stand 6 to 10 feet from the net, diagonal side from the server. The variation in distance from the net depends on her reactions and her height. If she has quick reaction time, she may stand closer. If she is slower in her reaction time, she will probably want to stand further back. Also, she may want to stand further back if she knows the receiver likes to lob.

The Receiver

The receiver should stand on the other side of the court from the server, almost on the diagonal, almost on the baseline. Once again, this is a judgement call for the receiver. She will have to judge how far to stand back and maybe move left or right, depending on how the server serves. (She might be able to determine this in the warm-up or during the first few games of the set.) This photo shows the basic positions.

Take your positions.

Photo Credit: Vicki Fort

The Receiver's Partner

The receiver's partner should stand on the service line across the net in front of the server. If the return is solid, she should be ready to move in. If the return is weak, she must wait for a good opportunity to move to the net. The positions described above are the starting court positions for all for doubles players. These may vary if the receiver and the receiver's partner discover they need to stand back to play a more defensive game.

Good court position in doubles is almost more important than your strokes. You have to be ready to react. Every action requires a reaction. The ball is going to be traveling fast and you must be ready. This means being in the ready position and in the right position.

The Importance of the Net

As I mentioned previously, getting to the net is one of your goals in doubles. Once at the net, you are in a position to finish the point with a winning volley or overhead. The team that comes to the net together gives their opponents more trouble. They are now faced with trying to pass both of you. The only thing that your opponents can do if you are effective net players, is to lob, giving you the opportunity to hit an overhead. Nine out of ten times, the team at the net will win the point.

Look at this photo and you will see all four players have tried to capture the net.

Grab that net.

Photo Credit: June Harrison

Poaching

Poaching means moving in front of your partner and volleying an opponent's service return or ground stroke. It is a very effective move in doubles. Your opponents need to anticipate a poach. This often causes them to make a mistake. You are also closer to the net and are more in position to win the point. The element of surprise will help win the point because your opponents have to regroup.

Many people do not poach because they are afraid of looking foolish by going for a ball and missing it. This is the wrong attitude. As long as you know when and how to move and where to hit the ball, you should go for it. You may miss a few, but you will probably make more than you miss. Look at this photo and you will see my partner should have taken this volley so that I did not get out of position.

> **Double Faults**
>
> Many times in doubles, when you lose your serve it is not your fault. If you have served mainly deep first serves then your partner should have been cutting off volleys and poaching to help win the game. Remember that doubles is a game of teamwork and confidence.

Yours, partner!

Photo Credit: June Harrison

Australian

"Australian" is the term used to describe a formation strategy that has both the server and the server's partner on the same side of the court. You should elect to play Australian if the receiver has a very strong crosscourt return. Changing the formation makes the receiver rethink his or her return.

Here is a photo of a typical setup for playing Australian. I am serving and my partner is standing in her ready position, but standing with me on the same side of the court, or in the middle.

Australian positions.

Photo Credit: June Harrison

When receiving a serve from your opponents, if they are in an Australian formation, you will still have various choices. Down the line is your best return, followed by a lob. Your normal crosscourt return is not as good because the net player may be in that very position. Down the middle is not advisable unless you can hit it perfectly low and hard.

Mixed Doubles

Mixed doubles is often played as a social event. Usually two couples decide that they would like to do something besides dinner and a movie. For the most part, fun is had by all; but there are those rare occasions when it may not be fun for all of the participants.

Problems may arise when couples are not used to playing together. The husband may give more direction than the wife wants. The wife may be better than her mate, and his male ego may get hurt. Or, one of the men may be very aggressive and hit hard shots at the woman on the other side.

So to sum it up, when playing social mixed doubles, remember you are out there to have a good time. If you want to put the ball away, aim *away* from the weaker player, not *at* him or her. And avoid criticism or, at the very least, keep it to a minimum.

Climbing the Ladder of Success

Most active tennis clubs have a *challenge-ladder* system for both singles and doubles and sometimes even mixed doubles. A tennis ladder usually operates on the premise that if you keep winning you will end up on the top of the ladder.

At my club, the ladder rules are more lax in the summer when many of my players go back up north. In season, players on the ladder must play a match every two weeks. They must either accept a challenge or challenge within those two weeks.

If you don't know if you would like the ladder, speak with your pro. Ask the pro how many players are on the ladder and how often you must play a match. Playing a ladder is a great way to meet other members and play matches against people who are about your same ability level.

Passing Shots

Challenge ladder is a match system designed for players of all levels so that they have a regular match against players of like ability.

Your pro will usually place you on the ladder where you belong. If you enter the ladder late, you will have to start at the bottom of the ladder and work your way up. Some ladders will let you challenge more than one place at a time, so it should not take you too long to find your level.

I would encourage all players to enter the ladder at your courts. It guarantees you a good match and you don't have to arrange it.

The Right Team or League for You

In Australia, I played in a team match at least three times a week. Even when I was going to high school, I played on Wednesday nights on a mixed team. On Saturday morning, I played on a junior team and then on Saturday afternoon, I played on an adult team. Some of the year, I even played on a Sunday afternoon mixed team. Our teams often played our home matches on my court in my backyard. This was not unusual for Australia because many people had their own home courts.

Team match often took the place of friendly doubles games. Some of the team matches were singles but most of the time they were ladies' doubles, men's doubles, and mixed. There were three divisions: A, B, and C. Each division was subdivided so that there were eight to twelve teams in each subdivision. There was A1 all the way down to A15. The B Division had B1 down to B20 and C had C1 down to C25. This meant that on any given Saturday, just in our little local district in Sydney, there were over 7,500 players participating in team play.

When I first started I was in C10. The last time I checked, the Australian teams went down to D30.

Passing Shots

About 40 years ago, tennis players in Atlanta, Georgia, took the Australian team system and started a team competition using the same rating system and format. It started slowly with about 20 ladies' teams. Every year it grew and the league expanded to the weekends and evenings. At last count there were over 40,000 tennis players participating in league play every week just in Atlanta.

At clubs with more than six courts, there will generally be some form of team competition. At most clubs the ladies' teams drive the tennis programs during the weekdays. Ladies usually form a team of at least twelve women all at the same level. These twelve women sign up to play matches on a regular basis on the same day every week. They have uniforms and, whenever possible, they try to play with the same partners all season long.

Some areas of the United States are more active in the ladies' leagues than others. Playing in leagues is a great way for women of all ability levels to enter a competitive arena. For some players, this is their first taste of competition. Some can't cut it. For some women it is not a pleasant experience because the team can get to be a political animal and may not be all tea and crumpets.

For the most part, league playing is keenly competitive. Some women play hard and then go to lunch together afterwards. Others take it too seriously. They replay their matches in their minds and get upset at their losses. I keep reminding my players that it is only a game—they should play hard and then forget about it.

We may not be #1 but we look great.

Photo Credit: Vicki Fort

Trish Says

At my club in Florida, some league players live for their match day. They talk about it all week prior to the match, and then they talk about what happened in the match for three days afterwards. But some of these players take it too far. I find it necessary to remind them that it is only a local competition and that they are talking about their friends and fellow members when they start to say disparaging things about their teammates.

All I can say to those players who play team tennis is: Support your partner, practice hard together, and don't divorce your partner after one or two losses.

Apart from the men's and women's leagues, most clubs offer USTA leagues, senior leagues, singles leagues, and mixed leagues. Basically, there is a league for everyone. The better you are, the harder it is to get into a league because fewer players make up the league.

In Atlanta, there are pro divisions and the standard of play is very high. Our club at BallenIsles has a very strong ladies' program and slightly fewer high-level men players. Location and programming will have a great deal to do with how active your club is regarding leagues and teams. It takes a lot of work to put the teams together, enter the team in the league, and keep all the team members happy for the season. Some leagues require membership in the USTA, so ask what is required before you join.

Just like playing the ladders, playing on teams and in leagues is a great solution for the busy tennis player. Other people, captains, and pros are organizing all the details for you. You just have to show up, play your match, hopefully win for the team, drink some iced tea or a beer, and go home.

Many leagues now feature playoffs out of your local area. Now, if you win your local event, you will more than likely be invited to participate at a district level, then a national level. This allows you to meet the best players in the country who play at your same level. One such event, The Phoenix Challenge for men and women over 50, brings over 2,500 winning teams together from all over the USA. Some teams even come from Canada, New Zealand, South Africa, England, and Australia to play in this event held in California each year. Even though it has retained the name Phoenix Challenge, named after where it was developed, the event is now played in Palm Desert, California, due to the need for a lot of courts. Players come away with great memories and sore muscles, and some even go home with World Championship titles.

Trish Says

In 1991, I coached a team of ladies from BallenIsles Country Club in Florida who made it to the finals of the Phoenix Challenge in Palm Desert, where they won the national title. They then went on to play Australia to win the world title. I was very proud of these seven ladies. They practiced hard, trained together, and really pulled for one another during the matches. A special bond was formed during this week for these women.

Some clubs even give team memberships, which restrict play to team matches and practices only. For some, this is enough tennis, and it is a cheaper way to participate in a nice club. If you don't belong to a club and you would like to play in a league or on a team, call your public facility. City courts or municipal courts often have these activities. They may not have your exact level, so do some checking. If you want to play, believe me there is a team out there for you.

Team and league play is not for everyone. It is competitive and some players don't want that pressure. If you feel that this additional pressure is not for you, don't worry—there are plenty of other tennis activities you can do without getting into this very focused setting.

How to Get Rated

Most countries have a specific rating system that allows each player to measure his or her abilities against those of others. At first, everyone said they were either an A, B, or C player (a rating of A being the best and C needing some help.) The USTA then embraced the NTRP rating system which we have outlined in Appendix C. This is partly a self-rating system with an evaluation by a tennis professional every two years.

The system ranges from 1.0 to 7.0, the highest rating being for the pros. A really good local club player might be a 5 or 5.5. Your average club player is either a 3.5 or a 4.0. This NTRP rating lets you travel anywhere in the USA and get a reasonable match with someone of your own ability if the pros match up the ratings.

Check the club notice board for the nearest NTRP rating clinics, or call your local USTA office and ask where the next rating session might be. Expect to be there for at least one hour. The pro will usually not be your club professional. So that the rating is impartial, a new pro is brought in to evaluate the players. It generally costs between $10 and $15 per person.

At the rating session the pro will give you a form to fill out and then ask you for a self rating. This is only an indication to them of where you think you belong in the big tennis world. The pro will still evaluate you and write a report. About four to six weeks after the evaluation date you will get your rating card. If you think it is wrong, you may appeal. If you don't play your best and you get a low rating, be careful. Some players have been thrown out of the league because they are better than their rating. Play fair. Get your best rating and carry your card. It is excellent for when you travel.

The Least You Need to Know

➤ Doubles is an exciting and social way to enjoy tennis.

➤ With four people on the court, everyone has a job to do and a place on the court during each point.

➤ The net is one of the most important places to play in doubles.

➤ Poaching makes the server's job easier.

➤ Australian doubles is a special formation for the serving team.

➤ Mixed doubles can be a fun experience but, as in all doubles matches, communication is the key.

➤ League and team play can be very competitive and time consuming. Ask questions before you commit.

➤ Get your NTRP rating—it will help you get games.

Part 6
Different Ways to Enjoy Tennis

You have done really well. You are winning tournaments and you are sought after as a doubles partner. The problem is now everyone around you wants to know what has gotten into you. Your son wants to learn tennis. Even your mother wants to see if she can get into a beginner's clinic. Don't worry. I have all the answers in this part. It is just as easy for them to get started as it was for you.

You are a different matter. You are finding it hard to concentrate during a lesson. You feel like you have heard it all before and you are now improving very slowly. All of this is normal. It is very hard to see improvement once you reach a higher level of ability. Just like anything else, if you do something often enough you get bored. You need a pick-me-up. You are looking for a change of routine. Your friends suggest a week away at tennis camp. Camp! You are 40 plus—it has been years since you went to camp.

Guess what! Tennis camp is a terrific way to meet new players and learn in a new environment. You will be surprised at the amenities at the resorts and camps. Sit back and watch as your family gets the bug, too, when you come back with a new backhand and a new outlook from your camp.

You and your friends have bought tickets to the U.S. Open and you can't wait to see the pros in action. You know you can learn a lot by watching the best in the world. Who knows, maybe you will get to meet some of the top players.

You are back in action and raring to hit the courts.

Chapter 22

Send Junior to Court

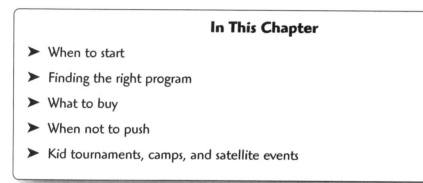

In This Chapter

➤ When to start

➤ Finding the right program

➤ What to buy

➤ When not to push

➤ Kid tournaments, camps, and satellite events

When I look around the club where I teach, I see many kids playing tennis. BallenIsles has a very active tennis program for children. I love watching the young children as they pick up the racquet for the first time and try to hit the ball over the net. Many of these kids have such a look of enthusiasm and excitement on their faces. It reminds me of when I first picked up a racquet.

My father told me that as soon as I could talk, I was pestering him to play "bat and ball." Because we lived behind a tennis court, I was exposed to the game before I even knew what it was. I only knew that as I watched others play tennis, they all looked like they were having fun, and I wanted to have fun, too.

Many of the kids that play tennis at my club are there because they enjoy tennis as an after-school sport. They have fun at all ages and they like the friendly competition the program offers them. Some of the children who play at the club have a deep interest in the game. These kids take tennis very seriously and have dreams of becoming pro

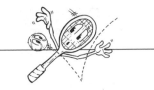

Double Faults

Play catch with your child to determine if she is ready to play tennis. It doesn't matter what sort of ball you use: tennis, baseball, basketball, football, or just a plain, old plastic ball. If your child can play catch, then she's ready to start tennis.

players. They go out weekly and play junior tournaments in their age divisions. These kids and their families are so dedicated that they devote their whole weekend driving sometimes hours away to participate in these tournaments. Tennis is their life. Most kids will not go on to join the pro circuit, but some will go to college on a tennis scholarship, and all of them will have a game they can enjoy for the rest of their lives.

Does your child express an interest in playing? If so, you should get some group or private lessons for the child. What about equipment? At what age should the child begin? How does a junior find the right program? All of these questions and more will be answered in this chapter. Getting the junior started is actually easy, and once he gets started in the right program, he will be hooked for a lifetime.

When Should a Youngster Start to Play?

It is very important that a child express an interest in learning to play tennis. If a child shows no interest in playing, he or she should not be forced to learn, because the child is not ready for the game. On the other hand, if a three-year-old asks you to hit tennis balls with him or her all of the time, why wait? The age a child begins to play is not really a factor. His or her interest level is more important. Introducing the child in a positive and fun way is a good start in developing a lifelong tennis player.

Make sure that when you do start the little kids in a tennis program, that it is fun and geared for your child. See the kids in the photo on the next page taking one of their first lessons.

Finding the Right Program

After determining your child's interest, investigate the local recreation department or tennis center. Finding the right program, one that will have a positive influence on junior's playing ability and attitude toward the game, is important. Investigate the instructor's teaching style and whether or not the pro is good with children.

Future stars.

Photo Credit: Vicki Fort

Each child, like each adult, is different. Children respond to different teaching methods and different people. I find the best person to determine who will be right for your child, is your child. You should know what motivates him, as well as what does not. Does he need a lot of praise? Does he have a short attention span, thus requiring the lesson to move very quickly and be over quickly? Does he get upset with someone who speaks in a loud voice? Is he easily distracted? If so, you might want to choose a very quiet atmosphere for lessons. These are all questions you should consider before choosing a pro for your child.

Double Faults

Start slowly when introducing your child to tennis. You want him or her to want more lessons and tennis time. Don't push young children.

If you do feel your child has talent, it is even more important to be very careful in choosing your tennis professional. Adults can adapt to changing professionals in mid season or year after year. Young players, particularly those who start to play in tournaments, are not usually mentally strong enough to have three or four people telling them what to do. You should look for a pro who will enable your very young child to learn the basics correctly while having fun. If this professional is not a full-service pro, then after your "prodigy" has grasped the basics, it may be time to look for a professional who specializes in developing good, young juniors. There are many pros out there, and if you choose the right one the first time around, your child and the pro will develop a very special bond. You will want to monitor this because you do not want the professional taking over your child's life.

Some children benefit from individual one-on-one instruction before becoming involved in a group lesson. In that case, a few private lessons might be the way to start.

Private lessons or group lessons? In a private lesson, all of the attention is focused on the junior. Sometimes too much emphasis can be placed on what they are doing incorrectly. This can change an enthusiastic junior into one who decides tennis isn't much fun. In a group lesson, the junior sees how everyone makes mistakes and this can encourage him or her to try harder and become more competitive and have fun. So, in deciding which programs to put junior in, do what is best for the individual.

Trish Says

I once knew a family with 12 children, many of whom played tennis. When the younger kids came out for the first time, they always wore hand-me-downs. The parents would wait about six weeks to see if the child was going to stick with the tennis lessons and practice. Then they would let the children pick their own special outfit. These rewards had nothing to do with ability, talent or winning. They were showing them that commitment was important.

Buying for Junior

A junior tennis player needs the right equipment. The right sized racquet is very important. The child's size will determine what size racquet is needed. Seek the advice of a knowledgeable tennis professional or have someone in the sporting goods store check the grip size. Have your child try several racquets to find the one that feels light enough.

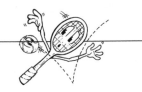

Double Faults

If you find you are dragging your child to her tennis lesson, put the racquet away for a while and let your child play another sport. Wait until she asks to play tennis again.

Tennis shoes are an important necessity for the tennis player. Since players do a lot of running on the court, your child will need a tennis shoe that is durable, stable, and comfortable. Running shoes would not be a good choice because they are higher off the ground, which could cause the foot to roll over, causing ankle injuries. A good, soft-soled shoe is recommended. Again, seek the advice of a tennis professional or sporting goods store for the best tennis shoe.

Well-dressed junior players.

Photo Credit: Vicki Fort

Tennis clothes for the junior can consist of a nice pair of shorts with pockets, and a tee shirt or collared shirt. The girls can wear a tennis skirt, tee shirt, collared shirt, or a tennis dress. See the photo above of what the junior kids are wearing today.

Practicing everyday after school and on the weekends might be too much for an older junior. Allowing other activities outside of tennis is important in keeping the interest of the child. Overall, it really depends on the individual player, because each junior is different and should be treated that way.

How to Make Tennis Fun

The important thing is to make tennis fun in order to keep children interested and enthusiastic. How do you keep it fun? A junior has to have a positive experience when on the court. Games that are used to teach the basic skills needed to play tennis help keep the junior interested. Another major factor in keeping the game fun is an enthusiastic and encouraging tennis instructor or parent. If drills become too repetitive and boring, juniors can lose interest very fast. The games should be challenging, fun, and interesting, so the junior doesn't even know she is learning. Using props and crazy-colored balls help keep the game fresh and interesting. Changing and progressing with each lesson so the junior is constantly learning something every time he walks out on the court is the key to a fun program.

Are we really learning?
Photo Credit: Vicki Fort

How Much Is Too Much?

If a child begins to show disinterest in going to a lesson or hitting with a parent, he may be bored or getting burned out. Evaluating the situation will help. If he has lost his motivation, cut back on the amount of time on the court, but concentrate on the quality of the lessons in some situations.

Depending on the junior's age, the amount of time spent on the court can be important. A younger child's attention span may be only 20 minutes or so, so keeping her on the court any longer than that can be more destructive than constructive. As soon as a junior begins to lose her attention, change the game, drill, or wrap it up for the day.

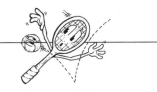

Double Faults

Some parents try to be both tennis professional and parent. There is a very fine line between the two, and it takes a mature parent to be able to serve his or her child well in both roles. Remember, you are always a parent first and a coach second.

Tennis Parents

One of the biggest problems that can turn off a junior to tennis is a parent who wants to compete more than the junior. A parent who encourages a junior to get into tournaments before a junior is ready, and wants the child to be a champion puts too much pressure on the child. Often the parent can want it more than the junior, which eventually causes the junior to want to quit.

Parents definitely need to play a supporting role in their child's tennis development—a role that is both positive and encouraging. Constructive criticism is also important. Often a junior has lost a match, comes off the court feeling upset, and sometimes discouraged. A parent can be supportive, listen to what the junior is feeling, and help her get beyond it. A parent should encourage but not push the child when she loses a match, and should be constructive, not overbearing. The parent's role should be as a parent.

Do You Have a Prodigy?

Unfortunately, many parents are looking at dollar signs when they push their children into tennis. I cannot impress on you enough how important it is to make certain that it is your *child* who wants to play tennis, not *you* who wants him to play. If you have a well-coordinated youngster, it is possible that he or she will take quickly to tennis. How do you know how good she is? Look around at other young children learning to play. Does she measure up? Does she move freely and smoothly? Does she react to the ball and not wait until the ball is right to her before making her move? The simple test is, again, the "catch test." If the child can catch a ball with two hands when he is very young (two to four years old), then you probably have a child with good coordination. The rest is up to you as a parent because putting a child into sports turns you into a chauffeur.

Trish Says

I know one young player from an Eastern Bloc country. Her parents were not very well off and they signed with a management company when she was 10 years old. Agents gambled on her abilities and capitalized on the parents' lack of funds. The girl went on to be ranked in the top 100 by the time she was 18, and she would have had more money at her disposal if her parents had not signed that contract.

By the time your child is 10 years old, you will begin to have some idea of how well he or she might be able to play tennis. If you started him at six, then you and the pro have now had four years to evaluate him. He should have played local tournaments. He should be steadily improving and still very eager to play tennis all of the time. He should be ready to play tournaments outside of your local club sphere.

The ages 12 to 14 are very important for a good young player. Your child should be growing and changing physically and emotionally, not to mention socially. The opposite sex comes into play. You may find that you will have to push your child to go to her lessons. Other interests now start to interfere with tennis. This is the time you will need to sit back, grit your teeth, and hope that your child will still see tennis as her main interest outside of school. Obviously, school now begins to play a bigger part. Grades become more important and homework takes up more time. Achievements are now based on junior rankings and who beat whom. There is a lot of pressure in junior tennis and, as I said earlier, don't put too much stock in winning. Good solid performances and great matches are what you should be looking for.

Double Faults

One good sign that your child has talent is if she is consistently winning junior tournaments in her age bracket, and also winning one or two age levels above her.

If you truly have a prodigy, this is also the time when you will be approached by the different academies. They are always looking for new talent. You must realize, as they do, that you need 100 could-be prodigies before you might find a Chris Evert or a Martina Hingis. I do not believe it is necessary to send your child to a total tennis environment unless, due to weather or financial circumstances, your child cannot play enough to reach his full potential. If you are unsure as to what to do, ask for advice. Find a former professional player who knows a lot about the current game, sit down, and ask questions. Speak with other parents. Ask your child—she often knows what she wants better than you do. Don't be tempted by promises of big money in the future.

Tournaments: When, Where, and Why

There is no set age for your child to start tournament play. The aspect you should consider most in deciding when to start is your child's maturity level. I've seen kids as young as seven who handle competitive situations with no problem.

There are a couple of programs designed to give younger players the opportunity to compete against other kids without playing in a really intense environment. The USTA offers junior team tennis, a program that falls under the category of Junior Recreation and does not put much pressure on the participant.

You should also be able to find small nonsanctioned tournaments in your area: local clubs, YMCA, or even some community centers. These types of tournaments don't focus on rankings and are therefore a great place to get started.

If your child is ready to start competing, the USTA is the place to start. Each region of the country is divided into sections. Each section has schedules of local tournaments in your area. The USTA tournaments are organized by age division: 10 and under are the youngest going up to 12 and under, 14 and under, 16 and under, and 18 and under. These tournaments are easy to enter but do require membership in the USTA.

Junior tournaments should be used for either development (working on improving your game) or just for the fun of competing. One of the negative aspects of the junior tournaments is the ranking system. Because of the ranking, there is a lot of pressure placed on winning. Anytime this occurs, the player will not perform at his or her best.

The USTA is currently working on a ranking system that doesn't penalize the player for losing, only points for each round won. This system will encourage the kids to play, while taking away the thought of a bad loss.

I've had parents say to me that junior tennis is evil, just like little league baseball and other sports for kids. My response was that it has nothing to do with the sport, but some of the people involved. One idea that is currently in the trial stage is holding tournaments where no parents are allowed. This concept will allow the kids to play without their parents getting involved. It will also give the kids the opportunity to be involved in all responsibilities of playing a tournament.

Trish Says

I witnessed one of the worst examples of parents pushing their kids during a junior tournament that was played at my club. One of the junior players in the 10-year-old division was being watched by his dad, who continued to coach his son, and tried to intimidate his son's opponent by questioning line calls that were obviously good. Every time his son missed a shot, he would yell at him to try harder. Finally the child just fell apart and left the court in tears.

Junior tournaments offer plenty of positive benefits to your child's all-around development. Learning how to compete is the first and most important. The competitiveness that the kids learn will help in all aspects of their lives. Dealing with adversity is also a useful tool for the kids to learn.

When your kids are ready, get them involved!

Different Levels of Tournament Play

The USTA has a great structure of tournament play for everyone. When your child has reached a level of consistent success at one level, there is another level waiting to challenge her.

The first level is the Junior Team Tennis. This program is under Junior Recreation with the USTA and offers a great place to start. The Junior Team concept offers the kids a team format, allowing the kids to have fun while learning to compete.

The next level is the Satellite Junior Tournaments. These tournaments are set up for kids with little or no ranking. Just like all other USTA tournaments, these events can count toward a state and/or sectional ranking.

The concept behind the satellite tournaments is that they allow the kids to play against kids of similar ability. Some parents feel their kids must play against better players in order to improve.

After a junior achieves a good ranking, he or she can start playing at regular sanctioned tournaments. These tournaments are where your junior can start playing some of the higher-ranked players in your area. In our Florida section, as well as in most other sections, you can find several of these tournaments every weekend within driving distance. These tournaments, as well as the satellite tournaments, normally offer a consolation draw. This means the child is guaranteed two matches.

Next, you have Junior Super Series tournaments. Each section has its own name for these tournaments. The main thing in common is that these tournaments are worth more ranking points. You will find the higher-ranked players participating while trying to accumulate points for ranking. It is not recommended that a junior play these tournaments until he or she has had quite a bit of success in the smaller tournaments.

Now we get into tournaments that are for junior players who have achieved top local rankings. The first set of tournaments is the sectional tournaments or qualifiers. These tournaments are designed to identify the top junior players in your section. These tournaments have limited draws and attract the top players.

Double Faults

If your child is traveling to other cities, towns, and states to play tournaments, encourage him to learn a little about where he is visiting so it can be a learning experience, too.

If your child has success in your sectional tournament, she can qualify for the National Tournaments. These take the top junior players from each section around the country to determine national rankings. There are different levels of national tournaments, so when your child is qualified, check with the sectional office on eligibility.

The final level for Junior Tournament play is the ITF (International Tennis Federation) circuit. These feature the elite junior tennis players in the world, the future touring pros. The ITF has different levels of play as well: Groups A, B, C, and Levels 1, 2, 3, with A and 1 being the toughest. Acceptance to these tournaments is based on the junior's ITF ranking. A junior player must have a high national ranking to enter.

The decision to enter a tournament should be determined by the commitment that it takes to participate and practice. Before entering a tournament, the junior should exhibit the desire to compete and the willingness to practice and get into condition to play. The novice player may choose to get into a novice tournament before diving into a tournament where juniors have more experience. This is a way for them to get their feet wet. There are many local tournaments that are offered in the community. It is not necessary to travel far to play competitively.

Tournaments are a great opportunity to travel to other cities and towns, which is a great way to visit other places and meet different people. It is also a great way to set goals and learn self-discipline.

Juniors learn how to deal with emotions under pressure and learn good sportsmanship. They learn to compete and deal with winning and losing. It can be a great way to help in other areas of their lives.

Camps: A Parent's Dream

Tennis camps can be for juniors of all levels. Camps provide a great environment for getting a good dose of tennis instruction. Camp can be as long as a week or an entire summer. Although tennis is an individual sport, your child will learn to interact with others and improve because of that interaction. Watching others can also be very motivating.

There are many camp programs across the United States that are designed just for kids who are very enthusiastic about tennis. Choose the program that is right for your child, be it one where the child will stay overnight or just spend the morning and return in the evening.

Double Faults

If you send your child to a tennis camp, make sure that it is not for too many weeks, because the days can be very intense and can turn counterproductive.

The Next Step

After participating in camps, a junior might express an interest in private lessons. In a private lesson, all of the professional's attention is focused on the one player. The professional will help the junior make the best use of his or her abilities. The attention that private lessons provides may help the junior to develop his stroke sooner. Group lessons once a week can also be an integral part of the learning process. Although the student may not get the personal attention he or she gets in a private lesson, there are many benefits with group instruction. The junior can do drills with other players, which can lead to actual point play. It can be more of a motivation to improve by watching others in the group. It can push the junior to higher levels by becoming more competitive.

Participating in camps, group and private lessons, as well as tournaments, will prepare the junior for more competitive tennis outside of lessons. High school tennis is a great way to get playing experience. For the junior who is interested in playing in college, this is a good stepping stone.

Tennis Scholarships

Tennis scholarships provide a great way for a player to get a college education without placing all the financial burden on her parents. By participating in junior tournaments, the junior can capture the attention of coaches who go to tournaments to recruit for their schools. There are many different scholarships and many different divisions of schools.

Passing Shots

Scholarships are now readily available in most schools for tennis. Even if a young junior is not going to be good enough to make it on the pro tour, tennis can give them a wonderful education. College tennis also provides excellent competition at a very high level, which is only one step below the pros.

Satellite Events

Open satellite tournaments, open to adults and juniors over the age of 14, are the step before the professional tournaments. By joining the circuit, the highly ranked junior player can travel all over the country and play at a very competitive, semi-professional level. By playing in these events, the tournament player can earn professional ranking points and prize money or expenses. The points earned can help those who are interested in playing in the "big leagues." The more tournaments the junior plays in and the better he plays, the better his chance of making it to the pro level. These satellite events are not only fun, but are also very challenging and a great way to see the world.

The Least You Need to Know

➤ Start your child in tennis when he expresses an interest and shows an ability to play catch.

➤ Be sure you pick the right program that fits your child.

➤ Your child needs only a racquet that is sized for her, a pair of sneakers, and comfortable clothes to play in.

➤ If your child seems to be losing interest in tennis, let him take a break from it.

➤ Do not be a pushy parent, because that is a sure way for your child to lose interest in tennis.

➤ Junior tournaments are a nice way to get your kids involved in a competitive environment.

➤ If your child is a good enough tennis player, a college might offer her a tennis scholarship.

Chapter 23

Ain't No Stopping Us Now: Tennis for Seniors and Those with Special Needs

In This Chapter

➤ When can I start?

➤ Act your age

➤ How to make new friends and stay fit

➤ Tennis for people with special needs

➤ How to play when you're pregnant

➤ Playing after surgery

According to the United States Tennis Association, at least 700,000 Americans over the age of 55 play tennis on a regular basis. Many of them are in their 70s and 80s, some even in their 90s. This goes to show you are never too old to play.

The USTA's motto is "Tennis, a sport for a lifetime."

A survey of senior tennis players found that 35 percent didn't start playing until they were adults over the age of 35. There are many reasons why players start so late. Most late starters give the excuse of being so busy raising a family, pursuing a career, or running a business that they didn't have time for fun. Many of the athletic ones say that they had run track or played football in college and they hadn't found a sport to replace these until they tried tennis.

Trish Says

I have the pleasure of running a tennis tournament for women over 40 once a year at BallenIsles. There are usually around 200 participants from all over the world. The divisions go from the 40s to the 80s. The level of tennis is wonderful. If you ever have the opportunity to watch senior players, you would be amazed at their shot-making techniques. Some of the women that play in this tournament never played competitively until the age of 40 or older.

Starting tennis later in life is not so bad. You have more time to devote to the learning process. You are smart enough to understand the necessary practice and commitment required to improve. You also have a more realistic idea of where you might take your newfound sport.

Who knows, you might be able take the national 70 and over title at my club if you start now.

Starting the Game at a Later Age

Take a look at the photo on the next page from this national tournament. With me I have the World 55-and-over champion, the world 70-and-over champion, Dodo Cheney, who would be the world 80-and-over champion if there were such a division, plus the national 70-and-over doubles champions. I feel honored to be in this photo. I held my own as the national 50s champion and world 50s number two.

Speak with many of these senior or veteran players and they will tell you how tennis has altered their lives. Many of these women who come to compete travel around the United States and play many of the National Seniors tournaments. As a matter of fact, there is a National Senior Women's Tennis Association (NSWTA) that oversees many local and national events. The NSWTA helps to rank the players, find sponsors, and even publishes a quarterly newsletter for its members.

What motivates these women to travel and play from state to state? Some do it to compete with their peers. Others do it for social reasons, because they have developed a whole network of friends from meeting at the tournaments. Whatever the reason, you can be sure they are all having fun and keeping active both mentally and physically.

An illustrious group.

Photo Credit: Vicki Fort

Older male and female tennis players find that tennis, more than any other sport, gives them the greatest all-around benefits both socially and in terms of cardiovascular activity.

According to the USTA, being 25 years old and over qualifies you as a "senior" player. Veteran competitions controlled by the International Tennis Federation (ITF) are for players 35 through 85. The ITF calls senior players "vets." Nowadays there are more tournaments both locally and internationally for senior players than there are for juniors.

Various parts of the country have senior leagues. Atlanta, which is the hotbed of league play and the ultimate city to live in if you are a league fanatic, has a league for everybody. Florida, Texas, and California have very strong senior men's and ladies' leagues for the over-50 club players.

In Florida, there is an organization called Les Grandes Dames and Les Grands Dukes. They assist in running tournaments for players over 35 throughout the state of Florida.

Double Faults

The NSWTA is not just for older women players. Anyone who loves tennis, male or female, may join. The organization is constantly growing and expanding its role in senior tennis. The senior men do not have an equivalent organization.

Dodo and another 80-year-old opponent at my tournament.

Photo Credit: Vicki Fort

You don't have to be really competitive to play in tournaments. You can just go out and have fun with your friends every week and know that you are getting great exercise, challenging your mind, and helping your heart.

Don't ever say you are too old to start. I have a man at BallenIsles who is taking lessons for the first time, and he is 83.

My professionals are aware that they need to approach a student a little differently if he or she is starting to learn after the age of 50. The older beginner is often unsure on his feet because his balance is suspect. He may already have some aches and pains, so I tell my pros to be understanding when asking a senior player to move to the ball. My staff works with seniors to choose racquets that will suit their pockets and their personalities. Let's face it, they don't need to spend a lot of money on their first racquet.

Be patient with yourself. It may take you a little longer to learn the basics if you did not play when you were younger. Ask your pro for the names of other senior players who might be taking up the game. It is nice to have another senior to practice with or even take lessons with.

Face up to the fact that you are no longer 21 and take precautions when you are out in the sun. Read through Chapter 16 where I talk about skin care and use products suited to your skin type. Wear a hat and bring at least two towels to the court. Make certain you have water to drink. When you first start, rest every 15 minutes. Ask your pro to sit and discuss the strokes with you while you catch your breath.

Passing Shots

Dodo Cheney now plays in the 80-and-over tournaments. Her mother was a Wimbledon semifinalist and Dodo has played tournament tennis since she was 10 years old. No one will ever catch her record of over 350 gold tennis balls from the USTA.

Take care of your skin— wear that hat.

Photo Credit: Vicki Fort

Social and Fitness Aspects

These are some of the benefits of an active lifestyle when you are a senior:

➤ Strength training keeps muscles strong—after the age of 45, you tend to lose muscle mass.

➤ Exercise helps prevent heart disease. As we age, the amount of blood we pump decreases. Exercise helps the heart pump out large volumes of blood.

➤ Regular exercise can reduce the rate of bone loss, which is a problem as we grow older, because our bone density diminishes with age.

➤ Exercise helps keep your weight down, because it builds muscle mass, which in turn increases your metabolic rate.

The psychological benefits of playing tennis and keeping active are:

➤ When you interact with people and share interests, your social circle expands.

➤ When you feel better physically, you feel better mentally.

➤ When you pursue lifelong interests such as tennis, you keep your mind active.

Double Faults

Breathing properly is very important in tennis. It is even more important when you are older. I always concentrate on breathing techniques with all my students and I especially take the time with my senior pupils. I teach them when to inhale, and how and when to exhale.

Senior champs.

Photo Credit: Vicki Fort

Different Equipment for Seniors

Racquet companies are now making products specifically for the senior market. Frames are longer, bigger, and lighter. They are made out of materials that help prevent tennis elbow and shoulder problems.

The ITF has changed the rules for the sizes of racquets. Now you can have a racquet at least two inches longer than the older models. They are also 4 ounces lighter.

Passing Shots

Senior champ Dodo Cheney, 80, holder of more than 350 gold balls symbolizing national championships, always wears pearls for luck. She also has a small duffel bag she puts on wheels to take to and from the court.

These new racquets have the following features:

➤ A larger "sweet spot," which will give you more power

➤ Frames with built-in vibration dampers to help prevent shock

➤ Lighter frames that are more striking in appearance

Other equipment for seniors include:

➤ Racquet bags with wheels so you don't have to lift all your heavy tennis paraphernalia

➤ High-top shoes to help stabilize the ankles

➤ New sunglasses to help you see the ball better on cloudy days

I've got the best racquet and I'm ready.

Photo Credit: Vicki Fort

Check with your pro to buy the right equipment for you personally. You may not be able to adjust to the newer frames. I doubt it, though. There is no comparison between the racquets of yesterday and the new whiz kids on the block.

Wheelchair Tennis

Rod Laver once said, "Part of the fun of the game is overcoming difficulties." Rod did not have wheelchair tennis players in mind when he said this, but wheelchair athletes who play tennis are an inspiration to us all because they are overcoming difficulties even before taking the court.

Wheelchair tennis is played with a special wheelchair that is pitched forward and designed with thinner wheels. If you are not used to it, you can fall out.

The major rule in wheelchair tennis that differs from regular tennis is that the ball is allowed to bounce twice. Even with the two-bounce rule, it is just unbelievable how wheelchair tennis players are able to get to the ball and hit it over the net.

I think it is just wonderful the way tennis has truly become a sport for anyone. If you ever have the opportunity to watch a game of wheelchair tennis,

Passing Shots

At one of the conferences on tennis I attended, they had the wheelchairs there for the pro to try; not one pro was able to maneuver the chair on his first try.

do it. You will be in awe of its players. Their ability to turn, change direction, and hit off both sides with forehands and backhands make them great athletes.

In 1980, less than 100 people played wheelchair tennis when the National Foundation of Wheelchair Tennis set up the U.S. Open Wheelchair Tennis Championship. Today, there are more than 10,000 wheelchair tennis players and U.S. Open Wheelchair Tennis Championships have topped more than 300 entrants.

The U.S. Open Wheelchair Tennis Championships are televised nationally in January of each year. There are also international ITF Wheelchair tournaments all over the world.

The Wheelchair Tennis Players Association merged with the USTA to administer the rules that govern the sport. Harry Marmion, President of the USTA, said, "This historic merger will help provide wheelchair tennis players with the resources they need and deserve." If you need more information on wheelchair tennis, turn to Appendix D at the back of this book.

There are also programs for players with handicaps and special needs. I have a young girl at BallenIsles who has cerebral palsy. Her parents have worked with her on the court and she has been in our junior program for about four years. She does amazingly well for a young player with only one strong tennis hand and one leg much shorter than the other. Take a look at this photo of Rachel and you will see how much she enjoys her tennis.

An inspiration. Rachel
Renaud has cerebral palsy.

Photo Credit: Vicki Fort

Playing When You Are Pregnant

Obviously, you need to have your doctor's permission. As a rule, if you have been playing tennis or have been active prior to your pregnancy, there is no reason to stop just because your condition has changed.

Trish Says

When I was pregnant with my first child, I did not put on much weight and my stomach muscles were tight. I borrowed a pair of shorts from a friend who was two sizes bigger than me, and I wore my shirts out. For months, my students thought I just looked a little sloppy. They were very surprised when I left for a month to have my first child.

You will need to buy some comfortable clothing. Some of the new dresses are perfect. Elastic-waist shorts and full tops are comfortable also; although as you become further along in your pregnancy, you may not want the feeling of elastic around your tummy.

You will also find as your pregnancy progresses your balance will change, so you will need to adjust on your volleys and ground strokes. Keep your feet a little wider apart to help adjust to your new weight.

The serve will be the hardest stroke to adapt as your body changes. Because you normally stretch up as you toss the ball, you will find you need to adjust the height of the toss to suit your new "nonflexible, already-stretched tummy."

Many players don't like to play against pregnant women because they feel hampered as to their shot selection and strategy. They feel if they hit a drop shot, they are being mean. Others feel they don't want to hit you, so they often try the wrong shot to avoid the pregnant player.

My advice is, if you are pregnant and you feel good and your doctor says OK, play as often as you want. If you are the opponent, don't worry; just play your game.

Courtside Quotes

"The hardest part about playing tennis when I was pregnant was picking up the balls."
—Evonne Goolagang

After Surgery

Follow your doctor's orders. Then, when the doctor says you can start playing slowly, do it. Don't rush out and play for two hours. I would suggest you take three half-hour hitting lessons with your pro. This will help you get your timing back and give you some idea of your fitness level. Next, book the ball machine for a couple of sessions. It is not nice to expect your normal partners to put up with you, while you are getting yourself back into shape.

Each surgery is different. After minor surgery, you may be able to come back immediately. Please remember that even if you were off the courts for only one week you will not be as fit and flexible as you were before.

Spend a little extra time in the gym stretching out and strengthening your muscles.

I have also spent some time working with stroke patients. Two of my pupils were good players prior to the stroke. This made it easier for them to play at a good level after they had done their physical therapy. But they also became very frustrated because they could not achieve the same level they had reached earlier in their tennis career. After a while they understood they would have some loss of motor skills and they resigned themselves to the fact they would not be as good as they were before. They still got great enjoyment out of the game.

Many doctors who are not athletes tend to be overly cautious, so make certain you make your needs and goals known to the doctor when asking when you can start running or playing tennis.

Most doctors will tell you to take it easy. I remember my friend Dr. Julie Anthony, who used to head up the Aspen Institute, told me it takes your body only one week to lose the fitness level it took six weeks to achieve. So start back slowly. Look for warning signs—if you don't feel good, stop until the following week.

Trish Says

A friend of mine, who plays senior women's tournaments in the 60-age division, has had two hip replacements. She credits good doctors, good genes, and common sense to the fact that she was able to come back and play at the same level she was playing prior to the operations. One year after her surgery she was in the semifinals of the national championships.

Most injuries or surgeries require rehabilitation and therapy following the operation. The correct rehabilitation therapy is a must if you are going to be able to use the part of your body that was weakened. If you do your exercises religiously and on a definite schedule, you will be back on the court in no time. Players who have had surgery often come back fitter than before because they have worked out and are strong.

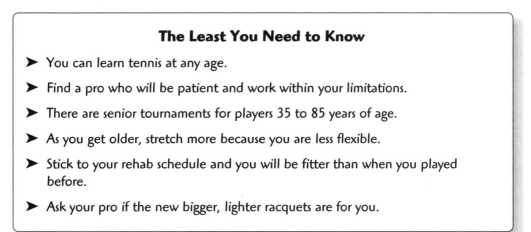

The Least You Need to Know

➤ You can learn tennis at any age.

➤ Find a pro who will be patient and work within your limitations.

➤ There are senior tournaments for players 35 to 85 years of age.

➤ As you get older, stretch more because you are less flexible.

➤ Stick to your rehab schedule and you will be fitter than when you played before.

➤ Ask your pro if the new bigger, lighter racquets are for you.

Chapter 24

Time Out—Tennis Vacations and Camps

> **In This Chapter**
>
> ➤ How to get your money's worth
>
> ➤ Resorts and camps—what's in a name?
>
> ➤ What should I spend?
>
> ➤ How long should I go for?
>
> ➤ How to pack for camp
>
> ➤ Have racquet and friend will travel

There are many reasons why you might want to go on a tennis vacation. Maybe you are just getting back into the game and you want to brush up on some strokes. Maybe you want to jump-start the learning process when you are just starting out. On the other hand, perhaps you and a couple of your tennis friends want to go somewhere to relax and have fun together. Whatever the reason, a tennis vacation can be a wonderful experience.

You will learn some new shots, get a great workout, and have fun. You will also meet many different people who are at your same level of play (or better), and be able to play games with them. I often tell my students that going to camp is a great way to improve their game and add to the enjoyment of their tennis experiences. Many students, after their tennis camp getaway, have a new excitement for the game.

Everything about a resort or camp is different: the drills, the players, the climate, the pros, and the courts. The experience will seem altogether new and exciting.

I once had a student who was playing many hours a day at the club where I was teaching. Her games were always with the same players, week after week. You could see she loved the game, but she seemed not to be enjoying it as much as she had in the past. I suggested that she take some time off and do something else; but the thought of not playing tennis for a while was not acceptable to her. As a compromise, I suggested a tennis camp not too far away. This experience would give her a change of climate. She went and had a great time, met new friends there, and even met someone with whom she entered some Florida doubles tournaments. She came back rejuvenated, with a new enthusiasm for her tennis game and a desire to practice and learn even more.

In this chapter, I will give you some idea of what to expect when you go to a camp or resort. I want you to get the most out of your experience, so you need to bring the right clothes, equipment, and the right attitude. I want you to do your homework, but I can tell you what to look for. Cost is also an issue but this time the old adage, "You get what you pay for," is very true. Don't be deterred by price. In many cases, the cost of the camp is all-inclusive; however, there are other camps that bill you for every extra once you get there.

Read your tennis magazines. Restring your racquets. Pack lots of socks and get ready for the vacation of a lifetime.

Maximum Bang for the Buck

To get the maximum out of your tennis camp experience, it is very important that you set certain goals before you even decide where you are going. These goals will vary from person to person. Below is a list of questions you will want to ask yourself when trying to determine where you want to go and how much you want to spend:

➤ Do I want to fix one particular shot?

➤ Do I want to concentrate on my physical fitness and endurance on the court?

➤ Am I trying to lose weight?

➤ Am I looking to meet new tennis players?

➤ Am I looking for a spa environment with a tennis program?

➤ Am I looking for a resort environment with a tennis program?

➤ Am I looking to get away to a new environment?

➤ Am I going because my friends and I think it will be time well spent?

➤ Am I going to give my tennis a boost?

Once you have set your goals for what you want to accomplish at camp, you will able to determine what type of program you want. When you arrive at the camp, be sure you and the instructors meet to discuss your goals so they have a clear understanding of why you are there. I had one student who attended one of the premier tennis resorts and arrived home disappointed because she did not learn anything new about strategy. She said she had concentrated on volleys, backhands, forehands, and serves, and had drilled repeatedly. She had not communicated her goals to her instructors.

Resorts and Camps: What's in a Name?

Once you have established your goals, you can easily decide where you want to go to achieve them. Resorts are usually in exotic places such as Hawaii, Palm Springs, and the Caribbean. In a resort, not only can you work on your tennis game, but you can usually work on your tan as well. The food at these resorts is four-star, and the facilities and amenities are top-notch as well. When you go to a resort, take some time off to enjoy the surrounding areas. If you want to be pampered after your tennis, choose a spa. Tennis camps, on the other hand, are places that exist primarily to enhance your tennis game. The programs are more intense than a resort's and the people who visit them go with the sole intention of improving their game. Tennis camps and tennis resorts have different functions, so decide what you want before going.

What a beautiful place.
Photo Credit: Vicki Fort

Trish Says

You will want to find out what sort of staff the camp has before booking your stay at a tennis camp. I feel this is a very important issue because many camps have non-English-speaking pros and sometimes, while they may be great pros, they may also be difficult to understand. Get all the information from the "horse's mouth," so to speak. Brochures and receptionists tend to paint a rosy picture—find out what it's really like.

I once had a student who wanted to go on a tennis vacation, and at the same time lose weight and get in shape for the upcoming season. I recommended she investigate the resorts in southern California that have spas as well as tennis camp. At these resorts, you can choose from a number of special diets with reduced calories and exercise programs to fit any need. The bonus is, you can also be pampered daily with massages, whirlpools, facials, and many other specialty treatments. These resorts often have some top-notch tennis facilities with world-class instruction, video analysis, and strategy sessions as well. Over the years, I've recommended these resort spas to many people who want good tennis, but also want the benefits of a spa/nutrition center with a highly knowledgeable staff. Your needs will be specially catered to. This is very important when you are on a diet and exercise program of any kind. There are also good tennis/spa resorts in Arizona and Florida.

For those not interested in, or not in need of, a spa treatment program, I recommend one of the many "tournament tough" camps. These intensive tennis camps will improve your game with training in fundamentals, drills, strategy, tactics, and the mental aspect of competition. In many of these camps, an emphasis is also placed on footwork, balance, speed, and agility, plus injury prevention. You can also expect video analysis, mental conditioning, and match play. These camps offer a great way for individuals to improve all aspects of their game. Because of the intensity of training— up to five hours of tennis a day—make sure you get into good shape if you are not already. Make sure you bring all of the supplies you might possibly need, including tape for taping up any old injuries. People prone to blisters should tape up as well, if they're not used to that much playing.

A general tip: Stop immediately if you feel you have injured yourself. Don't make it worse by trying to tough it out. Get some therapy and try it out the next day.

It is always wise when choosing a camp to inquire if any guarantees are offered. One company I know of says if you do not improve within one week, they will give you a free stay at any of their affiliated camps. One fellow, who went to many of these camps, was much better in terms of ability than most of the other campers. He was disappointed because of the disparity in levels and complained to the camp director. He was given a free week at the camp of his choice where his needs could be met.

Double Faults

If you find when you get to the camp that you are placed on the wrong court for your ability, talk to the pro. Don't waste your time or the other student's time. Make the court change immediately.

So, it's important to read all about the camp before you choose! Each camp usually has it's own philosophy. Find out what it is before you go. Most camps offer a teacher/player ratio of 4 to 1. In a hot or humid climate like Florida or Arizona, since you'll be hitting thousands of balls, begin with a shorter session of two hours as opposed to four hours. It's best to acclimate slowly and raise the number of hours later in the week. One girl I knew planned to do this when she attended her first camp. She was having so much fun the first day, however, that she decided to extend her time. Shortly thereafter, she went to get some water and take a break but ended up collapsing from heat exhaustion. So, make sure you don't overdo it and pace yourself at a leisurely rate. Drink plenty of fluids before, during, and after play. Remember, if you wait until you are thirsty, it is already too late. Your body is dehydrated.

Another option would be to plan on other activities as well as a two-hour tennis program. Strategy classes, video analysis, or classes on injury prevention and nutrition are usually offered. There is plenty to learn off the court as well, so you can keep busy. Remember to pace yourself.

I look like that?
Photo Credit: Vicki Fort

When choosing a camp, the philosophy, teaching staff, player/pro ratio and off-court programs are usually given the most consideration. Location and special activities are also important since most people want a tennis vacation where they have lots of options. So, whether you like to waterski or bike, check out what they offer. There is a wide range of prices to fit any budget, so do some research and have a great time doing whatever you choose!

How Much Will It Cost?

The average cost of a week in a tennis camp is around $800, and includes room and board, morning instruction, and afternoon game. Private lessons are available, but at an extra cost. Look for special rates during the off-season—many people find this a good time to go, learn, and save money.

The average cost of a resort is $1,500 per week. Again, this includes room and board, some instruction, and games. The price will vary depending on your accommodations. Many resorts, especially in the Caribbean, run special rates during the off-season. If price is an issue, I recommend you go during the off-season. The instruction is still top-notch and the accommodations are still wonderful.

If you go to a spa combination that has everything, you should expect to pay $2,000 a week. That will include everything—meals (if you can call them that), sporting activities, and accommodations. If you are not used to all this tennis, you will lose weight anyway. You will, however, love the massages and extra goodies you will find at the full service resorts.

After a hard day on the courts, make the most of all the amenities.

More Is Not Better

You will also need to decide how much time you want to spend traveling to the resort or camp, as well as how long you will want to stay. I recommend a minimum of three days and no longer than two weeks. One week is optimal and gives you time to settle in and acclimate yourself to the program. Any longer than two weeks is counterproductive, and any less than three days will not give you time to achieve your goal.

Double Faults

Pack light. Never bring more than you can carry. All these resorts have laundries or laundry services.

What to Bring

Plan to bring at least two pairs of sneakers, a warm-up suit or two, and comfortable tennis attire. Remember that you are going to improve your game, not make a fashion statement. Also, bring some exercise outfits for stretching and for off-the-court fitness workouts. A bathing suit is a must for the cool down after your tennis workout. Two to three racquets are also a necessity, as well as a couple extra packs of your tennis strings in case they don't have what you use. Dinner clothes are also necessary, depending on the location, because resorts may have a dinner dress code that may require jackets and ties for the men. Do yourself a favor and research the facility before you go.

Tournament Travel

The other tennis traveling you can do is going to tournaments outside your area. There are always local tournaments but sometimes it is fun to pick a few tournaments out of town. You and your partner can decide how far you want to go and whether you want to drive or fly.

Depending on your ability and age, you will find a tournament or two every week in your part of the country. In the winter, due to limited court time, there are fewer events. I don't think you want to travel to Boise in the middle of winter, so let's pick a nice location, a fun tournament, and plan on some competitive tennis.

Trish Says

I mentioned my Les Grandes Dames tournament at BallenIsles in another chapter. It is for women 40 through 80. Held in January, it is an ideal getaway for many tennis players snowed in for the winter months up north. Many of the entrants are never going to win a national title. They come with friends for a nice week in the sun, and to top it off they can play in a tennis tournament where they are guaranteed four good matches.

If you play in a local league, there is often a sectional and national championship for that league. The USTA leagues in particular play off all the way up to the national championships. This means you can win in Toledo, then go to your Midwest section tournament, then if you win there you might end up in Palm Springs, California, for the team finals. If you like to travel, play tennis, and make new friends, this is a great way to do all three.

A winning team.
Photo Credit: Vicki Fort

The Least You Need to Know

➤ Camps and resorts offer a great way to improve your game and heighten your enjoyment of tennis.

➤ Set your goals before deciding what kind of program suits you.

➤ Plan to spend at least $500 plus, per week.

➤ Spend a minimum of three days and no more than two weeks at a program.

➤ Play in local tournaments and leagues before entering events out of state.

➤ Once a year, take a special tennis trip.

Chapter 25

To Dream the Impossible Dream: The Pro Circuit

In This Chapter

➤ A couple of Panchos and a Jack; the first pro circuit

➤ I can get paid for doing what?

➤ Men at work; how the men's pro circuit got started

➤ "You've come a long way, baby!"; the women's circuit

➤ The Grand Slams

Most of today's tennis professionals pay homage and tribute to those great players who paved the way so that tennis could become the tremendous sport that it is today. As you will have read in our history chapter, there were many names who contributed to the game's growth and popularity. In the last 50 years the two names that should come to every tennis player's mind, as they say their thank-yous, are those of Jack Kramer and Billie Jean King. Kramer really started the men's professional tour and Billie Jean King spearheaded the women's tour.

It was a slow process but the purses got larger and the crowds came to watch. The men and the women separated and then came back together for the major events. Rivalries developed and the top players became personalities both on and off the court.

Television helped spread the word and sponsors jumped on board to help bring the purses up and make the top players household names and millionaires. There are now over 300 prize-money tournaments throughout the world. The men's computer ranking lists over 1,000 players and the women's list has over 600. The tour is very tough and very competitive—it is also a lonely existence and not as glamorous as it sounds.

Passing Shots

Billie Jean King was heralded as the first female athlete to win over $100,000 in a single year. Nowadays, this seems like a paltry amount, because players win more than this in a single tournament. But BJK paved the way for many women athletes because she pushed for equal rights and equal prize money.

Most tennis players dream of playing Wimbledon, or returning Pete Sampras's serve, even if it is a far-fetched thought. This is one of the greatest things about tennis. You are playing the exact same game as the pros with all the same rules, and if you practice hard enough—who knows—you might just achieve your dream.

At many professional tournaments, they hold drawings and competitions where the prizes are a chance at returning one of the pro's serves, or playing a doubles match with some of the top players. Many spectators are too timid or embarrassed to try these things and they miss out on some once-in-a-lifetime opportunities. I encourage you to enter everything because you will never know when your name will be drawn to play a game of doubles with Virginia Wade or Stan Smith.

I also want you to watch as much top-level tennis as you can. You will learn a great deal by watching all the different styles and personalities. You will be able to incorporate many of the same tactics and you will learn from their mistakes.

Let's go to the pros.

How It All Started

Actually, it was Bill Tilden and Suzanne Lenglen who were the first real professionals because they received quite a lot of money to play exhibitions during the late 1920s. But American Jack Kramer started the first real professional tour in 1960. He nabbed Pancho Gonzales, Pancho Segura, Frank Sedgman, and some of the other European players and started arranging exhibitions. First they played in the United States and then they went all over the world. Kramer signed more name players as the tour grew. But in the long run, the pro tour was in sorry shape because the fans did not come out and watch.

Then George McCall, an American businessman, underwrote the professional men's tour and created a series of tournaments for men and women that rivaled those events sponsored by the USTA. These players were making good money for tennis players in those days. It was not an easy time, traveling from one city to the next playing one-night stands. The best thing that occurred from all of these exhibitions was getting big-time tennis into some smaller cities.

The tennis institutions banned all these players who played for money. They became known as "registered players" and the lines between amateurism and professionalism became very muddled. By 1970, however, the groundwork was laid for the framework of today's men's and women's professional circuits.

A battle started to rage between the ITF and the WCT, in the men's game. The men's Grand Prix Series got off the ground. Pepsico was the first sponsor and the tour purses were worth $1.5 million. For the first time ever, Rod Laver won more money than Lee Trevino in a single year.

Lamar Hunt got the WCT World Championship Tennis Tour off to a good start and so did the USTA circuit headed by Bill Riordan. Everywhere the men turned, there was conflict.

The women were not happy either. In the few Open tournaments, the women's prize money was only one-eighth of the men's purses. Billie Jean and her friends were playing on one circuit and being ostracized by the USTA. BJK has always been a great pioneer. Her personality, both on and off the court, was aggressive. She changed the face of women's sports forever.

Our leader-Billie Jean King.

Photo Credit: June Harrison

Basically, the entire game was a mess. The public didn't really know what was going on inside the tours. It was probably just as well.

Nikki Pilic, the number-one player from Yugoslavia, was banned from Wimbledon by the ITF in 1973. He had committed to play the Davis Cup and then reneged to play an exhibition. His player friends took a stand with him against the ITF. That year, Wimbledon was very weak because many of the top players did not play. This prompted some major changes in the game for both men and women.

The true era of open tennis had begun.

Trish Says

One of the first women's pro tournaments sponsored by Virginia Slims was held in Detroit, Michigan, in 1972. What surprised everyone who worked the tournament was the willingness of the players to help with the promotions. Billie Jean and Rosie Casals did radio show after radio show. Wendy Overton gave so many free clinics she barely had strength left for her matches. The players were great and the public responded by coming out to watch. We were on our way, baby!

The women found a savior in Gladys Heldman. She was a great supporter of tennis and she managed to get Lionel as a sponsor for the first women's professional tournament. The first event, in Houston, in 1971, was very successful so Heldman approached Joe Cullman from Phillip Morris. With Heldman's persistence, Cullman didn't have a chance and he agreed to sponsor a series of women's tournaments. To help bring spectators to the sites, the players helped promote the events by wooing the press and the public every way they knew how.

Joe Cullman was the greatest supporter of women's tennis in the 1970s, 1980s, and well into the 1990s.

The women couldn't have done it without him—Joe Cullman.

Photo Credit: June Harrison

Slowly but surely, the tournaments got bigger and more popular. The players became stars and the sponsors poured more money into the events. During the 1970s and 1980s, tennis was in its heyday. The International Tennis Federation also put more money into the four major events known as the Grand Slams (the Australian Open, the French Open, Wimbledon, and the U.S. Open), so everyone was happy.

The Professional Tours

The men and the women divided into two separate groups when the professional tours first started. It took some time but the renegades and the establishment finally came together and the two circuits merged. This only strengthened the game and the matches featured all the top players, and the need for exhibitions diminished. Exhibitions have a place in the sport but they do take away from the regular tournaments.

The women's tour expanded even more with the advent of the *Avon Futures Tour*. This was a series of tournaments open to all women players who wanted to try to work their way up the rankings. It was the best thing that could have happened to women's tennis because it allowed players like Pam Shriver and Tracy Austin to quickly rise to the top level of the women's game.

The men's tour did not have a sugar daddy like Virginia Slims who poured money into promoting the women's tour, not just into the purses each week. They did, however, have some strong sponsors like Commercial Union Assurance, Colgate, Mercedes, and IBM. In the 1980s, tennis was booming, racquet sales were on the rise, and more and more people were taking up the sport.

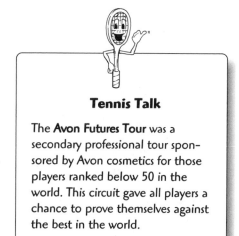

Tennis Talk

The **Avon Futures Tour** was a secondary professional tour sponsored by Avon cosmetics for those players ranked below 50 in the world. This circuit gave all players a chance to prove themselves against the best in the world.

The players had the power and the talent. They also wanted some say in their own future. Where once the player associations were just involved in decisions that affected the players, such as draw sizes and distribution of prize money, they now wanted more say. There followed some power struggles on both the men's and women's side as the players attempted to wrestle power from the ITF and the stronger national associations. What ensued was a redistribution of power and a reorganization of the two councils that governed the sport. Today, you have the ATP Tour and the Corel WTA Tour as the major forces in the game.

ATP: It's a Man's World

The Association of Tennis Professionals (ATP) is the player association for the men's tour. Founded in 1972, it is headquartered in Ponte Verde, Florida. The club has all the surfaces so the players can practice for all their tournaments. It also serves as a regular club and a place where some of the pros can teach to earn money during their off time.

Passing Shots

In the men's game, very few events pay any prize money for playing the qualifying event. You have to get through to the last four players and get into the main draw before you see any cash. So why do they play, you ask. For ranking points, and so they can get some good tournament experience and hopefully have some good results.

Passing Shots

Todd Martin, an American player, went to Northwestern University. Many people say that his game developed only later because he did not have the opportunity to play full time on the circuit as his peers did. Supporters say that he was not mature enough to compete on the circuit and that he has become a better player because he did not put pressure on himself too early. Whatever spin you put on it, playing in college improved his game.

It features a rehab center and a full fitness center, so that players can come there to rest or recuperate.

In 1990, the ATP took over the running of the tour. The association has an executive director and a board of directors. The board, comprised of players and former players, governs what happens to the players. They have instituted insurance and pension plans, and they help regulate the tournaments. The tournaments are like franchises. You own a week on the men's tour calendar and, unless you run a bad event or don't pay out all your prize money, you own the event in perpetuity. It is very difficult to start a new event. Most of the time, you have to start small and that means lower prize money. A smaller purse means no big-name players, which means no marquee appeal. Unless you are in a mid-size city, a smaller tournament will never make enough money to cover the cost of staging the event. These would-be promoters then turn to exhibitions.

The men players worked hard to secure their future in the sport. Players like Arthur Ashe, Butch Buchholz, Nikki Pilic, and Stan Smith dedicated a lot of time organizing behind the scenes so that today, players like Sampras and Rafter can win the big bucks and not have to worry about the state of the game.

Thanks to their forefathers in the tennis world, Rafter and Sampras (pictured on the following page) don't have a thing to worry about except their next opponent.

It is even hard to get on the calendar for an exhibition, because the dates all have to be approved by the Men's Pro Council. Players can play only a certain number of exhibitions each year. Each player must commit to a certain number of tournaments each year so that the ATP can promise the tournament directors a certain number of top players at each stop on the tour.

How does a player get onto the ATP rankings? The men's game is more difficult to break into than the women's. There are satellite events all over the world and if you win one of these you are well on the way to getting the computer points needed to get you on the rankings. Most men players spend about two years working their way onto the computer and from that point, they can then be accepted into tournaments. Not until a player is in the top 100 is he assured of getting into the major tournaments on a consistent basis.

Possibly the best ever.

Photo Credit: June Harrison

The new breed: strong, talented, and handsome.

Photo Credit: June Harrison

Many American male players elect to play college tennis. This gives them a great college education on a tennis scholarship and it also allows them time to play quite a few tournaments. It does not allow them to take any prize money above their expenses, but they get their education while still trying to work their way up the rankings. It also gives them a lot of competition without having to pay to travel all around the world. Many young players from other countries also seek to get college scholarships in the United States so that they can further their education and play a high level of tennis. The United States also has a great number of Challenger or Satellite tournaments where young players can try to get ranking points without traveling all over the world.

It is the ATP's role to find a sponsor for the men's game. Sponsoring tennis these days means big bucks. Staging men's tournaments requires a great investment of time and money. Most promoters finish one event and then immediately start planning for the following year's event. If the prize money is $500,000, then the rule of thumb is to make certain that all expenses are paid and the prize money is covered before opening the doors. It will take at least another $500,000 to stage the event. There are a lot of hidden costs because the contract with ATP requires the event provide certain amenities to the players, not to mention officials and ball-persons. This is the same on the Corel WTA Tour as well.

WTA: Women's Work

The WTA was founded in 1973. The Corel WTA Tour has its player headquarters in St. Petersburg, Florida, and its main business office is currently in Connecticut. There is also a small European office. The WTA operates with a president and a board of directors, some of whom are current players and others are business advisors. The board advises the Women's Pro Council which is the main governing body for the entire sport. As in the men's game, the WTA is primarily responsible for all player issues and they have their representatives on the Women's Pro Council, which determines all the rules that regulate the entire tour. The Women's Council also approves certain exhibitions so that the players can play a couple of these types of events without having them interfere with the real tournaments.

Trish Says

I once knew a very good junior player who did particularly well in doubles. She chose her tournaments very carefully because her goal was to get as many computer points as she could and still not play any more tournaments than necessary. She chose them well, and eventually became a highly ranked world junior and she was also in the top 200 on the WTA rankings. She now plays full time and is in the top 20. As a young player, you need advice as to how to understand the computer rankings.

The women's tour went through the same power struggles as the men's. The players wanted power over their sport, yet they did not control the events—certainly not the major events. After a period of negotiations, the WTA allowed the Pro Council to run the tour, with advice from their board delegates.

It is a little easier to get onto the women's computer rankings because players gain points simply by winning a few matches in any event with over $25,000 in prize money. Although players need to play at least 10 tournaments a year to maintain a decent ranking, it is easier to get into the smaller tournaments.

The women's tour has a school for their younger players. It focuses primarily on the tour and what playing in the tour entails. It was introduced because of problems with the younger players such as Jaeger, Capriati, and Austin. The WTA felt that there was too much pressure on the young players and they wanted to educate the players and their parents on the pitfalls of the professional game. The older players also felt it was important for the new players to understand the history of their sport. These players today are making thousands of dollars even if they lose in the first round of tournaments, so the former stars wanted the younger ones to know how they got into that position.

Jennifer Capriati, pictured here, went through some tough times but she is back on the tour trying to make up for lost time.

Can she come back?

Photo Credit: June Harrison

It is important that the two associations care about the players, particularly in women's tennis, where players can come into the professional ranks at age 14 with very little worldly knowledge. Many players can be taken advantage of and given poor advice. Look at the problems Steffi Graf encountered and this was her father who misused her money. The ATP and the WTA need to communicate with the players at the junior level before these players get caught up in the glamour and the money. Some of the major tournaments have had seminars for the parents, which I feel are a must if the family is to know what lies ahead for them.

Finally, the player councils have stopped adding new tournaments. Players can now comfortably take some time off without worrying about their computer ranking. Both the ATP and the WTA have put a stop to all the one-night stands for the top players. The sport is very healthy. Both tours have good players representing the game at the top. All players should still remember those pioneers who paved the way for them. Let's hope a 12-year-old top junior today knows what Kramer, Laver, Connors, Ashe, and on the women's side, King, Casals, Navratilova, and Evert put into their sports while they were still top players.

The International Tour

Pick up a newspaper, turn to the sports section, and you will find results for at least four tournaments somewhere in the world. Many times, it will be three men's tournaments and one women's event, but often it will be two and two. There might be a $750,000 event in Germany and a $200,000 event in Spain for the men. For the women, there might be a $350,000 event in Los Angeles and a $175,000 event in France.

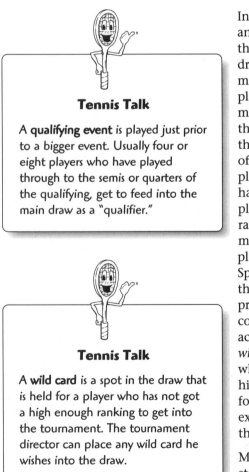

Tennis Talk

A **qualifying event** is played just prior to a bigger event. Usually four or eight players who have played through to the semis or quarters of the qualifying, get to feed into the main draw as a "qualifier."

Tennis Talk

A **wild card** is a spot in the draw that is held for a player who has not got a high enough ranking to get into the tournament. The tournament director can place any wild card he wishes into the draw.

In some of these events, there will be a qualifying, and the last four players in the draw will be fed into the main draw. Some tournaments are 64-player draws but most cater to only 32 players. Take the men's event in Germany with 32 players: It may be played indoors on a couple of courts. The top seed might be Sampras with maybe four other players in the top ten playing in the draw because of the size of the purse. The bigger the purse, the higher the rating of the tournament, which means that the better players will enter that event. The German event will have players ranked 1 to 50 because not everybody plays each week. But that does mean that a player ranked 51 will not be able to get into this tournament so if he wants to play that week he will have to play in Spain. This means that the smaller event in Spain will not have more than maybe one player in the top ten; but many of the Spanish players will probably enter it because it is an event in their home country. In this case, players ranked 5 to 75 might be accepted into the draw. All tournaments are allowed a *wild card* entry. These are reserved for marquee names who have been injured and who might not have a high enough ranking to get into the tournament, or for the latest junior sensation who might sell some extra tickets. The owner of the tournament selects these wild cards.

Mary Pierce, pictured on the following page, got her start on the pro tour by being given wild cards. After five years she is now in the top 10.

Going wild...and making it.

Photo Credit: June Harrison

The prize money is divided up into singles and doubles. For example, if it is a 32 singles draw, then it will be a 16 doubles draw. The singles will receive about 70 percent of the purse and the doubles the rest. In some cases, where there is a qualifying, the women always allot some prize money to qualifying to help these players pay expenses. It may be only 5 percent of the purse but a player could win $400 in qualifying which would help pay some bills. In all of the events, the winner will probably take home about 55 percent of the singles purse. Not bad for a week's work, or five matches if it is a 32 draw.

The finalist will receive about 25 percent, and then the rest is split up through the remaining rounds. Even first-round losers receive prize money for both singles and doubles.

The same holds true for the women's events, although almost every women's tournament has a qualifying on site so they take care of more players at each tournament. The tournament directors don't like the qualifyings because it means more players to take care of and more expenses. However, these players are also willing to do more PR, clinics, and pro-ams to help promote the event.

A player ranked in the top 20 should be able to take home over a million dollars in prize money in a good year. On top of this, that player will also earn bonuses for clothing contracts and other endorsements he or she might hold. Plus, the player will receive money for exhibitions, personal appearances, and clinics. It pays well if you are a top player.

Trish Says

One of my junior pupils goes to Saddlebrook in Florida every summer to really just immerse himself in tennis. One summer, he said that Jennifer Capriati had been at the camp working out with his tennis instructor and he often watched them work out. He came home renewed in his love for tennis. He said, "If Capriati still has to work that hard, then there's hope for me."

As I said before, over 1,000 men and 600 women have computer rankings. The two systems are not the same for both but they are similar. A player ranked 100 might make $100,000, but it drops off from there because the lower-ranked players cannot get into the bigger tournaments and they do not have a chance to earn the big bucks. It takes a good win, a lucky draw, and the ability to maintain that new level, to bump yourself up the rankings fast. A win over a top-ten player is your ticket to a new tournament level if you are a journeyman, as they call the Satellite players.

It is rare in either men's or women's tennis for a player to appear out of nowhere. These days, before a player is 12 years old, she or he has been scouted by the management companies. If these young players are good enough, sponsorship arrangements are offered to the parents to ensure that the young player can travel, receive good coaching, and have a nice place to live.

Full-time tennis academies have sprung up all over the world. Probably the most famous belongs to Nick Bolletieri in Florida. International Management Group (IMG), the largest sports management agency in the world, owns this academy. Bolletieri runs the academy, which caters to promising juniors from all over the world. Some of the really outstanding young players are given scholarships while others pay to attend. You are immersed in tennis and, although academic schooling is arranged, your tennis comes first. Many of our future champions on both the men's and women's tours will come from academies like this. Andre Agassi and Monica Seles were both Bolletieri pupils. Many top players still go back there to train during their off weeks.

Monica Seles (pictured on the next page) chose to work out at Bolletieri's Academy when she was ready to come back onto the tour after her stabbing.

Hard at work.

Photo Credit: June Harrison

So, what is it like playing on the professional tour today? I can assure you it is very competitive and it can be lucrative. It can also be very lonely and depressing, particularly if you are not winning a lot of matches, which means you are not winning a lot of money. It costs about $25,000 a year to play the circuit. Add more if you come from places like Australia or South Africa. Because airline expenses are high, many players from those countries do not go home very often, so they find a home away from home at one of the tennis academies or popular training centers with condos. Some simply stay with friends they have met in their travels.

For the top players who travel with an entourage, it can cost almost $100,000 just to get to the tournaments. Many of the tournaments offer free accommodations to the top players. Of course, the lesser players tend not to stay in the first-class hotels or eat in the fine restaurants.

The top players play about 18 major tournaments a year. The lower-ranked players can play more, because they are not playing until Sunday every week so their bodies do not have the same wear and tear. Most top-20 players go for three weeks in a row and then take one or two weeks off. During their off weeks, they usually rest completely for two days, then start practicing and working out twice a day. When playing an event most players like to get in to the city about two days before to acclimate themselves to the courts, the weather, the balls, and sometimes the altitude.

Trish Says

Martina Navratilova used to travel with her friends, parents, massage therapist, coach, and her dogs and cats. She also liked to bring her own pillow and comforter. One year Martina stayed at my house in Key Biscayne, Florida. She had three dogs with her and I had two cats and two Yorkshire terriers. She liked having everybody around. It made her more relaxed and she actually played better when she had all of her friends. She was miserable when she traveled alone.

The three most frequently asked questions at a tennis tournament are:

➤ "What time is my match?"

➤ "When can I practice?"

➤ "When is lunch?"

Players vary in their practice routines depending on whether or not they have a match that day. Before a match most players will stretch, warm-up off court for 10 minutes, then hit the court for half an hour or 45 minutes before their match. They will usually eat two hours before they have to play. On a nonmatch day during a tournament, most players will practice for two hours. If just playing doubles, players will usually hit in the morning for an hour or more and then, if the match is late in the day, they may hit briefly to warm up again. At indoor tournaments, practice is hard to book, because the court time is limited.

Many parents ask me what to do with their tennis-playing children. My answer depends a lot on the age of the child and how much talent the child has. If the child is winning local tournaments at the age of eight or ten, then the parents definitely need to enter him into regional events. Players who are ranked in the top five in their age group in their state rankings are certainly talented players. I always tell the parents that they really cannot tell how good a child will be until she is at least 14 or 15 years old. By then, the child will have played all the other good players in her age group, and the parents will have a good indication of where she will be ranked nationally. By the time a child is 16, he should have played in some of the international junior competitions, such as the Orange Bowl or the Easter Bowl. If your child is not ranked in the top 20 in his or her age group, then your child is probably not going to be a world champion. Don't despair! Your child has reached a level in tennis that will take him a long way both socially and economically. Your child can earn a college scholarship. She can use her skills in business. She can put her competitive spirit to good use in the game of life. She will have a talent that will give her joy for the rest of her life.

Should your child go to a *tennis academy?* Maybe—if the child is self-motivated and has a lot of initiative, then he will do well in an academy setting. If you send him when he is too young, he will get homesick and his schooling will suffer. Most parents today have read enough about the problems of tennis parents and are better informed of the possible problems than their predecessors.

On both the men's and women's tours, it is very hard for the players to know when to retire. Although it is a tough life, it is exciting and you get to travel the world getting paid to do something you love. When I was head tour director for the women's tour, one of the most frequently asked questions came from the older players who knew me very well.

After a poor match, they would come in to my office and say, "It's time to pack it in." They would seek my advice and I would always say the same thing: When you stop enjoying it, don't do it any more. When it becomes a job—even a well-paying job—that you don't like, then it is time to look elsewhere. The problem is, 30-year-old tennis players find it hard to get a job paying the money they are used to winning each year. After being the best at anything, it is hard to start at the bottom and work your way up. Really good tennis jobs are hard to find. Most of the better jobs are taken by experienced directors. Just because you are a great player doesn't mean you are a great coach or a good business person.

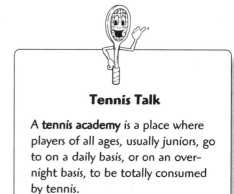

Tennis Talk

A **tennis academy** is a place where players of all ages, usually juniors, go to on a daily basis, or on an overnight basis, to be totally consumed by tennis.

I hope that the middle-of-the-road players, those who cannot retire on their winnings, have a plan for "after the tour." Some go back to school and start a whole new existence. This is hard because you are so much older than all the other students, but it is a good move. Not all tennis professionals want to stay in tennis. I have been lucky, because I have stayed in the sport in various positions. I continue to love what I do but others have not been so lucky.

The Grand Slams

Prior to 1960, the only major event that players really went after and held in high esteem was Wimbledon. Not that the other major tournaments in the USA, France, and Australia were not important, but they did not have the prestige that they have today. Not a lot of players went to Australia because of the cost to get there. The French Championships were always popular and most top players played it because it was close in time to Wimbledon, so foreign players could come to Europe and play both. At that time, the U.S. Championships were played on various surfaces and not a lot of foreigners came to New York to play.

Trish Says

Ask any tennis player what the worst tournament in the world is and they will all answer the same thing—Wimbledon Qualifying. Only a certain number of players can get into Wimbledon every year. The rest of those 128 world-ranked players must play, or face, a world-ranked player for at least three rounds to get into the main draw. This is the dreaded Wimbledon Qualies.

When the Open era arrived, the International Tennis Federation made it imperative that the Grand Slam Tournaments have a special place on the tennis calendar. The ITF increased prize money, made the draws larger, and improved the amenities at the four sites. Wimbledon and the French could not really move their sites but they did expand and give the players better changing rooms, restaurants, and lounges. Both the Australian Open and the U.S. Open built new stadiums, and all four venues have made improvements every year.

Ask a tennis player which Grand Slam she would like to win and, in most cases, the answer will be Wimbledon. Experiencing the tradition, prestige, and overall regard gained from winning a Wimbledon Championship is the prize of a lifetime. Walking around center court holding the Wimbledon trophy is something every tennis professional dreams about. Not that we wouldn't settle for any other Grand Slam title, but Wimbledon epitomizes all that tennis stands for.

Look at the next picture and imagine yourself there.

The granddaddy of them all. All-England Club–Wimbledon.

Photo credit: June Harrison

I remember playing Wimbledon one year when it must have rained for four straight days. We sat around waiting to play, trying to find practice courts, eating too much, drinking tea, and generally trying to stay warm and dry. When I did finally get on for my matches, the court was slippery, the balls were heavy, and it was still freezing. I certainly was never good enough to win a Wimbledon title, but I liked playing on grass and I always played well in England. After one of these long, wet days of waiting to play, I caught my car so that I could go back to my friend's house where I was staying. As we drove out of the gates at 7 P.M., there were long queues of spectators waiting in the rain. I looked at these people and thought they had to be mad, but I knew it was the only way that regular tennis fans could hope to get tickets to see tennis. People waited for days to try to buy tickets to the finals. As cold and wet as I was, I got a warm feeling to know that people wanted to watch tennis so much that they would stand all night to get tickets for the next day—which might be rainy anyway. It was experiences like this that helped make Wimbledon special for me and many other players.

Each Grand Slam event has a special feeling. In Paris, it is the fans and of course the city itself. How can you not feel wonderful when you are playing in a beautiful old stadium in the middle of the Bois du Boulogne, on a balmy spring afternoon. The French tennis fans are very knowledgeable and very boisterous, particularly when a French player is on court. I love watching men's tennis on the slow, red clay courts of Stade Roland Garros. With heavy topspin, deft drop shots, and long rallies, the men's singles matches turn out to be a test of strength, stamina, and endurance. Some matches last more than four hours and it boils down to the fifth and final set when both players are spent but fighting for the win. The French Open has that special feeling, and it isn't just the wine served at lunch.

The Australian Open, which kicks off the tennis year after a few smaller tournaments down under, is more laid back and it has a "take it easy, mate" feeling. The weather is always very hot and the surface is rubberized asphalt that gets a little soft and sticky. Regardless of where you are coming from, getting to Australia requires a long flight, so the players try to get there well in advance of the tournament. Most of them play in Sydney the week before and then go to Melbourne for the Open. For many years, the Grand Slams, except for the French Open, were on grass. Over the years, the surface has changed to suit the climate and the necessity for variety in the Grand Slam tournaments. The new Melbourne stadium has underground walkways, retractable roofs, and plenty of space for sponsor entertainment.

Passing Shots

In 1991, after winning the Australian Open for the first time, Boris Becker ran off the court before the presentation and threw himself in the river Yarra which ran by the stadium. Asked why he did this, Becker replied, "I was so excited I needed to cool off and regain my composure."

Boris Becker, pictured here, was a very popular figure at the Grand Slams.

The fans loved Boris.

Photo Credit: June Harrison

Probably one of the hardest Grand Slams to win is the U.S. Open. First, you have to conquer New York, the city, the traffic, the heat, and the rowdy fans. Once you have that figured out, you then need to block out the noise and get down to winning tough tennis matches. Winning this title is like going out for a heavyweight championship. It is two weeks of trying to play your best tennis every time you step on the court. At most Grand Slams it is hard to get to your match court, at Flushing Meadows, you have a long walk and a lot of pushy fans to get through. Most of the top players are escorted to their match courts by security guards. Since the Monica Seles stabbing, security has tightened at all tennis events around the world. Just like the Australian Open, the U.S. Open has been played on many different surfaces. I have played the event numerous times, on grass and on hard courts. When the event moved from the Westside Club in Forest Hills to Flushing Meadows in Flushing, it was able to expand and build more hard courts. They have just finished another new stadium so more fans can see their favorite sport played by the world's best.

All players work toward peaking for the four Grand Slams. Some of the European and South American clay-court specialists skip Wimbledon because they don't play well on the grass, but most of the time, every top player, if he or she is fit, will play the Grand Slams. Thanks to television, we can now watch all the best matches and learn a lot about the sport right in our own homes!

Trish Says

One year when the US was held at the Westside Tennis Club in Forest Hills, I had to get from the qualifying site to the Westside Club to check in. This was almost impossible without catching a taxi, but getting a taxi was difficult. Finding a driver who knew where the club was, was even harder. I didn't know New York and apparently my taxi driver didn't either. I finally reached the club, but talk about being frazzled and not relaxed before I had to play!

How to Learn from the Pros

Ten years ago, you were lucky to get any tennis on television; maybe the finals of the Grand Slams, but that was about it. Now, most major matches and even team events like the Davis Cup and Federation Cup are televised. If they are not on the networks, then channel surf over to one of the sports networks like ESPN, USA or PRIME. All the commentators are very knowledgeable. Some are former players, while others like Bud Collins or Dick Enberg are great analysts who have come to know a great deal about the sport over the years.

Although camera angles and closeups can give you a great view of the players and their styles, there is nothing to compare to being courtside. You cannot imagine the power of Sampras's serve or the speed of Venus Williams's forehand until you have heard the sound and seen the ball travel at over 140 miles an hour. But that is not something you will be able to relate to—you must simply admire and enjoy their extraordinary talents. You can, however, watch certain parts of their games and transfer what you see into your own game.

Passing Shots

Bud Collins is a great friend of tennis, particularly women's tennis. He is very highly regarded, both as a person and a commentator. However, he is known for wearing very loud, checkered pants at every tournament. So, if you don't know Bud, but you see a man wearing very loud, sometimes ugly trousers at a tennis tournament, chances are it's him.

First, take their service preparations. I don't expect you to hit the ball like Goran Ivanisovic, but you should watch the way the pros ready themselves before they begin their service motion. Remember I told you about routines. They all have them. They are all different. Pick one you like and copy it. Take the one that you think will get you personally focused and loose.

Then watch their follow-throughs. See how long and smooth their follow-throughs are when the players are deep in the court, and how they are shorter and more compact when the players are in close or in trouble. Imagery is helpful, so pick a player whose style you like and picture that player every time you hit that stroke.

More than anything else, I want you to watch their feet. Although some players have better footwork than others, they all move magnificently. If they don't, they are probably injured or sometimes out of shape, and they will lose because footwork is often the only difference in a close match. Make yourself watch only their feet for four games and see how many steps they take to set up for a shot or simply return serve. How do they pivot? How do they recover after their opponent has them out of position? How much are they off their heels and yet still balanced? Great footwork can turn you into a better player even if your strokes have not improved.

Trish Says

At my tournament in Albuquerque, New Mexico, we had stands around all four sides of the center court. There were two rows of boxes around the sides and both ends had sponsor boxes and media seating. The match featured Brenda Schultz from the Netherlands, who has a serve clocked at 123 miles an hour. At one point, she hit a boomer straight down the middle that her opponent did not get. The ball flew straight into the sponsor box seats, knocking cocktails, hamburgers, and hot dogs all over the place. Both players had a good laugh and I can guarantee you the spectators seated in the ends paid closer attention to the match from that point on.

Now watch their bodies. Can you tell whether they are winning or losing? You should not be able to detect this. Remember, I told you in Chapter 18 to never let your opponent see your emotions—particularly if you are down on yourself. If you have never seen Chris Evert or Steffi Graf play, try to find some of their matches on tape. They were both superb at hiding their true emotions. You can learn a lot from these two just by copying their body language and eye movement after they have lost a long rally or received a bad call. Their quiet calm was always unnerving to their opponents.

I love to watch tennis from the back of the court. From there you can see the point unfold and you don't have to swivel your head every time the ball goes over the net. You can see the spin and pace on the balls. You can read the direction of the serve sometimes even before the receiver can see where it is going. In doubles, it is wonderful to watch the players move in tandem to cover the angles and the middle. If they give signals, you get to see what they are trying when they are serving from your end.

Even at your own courts, if you see some good players playing, don't just wish you could play like them—watch them for a while. They are probably amateurs like you. Maybe they have just played longer and have more experience. If they are playing doubles, look at their court positions and their communication with their partners. Look at something as basic as the make of their racquet. What are they doing that you are not? The next time you go out to play, imagine moving your feet like Michael Chang. Keep your mind focused like Chris Evert and get ready to hit your ground strokes like Agassi. You can do this, I know you can.

The Least You Need to Know

➤ Jack Kramer and Billie Jean King started the men's and women's pro tours.

➤ If you are not going to be a top-50 ranked player you need to have another career planned after pro tennis.

➤ The four Grand Slams are the championships of Australia, France, Great Britain, and the United States.

➤ The rankings for both the men's tour and the women's tour are done by computer.

➤ Watch good tennis as much as you can—you can learn through osmosis.

Tennis Terms

ace   A service that lands in the proper court and is not touched by the receiver.

ad   Short for advantage, the first point scored after deuce.

ad court   The left half of the court. The left-hand service court so called because an ad score is served there.

ad in   Game score when the server wins the point after deuce.

ad out   Game score when the receiver wins the point after deuce.

all   A tie score—30–all, 3–all, for example.

alley   The area on either side of the singles court that enlarges the width of the court for doubles. Each alley is 4 1/2 feet wide. All shots in the alleys are in play for all shots after the serve in doubles.

amateur   A person who does not accept money for playing or teaching tennis.

American twist   A spin serve that causes the ball to bounce high and in the opposite direction from which it was originally traveling. A right-hander's American twist serve produces left-to-right spin on the ball.

angle shot   A ball hit to an extreme angle across the court.

approach   A shot that the hitter follows to the net.

ATP   Association of Tennis Professionals, an organization comprised of most of the leading male players in the world.

attack drive   An aggressive approach shot.

Australian doubles   Doubles in which the point begins with the server and server's partner on the same right or left side of the court.

backcourt   The area between the service line and the baseline.

backhand   A stroke hit by a right-handed player from the left side of the body; by a left-hand player from the right side of the body.

backhand court   For a right-handed player, the left-hand side of the court; for a left-handed player, the right-hand side of the court.

backspin   Spin that causes the ball to rotate backward and to bounce.

backswing   The initial part of any swing in which the racquet is drawn back before being swung forward.

balance point   The point in the shaft of a racquet where the head and the handle are balanced.

ball person   A person who retrieves balls for the players during competition.

baseline   The line that marks the boundary of the court farthest from the net. It runs parallel to, and 39 feet from, the net.

baseline game   Style of play in which a player stays in the backcourt.

bevel   The tilt or slant of the racquet face.

block   The return of a ball with a very short swinging motion.

boron   An expensive, extremely durable material used to manufacture racquet frames.

break service   To win a game in which the opponent serves.

bye   An opening in the draw that enables a player to advance to the next round without playing a match.

cannonball   A hard, flat serve.

carry   A shot that carried on the racquet strings or hit twice as the ball is returned. Carries are legal unless the player makes two or more deliberate attempts to hit the ball over the net; they may be called by the umpire or by the player who hits the ball.

center mark   The short line that bisects the center of the baseline. The server may not legally step on the center mark before striking the ball.

center service line   The line that is perpendicular to the net and divides the two service courts.

center strap   A two-inch-wide strap in the center of the net, anchored to the ground to hold the net secure at a height of 3 feet.

chair umpire   The lead on-court official during a match. The chair umpire's duties include calling and resolving disputes. The chair umpire sits adjacent to the net post.

check pause   The moment when both feet land together and split apart when approaching the net as the opponent is returning the ball.

chip   A modified slice, used primarily in doubles to return a serve. A chip requires a short swing, which allows the receiver to move in close to return.

choke   To play poorly because of the pressure of competition.

choke up   To move the hand up on the racquet to make it lighter or more easily handled.

chop   A sharp downward stroke producing heavy backspin to any part of the court.

circuit   A series of tournaments at the state, sectional, national, or international level.

closed face   The angle of the hitting face of the racquet when it is turned down toward the court.

closed stance   A position in which the toes of both feet form a line parallel to either sideline.

closed tournament   An event open only to members of a particular group or area.

Code of Conduct   A supplement to the rules of tennis that specifically defines etiquette parameters such as gamesmanship and line call responsibilities.

composite   A racquet frame reinforced with graphite, fiberglass, or boron.

consolation   A tournament in which first-round losers continue to play in a losers' tournament.

continental grip   A way of holding the racquet so that the player does not have to change grips between the forehand and backhand strokes; the wrist is directly over the top of the grip for the forehand and backhand volley.

counter-puncher   A player whose style of play emphasizes reacting to the other player's shots.

crosscourt shot   A shot in which the ball travels diagonally across the net, from one sideline of the court to the other.

cross strings   Strings running horizontally from one side of the racquet head to the other.

Davis Cup   An international team tennis event for male players.

deep shot   A shot that bounces near the baseline (near the service line on a serve).

default   A match won because the opponent did not show up to play or was disqualified. Synonym for forfeit.

deuce   The score when both players or teams have won three or more points apiece.

deuce court   The right court on one's own side of the net, and the left court on the other side of the net.

dink   A ball returned so it floats across the net with extreme softness.

double elimination   A tournament in which a player or team must lose twice before being eliminated.

double fault   A lost point resulting from the server missing two serves in succession. It costs a point.

doubles   A match played with two people on each team, four players total.

down the line   A straight shot hit parallel to the sideline.

draw   The means of establishing who plays whom in a tournament. The bracketed lineup indicating which players will be paired in each round of a tournament. Seeded players are spaced at even intervals throughout. Unseeded players are drawn by lot and placed in the remaining spaces.

drive   A forehand or backhand shot normally hit from anywhere behind the service line. It is an offensive ball hit with force.

drop shot   A softly hit shot that lands close to the net and bounces low.

drop volley   A volley that lands close to the net and bounces low. Hit softly and with backspin.

earned point   A point won through skillful playing rather than through an opponent's mistake.

Eastern grip   A handshake grip most commonly used for the forehand. The V between the thumb and index finger is slightly to the right on the racquet grip, with the racquet face perpendicular to the ground.

elimination   A tournament in which a player is eliminated when defeated.

error   A point achieved through an obvious mistake rather than through skillful playing.

face   The strung, hitting area of the racquet.

fast court   A court with a smooth surface, which causes the ball to bounce quick and low.

fault   Failure on an attempt to serve into the proper court.

Federation Cup   An international team tennis event for female players.

feed-in consolation   A tournament in which players who lose in the early rounds of a tournament reenter the championship draw and may finish as high as 5th place.

fiberglass   A somewhat flexible form of glass fiber used in some racquets.

fifteen   The first point won by a player or team.

finals   The match played to determine the winner of a tournament.

flat shot   A shot that travels in a straight line with little arc and little spin.

flexibility   How much a racquet bends from head to shaft or from one side of the head to the other when contact with the ball is made.

floater   A ball that moves slowly across the net in a high trajectory.

follow-through   The part of the swinging motion after the ball is hit.

foot fault   A service fault that occurs when the server touches the baseline with one or two feet before the racquet hits the ball.

forcing shot   A ball hit with exceptional power. It is a play in which, because of the speed and placement of the shot, the opponent is pulled out of position.

forecourt   The area between the net and the service line.

forehand   A stroke hit by a right-handed player from the right side of the body; by a left-handed player from the left side of the body. Any shot hit on the right side of the body for a right-handed player or the left side for a left-handed player.

forehand court   For a right-handed player, the right-hand side of the court; for a left-handed player, the left-hand side of the court.

forfeit   The awarding of a match to one player or team because an opponent fails to appear or is not able to complete a match. Synonym for default.

forty   The score when a player or team has won three points.

frame   The part of the racquet that holds the strings, but does not include the strings.

game   That part of a set that is completed when one player or side wins four points, or wins two consecutive points after deuce.

grand slam   The winning of the Australian Open, French Open, Wimbledon, and the U.S. Open in a single year.

graphite   A man-made, carbon-based material 20 times stronger and stiffer than wood, often used in racquets.

grip   The handle of the racquet. Also the method of holding onto the handle.

grommet   A small, round plastic sleeve in the frame, through which the strings pass.

ground stroke   Forehand or backhand stroke made after the ball has bounced.

gut   Racquet strings made from animal intestines.

hacker   A person who does not play tennis well.

half volley   A shot hit with a short volley stroke near the service line after the ball has bounced. Contact is usually made below knee level.

handle   The part of the racquet that is gripped in the hand.

head   The part of the racquet used to hit the ball; includes the frame and strings.

head-heavy   A reference to a racquet whose balance point is more than 1/4 inch from the center (midpoint of the racquet's length) toward the head.

head-light   A reference to a racquet whose balance point is more than 1/4 inch from the center (midpoint of the racquet's length) toward the handle.

hitting surface   The flat surface formed by the strings.

hold serve   To win a game in which one was server.

invitational tournament   An event open only to a select group, by invitation.

ITF   International Tennis Federation, an organization that governs international amateur competition and has some jurisdiction over professional tennis.

junior   A player 18 years old or younger.

Kevlar   A synthetic fiber used to strengthen tennis-racquet frames.

kill   To smash the ball down hard.

kill shot   A shot hit so hard or placed so well that the opponent cannot reach it.

ladder tournament   A type of competition in which the names of participants are placed in a column; players can advance up the column (ladder) by challenging and defeating players whose names appear above their own.

let   A point replayed because of interference, or a serve that hits the top of the net but is otherwise good.

linesperson   In competition, a person responsible for calling balls that land outside the court.

line umpire   An official who watches a line or lines and decides whether balls bounce in or out.

lob   A high arching shot. A lob can force an opposing volleyer away from the net or give a player at the baseline time to recover when out of position.

lob volley   A lob hit with a volley.

love   Zero. A player can win a love game, where the winner never loses a point (4 points to 0), a love set (6 games to 0) or a love match (two love sets, or 6 games to 0, 6 games to 0).

main strings   The vertical strings, running from the top to the bottom of the racquet head.

match   Singles or doubles play consisting of two out of three sets for all women's and most men's matches, or three out of five sets for many men's championship matches and tournaments.

match point   The final point needed to win the match. This term is used by spectators and television announcers during a match and by players after a match; it is not, or should not be, used by the umpire or players in calling out the score.

mid court   The general area in the center of the playing court, midway between the net and baseline. Many balls bounce at the player's feet in this area making the player unusually vulnerable.

mid-size   A racquet head of approximately 85 to 100 square inches. Smaller than an oversize racquet.

mixed doubles   A doubles match with a man and a woman on each team.

mix up   To vary the types of shots attempted.

National Tennis Rating System (NTRS)   A description of different tennis skills that helps the player to ascertain his or her correct ability level. Same as NTRP.

net game   Playing in the forecourt.

net person   A player positioned at the net.

net umpire   An official responsible for calling net serves.

no   An informal expression used by some players to call shots out.

no ad   Scoring system in which 7 points constitutes a game. For example, if the score is tied at 3 points for each player, the next player to win a point wins the game. Also called VASS scoring for Van Allen Simplified Scoring system.

no man's land   The area of the court between the service line and the baseline. This area is usually considered a weak area from which to return shots during a rally.

not up   An expression used to indicate that a ball has bounced twice on the same side before being hit.

NTRP   National Tennis Rating Program, which rates players from 1.0 (beginning) to 7.0 (touring professionals). Same as NTRS.

nylon   A type of synthetic racquet string.

open face   The angle of hitting face of the racquet when it is turned up and away from the court surface.

open tennis   Competition open to amateur and professional players.

opening   A court position that allows an opponent a good chance to win the point.

orthotics   An artificial material that is inserted into footwear to add support to the arches of the feet and align the body more efficiently.

overhead   A smash shot hit over the head, usually in the forecourt, after the opponent lobs. This technique is similar to the service motion.

out   A ball landing outside the playing court.

overgrip   A one-piece grip that slides over the original racquet grip.

overhead smash   A hard, powerful stroke hit from an over-the-head racquet position.

oversize   Refers to the largest of racquet heads, which are 100 square inches or more. Larger than a midsize.

pace   The speed or spin of a ball, which makes it bounce quickly.

passing shot   A ground stroke hit out of reach of a net player.

percentage shot   The safest, most effective shot hit in a particular situation.

percentage tennis   The art of hitting the shot most likely to land safely in the court at a given time. This is conservative tennis that emphasizes cutting down on unnecessary errors and on errors at critical points.

placement   A shot aimed at a particular place on the court that the opponent cannot return.

playing pro   A person who makes a living playing tennis.

poach   A doubles strategy in which the net player moves over to the partner's side of the court to make a volley.

point   One unit of scoring.

point penalty system   A penalty system designed to enforce fair play and good sportsmanship.

power zone   The area of the racquet's hitting surface that produces controlled power with no vibration.

pronation (wrist pronation)   The inward rotation of the forearm and wrist that occurs at the moment of impact during a serve. It causes the racquet to move up and over the top of the ball.

pro-set   An abbreviated way to score a match. Instead of playing the best two-out-of-three sets, the match consists of one set of 8 or 10 games, with a margin of at least two games needed to win.

pusher   A type of player who is consistent, but who hits with very little pace.

put-away   A shot that is literally put away (out of reach) from an opponent.

qualifying round   A series of matches played to determine which players will be added to a tournament field.

rally   The exchange of shots after the serve.

ready position   The position in which a player stands while waiting for a shot.

receiver   The player who is not the server.

referee   The head administrative official at tournament. This referee oversees the making of the draw and all other aspects of a tournament, and is the final judge on questions of law.

retrieve   A good return of a difficult shot. A retriever is a player who plays a defensive style, focusing on returning all shots. Much like the pusher, who gets everything back but does not play aggressively.

round robin   A tournament in which every player plays every other player.

rush   To move forward toward the net following a forcing shot.

second   An informal expression used by some players to indicate that the first serve is out.

seeded players   Players who are judged to be the best entering a tournament and who are placed in the draw in a way that prevents them from meeting each other in the early rounds. The usual pattern is to select one seed for every 4 entries.

semi-Western grip   A forehand grip used by many players where the hand is turned extremely toward the right on the racquet handle. This grip encourages extra topspin on the forehand.

serve   The shot that initiates a point. Also called service.

serve-and-volley player   A player who comes to the net immediately after serving.

service   A stroke hit over the head and used to put the ball in play. A player is allowed two attempts to serve the ball into the proper court.

service box   The rectangular area where the serve must land.

service break   When the receiver wins the game.

service line   The line that marks the base of the service court: parallel to the baseline and 21 feet from the net.

service return   A stroke hit by a player receiving serve.

service winner   A good service that the receiver is unable to return.

set   A group of games. To win a set, a player must win at least 6 games, with a minimum advantage of two games. A set score does not go higher than 7–5, except in Davis Cup play or special events. At 6–all, a tiebreaker is played in most situations.

set point   The last point needed to win the set.

shaft   The part of the racquet between the head and the grip.

sideline   The side boundary of the court for singles or doubles play. The singles sidelines are closer to the center of the court than are doubles sidelines.

sidespin   A shot in which the ball spins to the side and bounces to the side. The sidespin slice is one of the most common types of serves.

single elimination tournament   A type of competition in which players' names are drawn and placed on lines in a tournament bracket roster. Matches are played between players whose names appear on the connected bracket lines. Players who win advance to the next round of competition; those who lose are eliminated from competition.

singles   A game between two players.

slice   A spin serve that curves from the left to right or vice versa. Also, a shot executed by chopping down on the ball with an open racquet face.

slow court   A court with a rough surface, which tends to make the ball bounce rather high and slow.

smash   A hard overhead shot.

spin   The rotation of the ball.

split sets   When each player has won one set in a match, forcing the play of a third set.

split step   A jump reminiscent of the two-footed landing in hopscotch. It should be executed every time an opponent makes contact with the ball.

straight sets   A match in which the winner has won all sets.

string tension   Describes the tautness of the racquet strings. Measured in pounds of weight.

stroke   The manner in which a ball is hit (forehand, backhand, volley, for example).

sudden death   In no-ad scoring, when the score reaches 3–all.

sweet spot   The area near the center of the racquet that is most responsive. The sweet spot allows for the most power and accuracy and the least vibration. The exact place on the racquet face that produces controlled power with no vibration.

synthetic gut   A racquet string composed of several fibers of a synthetic material (not actually gut) twisted together.

take two   An expression meaning that the server should repeat both service attempts.

tape   The fabric band that stretches across the top of the net. The lines of a clay court. Lead tape is a weighted tape that is applied to the head of a racquet to make it heavier.

teaching pro   A person who teaches people to play tennis and is paid for the service. Teaching pros are usually distinguished from playing pros, although some professionals teach and play for money.

tennis elbow   A painful condition of the elbow joint commonly caused by hyperextension of the elbow or by excessive wrist action in tennis play.

thirty   The score when a player or team has won two points.

throat   The part of the racquet between the handle and the head.

tiebreak   A tiebreaking game played when the set score reaches 6 games all. A player must win at least seven points to win the tiebreak and must win by a margin of two.

titanium   A strong, lustrous, white metal used in the construction of some racquets.

topspin   Spin of the ball caused by hitting up and through the ball. It makes the ball bounce fast and long and is used on most ground strokes.

toss   Lofting the ball into the air with the free hand during the serve.

touch   The ability to hit a variety of precision shots.

trajectory   The flight of the ball in relation to the top of the net.

umpire   The person who officiates matches between two players or teams.

undercut   A backspin caused by hitting down through the ball.

underspin   Spin achieved by hitting through the ball with an open face. A ball hit with underspin bounces low and tends to skid.

unforced error   A point lost with absolutely no pressure having been exerted by the opponent.

unseeded   The players not favored to win nor given any special place on draw in a tournament.

USPTA   United States Professional Tennis Association is the leading organization for teaching professionals world-wide.

USTA   United States Tennis Association, the sport's governing body in the U.S.

VASS   Van Allen Simplified Scoring system, a no-ad, sudden-death scoring system used extensively in the 1970s and 1980s (no longer used in international competition).

vibration dampener   A rubber or plastic device inserted at the base of the racquet strings (near the throat) to reduce the vibration of the strings upon impact with the ball.

volley   A shot hit before the ball bounces, usually between the service line and the net.

Western grip   A way of holding the racquet in which the wrist is positioned directly behind the handle, making it possible to hit heavy topspin.

wide   A shot landing outside of the sideline boundary.

widebody   A racquet frame with a head substantially larger (thicker than its throat).

Wimbledon   A tournament in England considered the most prestigious in the world.

winner   A shot your opponent cannot touch.

wrong-footing   Hitting a volley or drive back to a point on the court from where the opponent has just moved. Entails hitting your shot behind your opponent.

WTA The Women's Tennis Association, an organization consisting of the world's leading female professional players.

yoke The part of the racquet immediately below the head; the upper part of the shaft; the throat.

USTA Code of Conduct

To ensure the highest type of sportsmanship, the United States Tennis Association (USTA) has established a code of conduct that every player is expected to follow. Excerpts from the official USTA publication The Code, whose principles and guidelines apply in any match conducted without officials, are as follows:

If you have any doubt as to whether a ball is out or good, you must give your opponent the benefit of the doubt and play the ball as good. You should not play a let.

Any out or let call must be made instantaneously (that is, made before either an opponent has hit the return or the return has gone out of play); otherwise, the ball continues in play.

If you call a ball out and then realize it was good, you should correct your call.

To avoid controversy over the score, the server should announce the set score (for example, 5–4) before starting a game, and the game score (for example 30–40) prior to serving each point.

If players cannot agree on the score, they may go back to the last score on which there was agreement and resume play from that point, or they may spin a racquet.

Wait until players on another court have completed a point before retrieving or returning a ball.

Intentional distractions that interfere with your opponent's concentration or effort to play the ball are against the rules.

Players are expected to maintain full control over their emotions and the resulting behavior throughout the match. If you begin to lose your composure during play, try the following: Take several deep breaths. Exhale as slowly as possible and feel your muscles relax. Concentrate on your own game and behavior while ignoring distractions from your opponent or surroundings.

Be your own best friend—enjoy your good shots and forget the poor ones.

Once you have entered a tournament, honor your commitment to play. Exceptions should occur only in cases of serious illness, injury, or personal emergency.

From the beginning of the match, play must be continuous. Attempts to stall or extend rest periods for the purpose of recovering from a loss of physical condition (such as cramps or shortness of breath) are clearly illegal.

Players are expected to put forth a full and honest effort regardless of the score or expected outcome.

Spectators, including parents, friends, and coaches are welcome to watch and enjoy matches. Their role, however, is clearly restricted to that of passive observer, with no involvement of any kind during the match.

Foot faults are not allowed. If an opponent persists in foot faulting after being warned not to do so, the referee should be informed.

At the competitive level, there is a three-pronged penalty system for violating the rules of behavior. The first violation incurs a warning; the second costs a point and the third results in a defaulted match. Although the pros do a certain amount of arguing with the officials, technically, arguing is not allowed, and it sets a poor example.

USTA Levels of the Game—the National Tennis Rating Program

To provide a better understanding of the levels of the game, the United States Tennis Association (USTA) has devised the National Tennis Rating Program (NTRP) to rate players as follows:

1.0 This player is just starting to play tennis.

1.5 This player has limited experience and is still working primarily on getting the ball in play.

2.0 This player needs on-court experience. This player has obvious stroke weaknesses but is familiar with basic positions.

2.5 This player is learning to judge where the ball is going, although court coverage is weak. This player can sustain a slow-paced rally with other players of the same ability.

3.0 This player is consistent when hitting medium-paced shots but is not comfortable with all strokes and lacks control when trying for directional intent, depth, or power.

3.5 This player has achieved improved stroke dependability and direction on moderate shots but still lacks depth and variety. This player is starting to exhibit more aggressive net play, has improved court coverage, and is developing more aggressive teamwork in doubles.

4.0 This player has dependable strokes, including directional intent and depth on both forehand and backhand sides on moderate shots, plus the ability to use lobs, overheads, approach shots, and volleys with some success. This player occasionally forces errors when serving, and teamwork in doubles is evident.

4.5 This player has begun to master the use of power and spins and is beginning to handle pace, has sound footwork, can control depth of shots, and is beginning to vary tactics according to opponents. This player can hit first serves with power and accuracy, can place the second serve, and is able to rush the net successfully.

5.0 This player has good shot anticipation and frequently has an outstanding shot or exceptional consistency around which a game can be structured. This player can regularly hit winners or force errors off short balls; can put away volleys; can successfully execute lobs, drop shots, half volleys, and overhead smashes; and has good depth and spin on most second serves.

5.5 This player has developed power or consistency or both as a major weapon. This player can vary strategies and styles of play in a competitive situation and hits dependable shots in stress situations.

6.0 These players generally do not need the USTA rating system. Ranking or past rankings will speak for themselves. The 6.0 player typically has had intensive training for 7.0 national tournament competition on the junior and collegiate levels and has obtained a sectional or national ranking or both.

6.5 This player has a reasonable chance of succeeding at the 7.0 level and has extensive satellite tournament experience.

7.0 This is a world-class player who is committed to tournament competition on the international level and whose major source of income is tournament prize winnings.

Tennis Reference List for Organizations and Publications

Tennis Organizations

Association of Tennis Professionals Tour (ATP Tour)
200 Tournament Players Road
Ponte Verde Beach, FL 32082
904-285-8000
Fax: 904-285-5966

The ATP Tour oversees the men's professional tour, with more than 90 tournaments in 40 countries and more than $60 million in prize money. The ATP Tour determines rules and policies for the Tour.

Intercollegiate Tennis Association (ITA)
P.O. Box 71
Princeton, NJ 08544
609-258-6332

The ITA, known as the Intercollegiate Tennis Coaches Association until 1992, is the governing body of collegiate tennis. The ITA promotes the athletic and academic achievements of the collegiate tennis community.

International Tennis Federation (ITF)
Palliser Road
Barons Court, London W149EN
England

The ITF, founded in 1913 as the International Lawn Tennis Federation, is the world's governing body of tennis. The ITF oversees many of the world's most prestigious events: the four championships that make up the Grand Slam (French Open, Wimbledon, U.S. Open, and Australian Open), the Davis Cup and the Federation Cup.

International Tennis Hall of Fame
Newport Casino
194 Bellevue Avenue
Newport, RI 02840
401-849-3990

This is a nonprofit agency committed to preserving the history of tennis worldwide. The museum on site is open to the public.

United States Professional Tennis Association (USPTA)
One USPTA Centre
3535 Briarpark Drive
Houston, TX 77042
713-978-7782

The USPTA, founded in 1927, is the world's oldest and largest association of tennis-teaching professionals, with more than 10,000 members worldwide. The USPTA strives to raise the standards of the tennis-teaching profession and to promote awareness of tennis. Its members work as teaching professionals, coaches, club managers, and marketing specialists and in other positions within the tennis industry.

WTA Tour Players Association
133 First Street NE
St. Petersburg, FL 33701
813-895-5000

Founded in 1973, the Women's Tennis Association is the governing body of women's professional tennis. The WTA, with approximately 600 members, oversees an international tour consisting of more than 60 events and offers more than $30 million in prize money.

United States Professional Tennis Registry (USPTR)
P.O. Box 4739
Hilton Head Island, SC 29938
803-785-7244

This organization also certifies tennis professionals and has an extensive training program to help first-time professionals learn how to teach.

United States Tennis Association (USTA)
70 West Red Oak Lane
White Plains, NY 10604
914-696-7000
Fax: 914-696-7167

The USTA, founded in 1881 as the U.S. National Lawn Tennis Association, is the governing body of tennis in the United States. The organization, with more than

500,000 members and volunteers, embodies 17 sectional associations from New England to California. The USTA sanctions amateur and professional tournaments, trains officials, and seeks to increase participation at the recreational level. The organization's most celebrated duty is to operate the U.S. Open at Flushing Meadows in New York.

To help govern tennis in the United States, the USTA is divided into 17 sections. Most of the sections publish their own periodicals to help get the word out to their tennis enthusiasts. You can get help quickly if you contact your section directly.

USTA Section	Area Governed	Telephone Number
Caribbean	Puerto Rico/Virgin Is	809-765-7711
Eastern	NY/NJ/CT	914-698-0414
Florida	FL	
Hawaii/Pacific	Hawaii/Guam/Pago Pago	808-955-6696
Intermountain	CO/NV/WY/UT/MT/ID	303-695-4117
Mid-Atlantic	VA/DC/MD/WV	703-560-9480
Middle States	PA/DE/NJ/WV	215-768-4040
Midwest	IL/IN/MI/OH/WI/KY	
Missouri Valley	MO/IA/KS/NE/OK	816-556-0777
New England	CT/ME/MA/NH/RI/VT	
Northern	MN/ND/SD/WI	
Northern California	CA/NV	510-748-7373
Pacific Northwest	AK/OR/WA/ID/BC	503-245-3048
Southern	GA/AL/AK/KY/LA/MS/NC/SC/TN	404-257-1297
Southern California	CA	310-208-3838
Southwest	AZ/NM	602-921-8964
Texas	TX	512-443-1334

Tennis Publications

The following publications are available from the United States Tennis Association, 70 West Red Oak Lane, White Plains, NY 10604-3602, Phone: 914-696-7000, Fax: 914-696-7167.

Tennis Week

This magazine founded in 1974 by Gene Scott, a former top ten player, is published twice a month except for January, October, November and December, when it is published monthly.

It is sold to tennis players, fans of the game and general tennis consumers by subscription or it can be bought in bookstores. Gene Scott, the editor-in-chief, still writes a very informative column every issue. It deals with the game in a very timely manner.

Tennis Week, 341 Madison Avenue, Suite 600, New York, NY 10017. Phone 212-808-4750. Fax 212-983-6302.

Tennis Magazine

This magazine used to be called *World Tennis* and was founded by Gladys Heldman in the late 60s. It is now published by the Miller Sports Group. It is a monthly geared to the avid tennis fan and amateur player. Many articles on the pro circuit and teaching tips make it an interesting and educational publication.

Tennis Magazine, 810 Seventh Avenue, 4th Floor, New York, NY 10019. Phone 212-636-2700.

Tennis USTA

Is a supplement to *Tennis Magazine*. It deals primarily with the USTA tournaments such as the U.S. Open. It also reports on the USTA sections, junior tournaments and senior events. It is packaged with the subscription to *Tennis Magazine*. If you are a member of the USTA, you will receive this magazine and *Tennis Magazine* as part of your membership fee.

Official USTA Tennis Yearbook

Contains up-to-date information on tournaments, committees, rankings, members, records, tournament regulations, and the official Rules of Tennis and Cases and Decisions.

USTA College Tennis Guide

For the college-bound tennis player, a comprehensive index to intercollegiate tennis teams and scholarships for both men and women. More than 1,000 American colleges and universities are listed alphabetically by state.

USTA Guide for Competitive Junior Players

Explains and clarifies the rules and regulations governing participation in USTA junior competitive events, provides information about rankings and special opportunities, and offers specific sources for additional information and assistance. Although parts of the guide will help those who have not yet entered their first tournament, it will be especially helpful to those advanced players who now compete at the national level or who will in the future.

"USTA League Tennis" Brochure

Contains information on all facets of USTA adult league play. Topics included general information, league program progression, and NTRP general characteristics.

Wheelchair Tennis: Myth to Reality

This publication covers every aspect of wheelchair tennis, from the equipment needed, to on-the-court technique, to strategies for winning at singles and doubles. Whatever the player's level, novice or advanced, this is written to improve technique and build confidence. The authors are masters at not only playing and coaching the game, but at explaining it, as well, in easy-to-grasp text and graphics.

Tennis in A Wheelchair

This is a practical manual of tennis playing techniques for the wheelchair athlete. Included are sections on basic strokes from a wheelchair, wheelchair mobility, singles and doubles strategy, advanced movement shots, advanced stroke techniques, and court surfaces. Readers will discover how enjoyable and challenging the game of wheelchair tennis can be.

USTA Guide to Teaching Sportsmanship

Encouraging good sportsmanship in tennis has been a major goal of the USTA. To reach this goal, tennis teachers, coaches, and tournament directors across the country must join in a concerted effort to promote this important component of the game. This book contains all the essential elements to promote sportsmanship, the basics of the rules, The Code and tennis etiquette.

Tennis Courts

Contains official USTA recommendations for the construction, repair, maintenance, and equipment needs of tennis court installations, indoors and out. Includes USTC and TBA guideline specifications for court construction and equipment.

"USTA Flexibility" Poster

A four-color poster featuring 30 illustrations: two poses of each of 10 stretches plus one anatomical drawing of each stretch. A quality conditioning program for tennis includes a flexibility component. Ignoring flexibility could result in one's inability to achieve one's performance potential and a greater risk of injury at some time during one's playing career.

"USTA Flexibility" Cards

The information found on the "USTA Flexibility" poster is also found on a $9^1/2$" by 5" two-sided laminated card. It is four-color and features 30 illustrations: two poses of each of 10 stretches plus one anatomical drawing of each stretch.

Friend at Court

A guide for tennis officials. Includes duties of officials, Solo Chair Umpire procedures, officiating techniques and tactics, USTA Tournament Regulations (including the making of a draw), the official Rules of Tennis and Cases and Decisions, and The Code.

Rules of Tennis and Cases and Decisions

The official Rules of the International Tennis Federation, of which the USTA is a member. Included are comments by the USTA Tennis Rules Committee, which amplify and facilitate interpretation of the formal code.

Illustrated Introduction to the Rules of Tennis

A summary of the rules and code of tennis in simplified language and with appealing illustrations. It is recommended for beginning tennis players from 8 to 80 years of age.

"Code of Conduct" Card

Unsportsmanlike behavior is a serious issue that is detracting from the sport of tennis today. To encourage and promote attitudes and conduct that are more positive, the USTA has produced a two-sided laminated "Code of Conduct" card. It is hoped that as many players as possible will carry a card in their racquet covers and refer to it when questions or problems arise on the court.

The Code

Rules, principles, and guidelines, which apply in any match, conducted without officials.

"The Tie-Break System" Information Sheet

The 12-point tie-break, the 9-point tie-break, and cases and decisions on the system from the Rules of Tennis and Cases and Decisions.

Basic Chair Umpire Handbook

You've been asked to serve as a chair umpire for a local tournament. Where do you start? What do you do? This booklet has been designed to provide guidelines and tips to help make this an enjoyable experience for both you and the players. It is not meant to replace USTA certification clinics.

The USTA Guide to Community Tennis

This guide contains information on organizing community-supported tennis programs. Included is detailed information on how to formalize the administrative structure with tax-exempt status. This book also gives an overview of instructional and competitive programs that will appeal to a wide variety of players.

Who's Who in Tennis

Andre Agassi (USA)   A player of tremendous flair and appeal who appeared on the professional circuit as a 16-year-old in 1986, Agassi beat Pete Sampras for the U.S. Open title in 1990, and Andres Gomes and Jim Courier for the French title in 1990 and 1991. Agassi was also a gold-medal winner in the 1996 Olympics in Atlanta, when he beat Spain's Sergi Bruguera in 78 minutes. In 1988, as the youngest member of the Davis Cup team, Agassi won all of his singles on Latin clay at Peru and Argentina. That same year, he made a marvelous effort at the French Open, a five-set joust with Mats Wilander, the defending champ; and a five-set win over Jimmy Connors, before losing in the singles to Ivan Lendl.

Arthur Ashe (USA)   The only black male to win the Wimbledon championship. Ashe made it to the finals at Wimbledon for the first time in 1975, but was a long shot to win. He was a number-six seed, had not been in a Grand Slam final in three years, and had not won in seven, since the 1968 U.S. Open. His opponent was Jimmy Connors, the number-one ranked player in the world. But Ashe came out smoking, winning each of the first two sets by a 6–1 count. The stunned Connors won the third set 7–5 and led 3–0 in the fourth and seemed ready to cruise to a come-from-behind win. Ashe turned up the heat again, however, and won six of the next seven games for the upset championship victory.

Tracy Austin (USA)   The youngest player to win a singles title at the U.S. Open. Austin became the youngest champion of all time at the U.S. Open in 1979 when she defeated Chris Evert in the finals, 6–4, 6–3. She was 16 years old. Austin also won again in 1981 in a pressure-paced championship match over Martina Navratilova 1–6, 7–6, 7–6.

Boris Becker (GER) The only unseeded player to win a singles final Wimbledon. Becker broke three barriers at Wimbledon in 1985. He became the first unseeded player to win a singles title, the first German man to win the event, and at 17 years old, the youngest-ever male singles champ. Prior to Becker, eight men and four women had been unseeded and reached the singles final, but none of them had even won a set. Becker won the match 6–3, 6–7, 7–6, 6–4 over Kevin Curran. He proved it was no fluke, winning the championship again in 1986 and 1989 and by reaching the finals in 1988, 1990, and 1991.

Nick Bollettieri (USA) A most renowned coach, Bollettieri runs an assembly line for champs at his training center in Bradenton, Florida. Among those he has taught are: Andre Agassi, Jimmy Arias, Carling Bassett, Jim Courier, Aaron Krickstein, Monica Seles, Mary Pierce and Iva Majoli.

Bjorn Borg (SWE) The only player to win the men's singles title six times in the French Open. Borg won the French Open in 1974, 1975, 1978, 1979, 1980, and 1981. He also won Wimbledon five times in succession beginning in 1976, but oddly, never won in men's singles in the Australian Open or the U.S. Open. His most memorable match was the five-set heartstopper against John McEnroe in the 1980 Wimbledon final. Borg won 1–6, 7–5, 6–3, 6–7 (16–18), 8–6.

Don Budge (USA) The only player to win six consecutive Grand Slam men's singles championships. Budge began his record run in the 1937 Wimbledon final with a win over Gottfried von Cramm. He defeated von Cramm again in the U.S. championship the same year, then swept all four Grand Slam events in 1938. Budge beat John Bromwich in the Australian, Roderick Menzel in the French Open, Bunny Austin at Wimbledon, and Gene Mako in the U.S. Nationals. Budge was so dominating that he lost only three sets in the six finals, winning 124 games while losing just 61.

Maria Bueno (BRA) The only woman to win the Grand Slam of women's doubles in one year with two different partners. Brazilian born Bueno swept the Grand Slam in 1960, winning with Christine Truman (Great Britain) in Australia and Darlene Hard (USA) in France, Great Britain, and the U.S. She also won the singles title at Wimbledon the same year. In all, Bueno bagged 20 Big Four titles in singles, doubles, and mixed doubles.

Jennifer Capriati (USA) The youngest player to win four Grand Slam junior championships. Capriati became the youngest ever to win a Grand Slam junior event in 1989 when, at 13, she captured the French Open singles title, the Wimbledon doubles championship, and the singles and doubles at the U.S. Open. She signed endorsements worth more than $1 million before she turned 14. At 15, Capriati reached the quarterfinals at Wimbledon and the semifinals at the U.S. Open. In 1992, she won the gold medal at the Olympics in Barcelona.

Mary Carrillo (USA) She played the women's tour, collaborated with John McEnroe in his first major title and the French mixed in 1977. She is best known as a tennis telecaster for ESPN, HBO and CBS.

Rosie Casals (USA)   The only woman threatened with expulsion from a Wimbledon match for wearing purple squiggles. Casals reached the singles semifinals at Wimbledon in 1972, but was ordered off the court during warmups because her dress had purple squiggles on the front and back that suggested the initials VS for Virginia Slims, sponsor of many women's tournaments. Casals was threatened with expulsion if she did not conform to Wimbledon's predominantly white sartorial code. She did, but lost the match 6–2, 6–4 to Billie Jean King.

Pat Cash (AUS)   A powerful Aussie right-hander, his career was shortened by injuries. A strong server, excellent volleyer, the high points of his career were winning Wimbledon singles in 1987, led Davis Cup victories in 1983 and 1986. He turned pro in 1982, winning six singles and 10 pro doubles titles.

Michael Chang (USA)   The only player to win a Grand Slam men's singles championship at age 17. Chang became the youngest male singles titlist ever in a Grand Slam event in the 1989 French Open. Seeded 15th, Chang stunned Ivan Lendl in the fourth round 4–6, 4–6, 6–3, 6–3, and advanced to the final where he downed Stefan Edbert 6–1, 3–6, 4–6, 6–4, 6–2.

Dorothy Bundy Cheney (USA)   A most enduring champ, playing from her teens to super-seniors tournaments. She won the Australian in 1938 and kept winning, straight on into her 80s with a 1996 win in the Hart Court singles. By the end of 1996, her career winnings included: 270 U.S. Senior titles from 40s age group up (45, 50, 55, 60, 65, 70, 75, 80) beginning in 1957.

Bud Collins (USA)   The most visible and versatile U.S. tennis journalist. He worked the U.S. Open for CBS from 1968 to 1972, signed on with NBC in 1972, and was thereafter closely identified with that network's presentation of Wimbledon and the French Open. Although he refers to himself as a hacker, he is an accomplished now-and-then-again player, known for his touch, tactical cunning, and preference for playing barefoot on grass courts. He won the U.S. Indoor mixed doubles in 1961, and was a finalist in the French Senior doubles.

Maureen Connolly (USA)   Nicknamed "Little Mo" for her big gunning, unerring ground strokes (Big Mo was the U.S. battleship Missouri), she was devastating from the baseline, and seldom needed to go to the net. She won her major singles championships as a teenager: three consecutive Wimbledons from 1952 to 1954, the U.S. Championship from 1951 to 1953, and, at 16, was the youngest U.S. champ until Tracy Austin won in 1979. Nobody has measured up to her perfect record in the majors after her early U.S. defeats in 1949 and 1950. She sailed through nine successive majors (three U.S., three Wimbledons, two French and one Australian) unbeaten in 50 matches. Her playing career ended in 1954 when, while riding a horse, she was severely injured when hit by a truck. She was inducted into the Hall of Fame in 1968, and is memorialized by the Maureen Connolly Brinker Cup, an international team competition between the U.S. and Great Britain for girls under 21.

Jimmy Connors (USA)   The only man to win 109 singles championships. From the time he burst onto the professional circuit in 1972 as a teen sensation, through 1991 when he made a valiant run at the U.S. Open title as an aging veteran, Connors won 109 singles championships. His Grand Slam titles include the U.S. Open in 1974, 1976, 1978, 1982, and 1983; Wimbledon in 1974 and 1982; and the Australian Open in 1974.

Jim Courier (USA)   A ruggedly built 6'1" right-handed player with a two-handed backhand. He parlayed ferocious ground strokes to French titles in 1991 and 1992; Australian Open titles in 1992 and 1993.

Margaret Smith Court (AUS)   The only player to win 66 Grand Slam championships. Tall and gangling at nearly six feet, Smith Court came out of Albury, New South Wales, Australia, to dominate tennis between 1960 and 1973. Her Grand Slam titles included 26 in singles, 21 in women's doubles, and 19 in mixed doubles. Twenty-one of her championships came in Australia, 13 in France, 10 at Wimbledon, and 22 in the U.S.

Lindsey Davenport (USA)   This 6'2" player has won 14 career titles, topped off by her first Grand Slam victory at the 1998 U.S. Open. She has won titles such as the Bank of West Classic, Toshiba Tennis Classic, and the Acura Classic. Lindsey is probably most famous for her gold-medal victory in the 1990 Olympics. This young, bright woman is becoming stronger each year, and finished the 1998 year ranked at number one.

Stefan Edberg (SWE)   The only player to lose a semifinal at Wimbledon without losing his serve. In a frustrating loss to Michael Stich of Germany in one of the semifinals in 1991 at Wimbledon, Edberg served 23 times and won the game each time, but lost the match in four sets because he could not win the tiebreakers. The match ended 3–6, 7–6 (7–5) 7–6 (7–5), 7–6 (7–2). Just two days earlier, Jimmy Van Alen, the man who invented the tiebreaker, died in Newport, Rhode Island, at the age of 88.

Roy Emerson (AUS)   The only individual to win the men's singles championship at the Australian National six times. Emerson first won the Australian championship in 1961, defeating Rod Laver in the final 1–6, 6–3, 7–5, 6–4. Emerson lost to Laver in the 1962 final, but then captured five titles in a row with championship matches against Ken Fletcher in 1963, Fred Stolle in 1964 and 1965, and Arthur Ashe in 1966 and 1967. Emerson is also the only man to win 12 Grand Slam singles titles, with wins at Wimbledon in 1964 and 1965, in France in 1963 and 1967, and in the U.S. in 1961 and 1964.

Chris Evert (USA)   The only player to win seven singles titles in the French Open. Playing on the clay surface of Roland Garros Stadium in Paris, Evert reached the finals of the French Open nine times and won seven. Her first victory came in 1974, and was followed by triumphs in 1975, 1979, 1980, 1983, 1985, and 1986. Evert also won six singles championships in the U.S. Open, three at Wimbledon, and two in the Australian Open for a total of 18 Grand Slam singles titles.

Zina Garrison (USA)   An American right-hander from Houston, Zina Garrison won Olympic Gold in doubles with Pam Shriver and Bronze in singles in 1988. She gave

Chris Evert her last defeat in 1989, and was the first black woman since Althea Gibson to win at Wimbledon. She was aggressive, quick, and a fine volleyer.

Vitas Gerulaitis (USA)   Dubbed the Lithuanian Lion, Gerulaitis is the only American to win the Italian Open twice. He also won the Australian Open in 1977. Gerulaitis comes from a family of winners: His father Vitas was a champion in Lithuania, and his sister Ruth was on the women's pro tour and ranked number 31 in 1980.

Althea Gibson (USA)   The first black player to win at Wimbledon and in Forest Hills, NY. A mark of her general acceptance was her 1957 selection to represent the U.S. on the Wightman Cup team against Great Britain for two years, winning three of four singles, and two of two doubles. In 1956, partnered with Great Britain's Angela Buxton in the doubles event at Wimbledon, Gibson was the champion, not only in the game, but also as the first black winner there.

Evonne Goolagong (AUS)   The only six-time Grand Slam singles champion of aboriginal descent. Goolagong made it to the singles finals of 17 Grand Slam tournaments, winning six: Wimbledon and the French Open in 1971, and the Australian Open in 1974, 1975, 1976, and 1977. Because Goolagong's grandfather was an aborigine from the outback of Australia, the South African government was disturbed enough by her ancestry to bar her from competition in that country due to its apartheid policies, claiming she was nonwhite.

Steffi Graff (GER)   The only woman to be ranked number one in the computer ranking 186 weeks in a row. Since the computer ranking began in 1973, no one has held the top spot for a longer period. Graff became number one on August 17, 1987, and held it until March 11, 1991. She is also the only player to win a Grand Slam and a gold medal in the Olympics in the same years, accomplishing the feats in 1988.

Gladys Heldman (USA)   For more than two decades, Gladys Heldman was the game's anchor, first as a founder/owner/publisher of *World Tennis* Magazine, and then later as the instigator and housemother of a separate professional tennis circuit for women, begun in 1970, now known as the Virginia Slims Tour. Although not a competitive player, she was a great supporter of women's tennis. Her daughter, Julie Heldman, became a top ten ranked U.S. player.

Martina Hingis (CZH)   Named Martina after tennis great Martina Navratilova, Hingis is fulfilling the promise. She is extraordinarily poised and thoughtful. She debuted as a pro at age 14 in Zurich and since then has become the youngest to win at Wimbledon at age 15, three days younger than Lottie Dod, the 1887 winner.

Harry Hopman (AUS)   Made his name as the most successful of all Davis Cup captains, piloting Australia to 16 Cups between 1939 and 1967. Following his last Davis Cup match as captain in 1969, he emigrated to the U.S. to become a highly successful teaching pro, counseling John McEnroe and Vitas Gerulaitis at the Port Washington Junior Tennis Academy in New York.

Goran Ivanisevic (CRO)   The only person from Croatia to play at Wimbledon, although he lost to Andre Agassi in 1992 and to Pete Sampras in 1994.

Andrea Jaeger (USA)   The youngest ranked player in the World Top Ten, she was ranked number five when she was 15. Finished by injuries just like contemporary Tracy Austin, Jaeger is best known for wins at Wimbledon in 1983, beating Billie Jean King. At 16, Jaeger and Jimmy Arias won the French mixed in 1981 and were the youngest team to win a major doubles.

Yevgeny Kafelnikov (RUS)   Born in Sochi, Russia, 6' 3" Kafelnikov reached the top 10 in the world by getting to the quarterfinals of the Australian Open. In 1995, he became the only player on the ATP tour to win four singles titles and four doubles titles during the year. In 1998, he won the French Open and also broke into the top 10 in singles and doubles. Kafelnikov has the potential to be one of the best players on tour in upcoming years. He is currently ranked number nine.

Billie Jean King (USA)   The only player to win 20 titles at Wimbledon. The daughter of a Long Beach, California, fireman, King won 38 Grand Slam titles, but the grass at Center Court at Wimbledon was especially kind; between 1961 and 1979, she won six titles in singles, 10 in women's doubles, and four in mixed doubles. King was extremely influential in gaining more recognition for women in tennis. She was in the vanguard in founding the Virginia Slims tour, a separate tour for women that greatly increased their visibility and prize money.

Anna Kournikova (RUS)   Anna is the 1998 Lipton runner-up, where she won four consecutive matches against top-10 players, until being defeated by Venus Williams in the finals. The young Russian made her pro debut at the age of 14. In 1997, she reached the semi-finals of Wimbledon. She is currently ranked 12th in the world, and is a young player with tons of potential.

Richard Krajicek (NET)   Born in Rotterdam, Netherlands, Krajicek started his career in 1994 with his first grass-court title in Rosmalen, and also defeated Boris Becker in the Sydney Indoor Event. In 1990, the 6' 5" Krajicek won Wimbledon by defeating Pete Sampras. He also finished as the Netherlands number-one player for the fifth consecutive year. In the future, Krajicek hopes to be a strong force in men's tennis. He is currently ranked 11th in the world.

Jack Kramer (USA)   The only man to win 130 of his 167 games in one year at Wimbledon in a relentless march to the 1947 Wimbledon singles championship. In the final, he beat Tom Brown 6–1, 6–3, 6–2. After winning the 1946 and 1947 U.S. Championship and leading his country to victory in the 1946 and 1947 Davis Cup, Kramer turned pro. On the professional tour, he dominated Pancho Gonzalez and Bobby Riggs. After his playing days were over, he became the most prominent promoter the game has ever known, acted as a television commentator, and helped form the male players' union.

Rod Laver (AUS)   The only player to win the men's singles Grand Slam twice. Laver swept the Australian, French, Wimbledon, and the U.S. Championships in both 1962 and 1969. The only other man to win a Grand Slam in singles was Don Budge in 1938. Laver hailed from Rockhampton, Queensland, Australia, and grew up on a cattle farm in the outback. Small and sickly as a child, Laver practiced incessantly until his left forearm became, like Popeye's, almost twice as large as his right. In all, Laver won 11 Grand Slam singles titles and dominated the pro circuit from 1963 through the advent of Open tennis in 1968.

Ivan Lendl (CZH)   The only player to win a championship after being down two sets to love in his fifth attempt to win his first Grand Slam final. When Lendl stepped onto the court for the 1984 French Open men's singles championship against John McEnroe, he was known as a player who choked in the big matches. Lendl had been in four Grand Slam singles finals and had lost them all. When McEnroe won the first two sets 6–3, 6–2, it looked as if history were about to repeat itself. But Lendl rallied and won the final three sets 6–4, 7–5, 7–5 to take the championship. Lendl went on to win 7 more Grand Slam championships.

Suzanne Lenglen (FRA)   The only three-time triple-crown winner at Wimbledon. Lenglen crossed the English Channel from her native France in 1919 to play at Wimbledon, and the international tennis scene was never the same. She was the first to wear dresses with sleeves above the elbow and hemlines only just below the knee, shocking attire that scandalized the Victorian mind-set of the era. In 1920, 1922, and 1925 at Wimbledon, Lenglen won the triple-crown championships in singles, women's doubles, and mixed doubles. In 1925, she dominated at Wimbledon in singles, winning 60 of 65 games.

Hana Mandlikova (CZH)   The only player to twice stop a single opponent's winning streak of 50 or more matches. Mandlikova squared off against Martina Navratilova in the Virginia Slims final in Oakland, California, in 1984. Navratilova had won 54 matches in a row, one shy of Chris Evert's all-time record, but Mandlikova won 7–6, 3–6, 6–4. Navratilova won her next 74 matches to obliterate Evert's record, and had another streak of 58 match victories when she faced Mandlikova again in the 1987 Australian Open final. Mandlikova again stopped a long winning streak 7–5, 7–6.

Conchita Martinez (SPA)   The only Spanish woman to win at Wimbledon, Martinez thwarted Martina Navratilova's bid for a 10th title. Martinez won a record three straight Italian Opens beginning in 1994. With Arantxa Sanchez Vicario, Martinez made Spain dominant in the Federation Cup from 1988 to 1996, and won a silver medal with Sanchez Vicario at the 1992 Olympics in Barcelona.

John McEnroe (USA)   The only player to win 57 matches for the U.S. in Davis Cup competition. Through 1991, McEnroe won 41 singles matches and 16 doubles for the U.S. in the Davis Cup. His other accomplishments include winning the singles title four times at the U.S. Open and three times at Wimbledon, and earning the frequent ire of umpires, linesmen, lineswomen, opponents and spectators for his unruly behavior.

Gardnar Mulloy (USA)   An eternal beacon in the game, Gardnar Mulloy held his first U.S. National title in 1936, and his most recent 60 years later in 1996: number 1 in the 80 and over singles and doubles. His was a complete game: His volleys and smashes lit up the left court as he and Bill Tilden became one of the finest teams winning four U.S. titles in 1942, 45, 46 and 48.

Thomas Muster (AST)   Called the Moo Man for his bellowing cow noises as he belts at the baseline, Muster, an Austrian player, seems indestructible in body and spirit. Winner of the 1990s on clay, he won the French Open singles in 1995 and the Italian Open in 1990, 1995 and 1996. After injuring his knee in 1989 in a car accident, Muster came back in 1990 as a winner. In 1995, he won 12 titles on 86–18 (with 40 straight on clay).

Martina Navratilova (CZH)   The only woman to win nine singles titles at Wimbledon. Navratilova won the women's singles title at Center Court at Wimbledon in 1978, 1979, 1982, 1983, 1984, 1985, 1986, and 1987 to tie the all-time record of eight championship sets by Helen Wills Moody. Navratilova desperately wanted her record ninth and made it to the finals in 1988 and 1989, but lost both times in three sets to Steffi Graf. She finally took number nine in 1990 with a 6–4, 6–1 win over Zina Garrison. Navratilova's other victims in the women's singles championship were Chris Evert five times, and Andrea Jaeger, Hana Mandlikova, and Steffi Graf, once each.

Martina Navratilova (CZH) and **Chris Evert** (USA)   The only pair to play each other in a Grand Slam singles final 14 times. Evert played in a record 34 Grand Slam singles finals and won 18. Navratilova played in 31, winning 19. They met 14 times, with Navratilova taking the title 10 times. Navratilova won the Australian Open in 1981 and 1985, the French Open in 1984, Wimbledon in 1978, 1979, 1982, 1984, and 1985, and the U.S. Open in 1983 and 1984. Evert won from Navratilova the Australian Open in 1982 and the French Open in 1975, 1985, and 1986.

John Newcombe (AUS)   Newcombe was one of the youngest Aussies ever to play in the Davis Cup. He was selected for the final to play singles against the U.S. He made his name by playing singles. He and Rod Laver are the only players to win the men's singles at Forest Hills and Wimbledon as amateurs and pros. Newcombe was the last amateur champion at Wimbledon in 1967, and repeated in 1970 and 1971 during the open era. Newcombe's serve, forehand, and volley were the backbone of his attacking game, which was at its best on grass. His heavy serve was possibly the best of his era. In 1967, he was the number one amateur in the world, and in 1970 and 1971, number one of all. He was one of the first to sign a contract to play World Team Tennis in 1974. His best pro season was 1971, when he won five of 19 singles tournaments on a 53–14 match record.

Yannick Noah (FRA)   The foremost Frenchman in accomplishment and popularity since the Four Musketeers, Noah attained all-time renown with his countrymen by winning the French Open in 1983 (beating Mats Wilander). He was the first Frenchman to win a male title since Marcel Bernard in 1946. He is a Davis Cup hero, winning 26–15 singles and 13–7 doubles between 1978 and 1990. He led the French to their first Cup in 49 years in 1982. He is an appealing net-rushing gambler, leaping volleyer and a big server, who was discovered in Cameroon in 1971, and recommended to the French Federation for development by touring pro Arthur Ashe.

Mark Phillippousis (AUS)   Born in Melbourne, Australia, 6' 4" Phillippousis is known for his rocket serve. He holds four career titles, and was the 1998 U.S. Open runner-up. His most memorable match was his stunning defeat of Pete Sampras in the 1996 Australian Open. He is currently ranked 18th in the world and definitely holds the characteristics of a true future champion.

Mary Pierce (FRA)   Among the all-time hardest hitting, baselining right-handers with a two-handed backhand, Pierce was born in Quebec to a French mother and an American father, and was raised in Florida. She holds American, French, and Canadian passports. She plays the Federation Cup for France. Known for bringing on the return of the tennis dress, Pierce won the Australian Open in 1995, and was ranked number five from 1994 to 1995. Coached by her demanding father until she obtained a restraining order against him, she turned pro in 1987.

Patrick Rafter (AUS)   Rafter is a 6' 1" Aussie who won his first Grand Slam in 1997 with a stunning victory over Greg Rugeoski in the U.S. Open. Since then, he has torn up the charts. In 1993, he was awarded the ATP Newcomer of the Year award. Leading up to the 1998 U.S. Open, Patrick went on to a winning splurge, winning two straight Mercedes Super 9 titles. He went on to win the U.S. Open, defeating Mark Phillippousis in the finals. Rafter is currently ranked number two in the world, trailing Pete Sampras.

Renee Richards (USA)   Born Richard Raskin in 1934, Richards, an opthalmological surgeon, played as an amateur male in 1955, 1956, 1957 and 1960, and as a female pro from 1977 to 1981. After a 1975 sex-change operation, she sought to play on the women's tour and faced opposition. She resorted to the court of law to gain entry, and in a New York Supreme Court ruling, gained entry to the WTA and USTA events. In 1977, she lost to Virginia Wade at Wimbledon, and lost again in 1979 to Chris Evert before returning to medicine.

Marcelo Rios (CHI)   Born in Santiago, Chile, Marcelo finished as the number one junior player in the world in 1993. He cracked the top 25 in 1995 and since then has become a power to be reckoned with. In 1998, Rios beat Andre Agassi to win the Lipton Championship. This victory allowed him to take over the number-one ranking, ending Pete Sampras' reign of 102 weeks. He is currently ranked number three in the world.

Ken Rosewall (USA)   Rosewall is the only player to lose a U.S. Open men's singles final in 20 games. The 1974 U.S. Open singles final between Jimmy Connors, age 21, and Ken Rosewall, age 39, marked the passage of time. Rosewall was playing in his last Grand Slam singles final, 21 years after winning his first in the 1953 Australian Open. Connors was in his first U.S. Open final. Youth prevailed, as Connors won 6–1, 6–0, 6–1. Rosewall had won 18 Grand Slam titles in singles, doubles, and mixed doubles, and would have won more had he not turned pro in 1957, becoming ineligible for Grand Slam play until 1967.

Gabriela Sabatini (ARG)   One of the finest Latin American players since Maria Bueno, Sabatini is known as the Divine Argentine. She has powerful topspin and ground strokes and played superb attacking tennis to win the U.S. Open in 1991. She won the silver medal in the 1988 Olympics, and retired in 1996 with 27 singles wins and 14 doubles pro titles.

Pete Sampras (USA)   Arguably the greatest men's tennis player of all time, Sampras is the youngest player to win the U.S. Open singles championship at age 19 in 1990. Seeded 12th when the tournament began, he pulled off upset after upset, culminating in a 6–4, 6–3, 6–2 shellacking of Andre Agassi in the final. He holds 49 career titles including five Wimbledons, four U.S. Opens and two Australian Opens. He is one shy of tying Rod Laver's record of 12. The only Grand Slam to evade him is the French Open, though he made it to the semifinals before losing to eventual champion Yafgenue Rabelnikov. His complete game matches his gentlemanly qualities on and off the court. He is a true champion.

Monica Seles (YUG)   The youngest player to win a singles final in the French Open. Seles won the first of what promised to be a long string of Grand Slam singles championships when at the age of 16 years, she became the youngest ever to win the French Open in 1990 by defeating Steffi Graf 7–6, 6–4. In 1991, Seles won the French Open and the U.S. Open and became the youngest ever to win the Australian Open with a 5–7, 6–3, 6–1 finals victory over Jana Novotna (CZH). Seles won three more Grand Slam titles in 1992.

Pam Shriver (USA)   Shriver became the youngest finalist ever in women's singles at the U.S. Open in 1978. At 16 years old, she scored a stunning 7–6, 7–6 upset over Martina Navratilova in the semifinal. In the final, she led Chris Evert before succumbing 7–5, 6–4. Oddly, Shriver never again reached a singles final in a Grand Slam event. She did win 21 Grand Slam doubles championships—20 of them as a partner with Navratilova.

Pam Shriver (USA) and **Martina Navratilova** (CZH)   The only pair to win eight consecutive women's doubles championships. Shriver and Navratilova were unstoppable between 1983 and 1985, sweeping eight straight Grand Slam doubles titles. No other women's doubles team has won more than three in a row. The duo won 109 consecutive matches from April 24, 1983 through July 6, 1985, when Kathy Jordan and Liz Smilie stopped their championship, run at Wimbledon.

Michael Stich (GER)   The only player to win an all-German final at Wimbledon. Stich defeated fellow countryman Boris Becker in the 1991 final, 6–4, 7–6 (7–4), 6–4. Along with Steffi Graf and Becker, Stich has been part of a revival of tennis in Germany. The country had produced several prominent players in the 1920s and 1930s, but the sport had been almost dormant in Germany for nearly 50 years.

Fred Stolle (AUS)   The only unseeded player to win the men's singles championship at the U.S. Open. Stolle stunned the crowds at Forest Hills with his march through the draw in 1966. He beat fellow countryman Roy Emerson 6–4, 6–1, 6–1 in the semis and

John Newcombe 4–6, 12–10, 6–3, 6–4 in the final. Prior to the match, Stolle's record in Grand Slam singles finals was one win and six losses.

Bill Tilden (USA)   The only player to win 16 titles in the U.S. Open. Some still consider Tilden to be the greatest player of all time. He won 16 U.S. titles from 1913 until turning pro in 1930. Tilden had seven titles in singles, five in men's doubles, and four in mixed doubles. He also played on seven Davis Cup championship teams. On his 27th birthday in 1920, Tilden had only three U.S. titles, all in doubles, but his devotion to improvement made him a terror at an age when most players struggle to win matches. In 1922 and 1923, Tilden swept the U.S. Nationals by winning all three titles.

Ted Tinling (ENG)   Called the Leaning Tower of Pizazz, 6' 5" Tinling entered the Hall of Fame in 1986 as a many-faceted benefactor of the game. He was couturier for the newly formed Virginia Slims circuit, and later the Slimsies' minister of protocol and emcee, a strong advocate of the women's game. An unmistakable bald-headed beacon, he was of immeasurable value late in life as historian and writer who had observed most of the game's luminaries, and as a liaison between the players and Wimbledon. He was outspoken and generous in informing and counseling newcomers to the game.

Arantxa Sanchez Vicario (SPN)   The only player to defeat Steffi Graf in a Grand Slam event in 1989. If Graf had defeated Sanchez Vicario in the championship match of the French Open in 1989, she would have become the first player in history to win the Grand Slam two years in a row. Sanchez Vicario won the French title 7–6 (8–6), 3–6, 7–5.

Virginia Wade (ENG)   As the singles winner at Wimbledon's Centenary (1977), Wade was presented with the women's prize by Queen Elizabeth, who appeared for the first time in 25 years to present at Wimbledon. Known as "Our Ginny" by her compatriots throughout the UK, she deposed 1976 champ Chris Evert in the semis 6–2, 4–6, 6–1. Wade had the longest and, considering the highly competitive age in which she sparkled, the most fruitful career of any Englishwoman. Her career spanned the amateur and open eras, and in 1968 she scored two notable firsts: As an amateur, she won the inaugural open, the British Hard Court; and five months later, captured the U.S. Open, beating the defender and Wimbledon champ, Billie Jean King, 6–4, 6–2.

MaliVai Washington (USA)   Washington was the first black U.S. Davis Cup participant in 1993 to play since Arthur Ashe. Washington was unseeded and played Wimbledon in 1996, making the semifinals.

Serena Williams (USA)   Born in Saginaw, Michigan, Serena is currently living in Palm Beach Gardens, Florida. She played her first Grand Slam event in the Australian Open of 1998 where she defeated Irina Spirlea in the first round before losing to her sister Venus in the second round. Serena is most noted for her stunning comeback against Lindsay Davenport in the 1998 Sydney Event. Her current ranking is 27th in the world.

Venus Williams (USA)   Born in Lynwood, California, Venus is an 18-year-old, 5' 11" powerhouse. A future star, she now holds two titles, including the 1998 Lipton in which she defeated Anna Kournikova. Venus was the 1997 U.S. Open runner-up, losing to Martina Hingis. She is currently ranked fifth in the world. She undoubtedly has the talent to be number one in the near future.

Natalia Zvereva (RUS)   Known as the Mother Freedom of Soviet tennis, Zvereva demanded full prize money in 1989, at a time when the country's players received a meager subsidy of the money they won from the federation. She earned public disapproval, but got her way, benefiting her colleagues. She was the first Soviet to win a major—the French Open in 1989 with Larisa Savchenko.

Important Events and Dates in the Tennis Calendar

The Tour

The Tour, or the Professional Tennis Circuit, is the high point of a tennis player's career. To make it to this level means you are among the top 200 players in the world.

Every January, both the Men's and Women's Tour start in Australia.

Every major city in the world boasts a tennis tournament; the bigger the city, the bigger the tournament. In resort locations, like Hilton Head Island, tournaments are held to attract tourists and place the site in the public eye.

There are only a few events where the men and the women play at the same site in the same tournaments. These include four Grand Slams: the Australian Open, always played in Melbourne in January; the French Open, scheduled in Paris every late May and early June; Wimbledon, a suburb of London, host to the world's most famous tournament every year on the last week of June and the first week of July; and the U.S. Open, which finishes off the majors in New York at Flushing Meadows every late August and early September. One of the newer events to host both sexes is the Lipton in Florida. This event is always played in March over a ten-day period.

A few other sites, such as Indian Wells, California, in February, and the Grand Slam Cup in Germany in October, also have men's and women's events side by side. This is great for the fans because they get double the value for their tennis-viewing dollar.

Each week there are at least three events somewhere in the world for both men and women professional players. There is a tier system, which is based on prize money. The bigger the prize money offered, the better the player commitment to the tournament.

The bigger tournaments such as the ones listed here are usually played on approximately the same date in the same city every year. The smaller cities have smaller tournaments. The bigger cities, like Boston, New York, Montreal, Cincinnati, Tokyo, Hamburg, Los Angeles, and London, for example, all have major events.

The Grand Slams have been in existence since tennis first became a popular sport in the late 1870s. These tournaments are owned by the tennis federations. The other tournaments are owned by individuals or corporations.

There is no off-season in tennis like there is in other sports. Tennis tournaments are held year round all over the world. Professionals have to pace themselves so they play only about 18 to 22 tournaments a year.

So, if you want to see your favorite players, call the WTA, Women's Tennis Association, in St. Petersburg, Florida or the ATP, Association of Tennis Professionals, in Ponte Verde, Florida. These Player Associations can tell you where the players will be playing at least six weeks in advance. Sampras may be in Japan, Davenport may be in Zurich, Switzerland, and your nephew who is just starting on the ATP Satellite Circuit may be in Canberra, Australia.

Index

in a set, 93
singles, 5
tiebreakers, 93
Garrison, Zina, 392
gauge levels (strings), 51
Gerulaitis, Vitas, 393
Gibson, Althea, 31, 393
gloves, 22
goals
for tennis camps,
planning, 338-339
for improvement, 81
Gonzales, Pancho, 30, 133, 346
Goolagong, Evonne, 333, 393
Gore, Spencer W., 27
Graf, Steffi, 353, 393
Grand Slam Tournaments,
359-362
grass courts, 74, 289
Omni courts, 74
Grays of Cambridge, 23
grips, 42
ambidextrous, 128
backhand, 124
two-handed, 126
choking up, 129-130
continental, 119, 120,
124, 175
backhand volleys, 168
flat serves, 190
forehand volleys, 167
serving with, 160
deathgrips, 131
Eastern backhand, 120-126
backhand volleys, 168
flat serves, 190
lobs, 169
slice serves, 192
Eastern forehand, 120-126
forehand volleys, 167
lobs, 169
forehand, 147
two-handed, 126
left-handed, 121-123
on racquets, sizing correctly,
121
right-handed, 121-123
semi-Western (topspin
shots), 177
serving, 160
Western, 120-126
groin pulls, 232
groin stretches, 107

ground strokes, 147-150
depth of, changing, 156
group lesson for children,
316, 323
gut strings, 50
gym workouts, 222-225

H

Hammer series racquets
(Wilson), 42
hamstring injuries, 232
hamstring leg stretches, 105
hands/forearm stretches, 109
hard courts, 10, 74
hash mark, 71
hats, 25
Head, Howard, 42
health
enhanced by tennis, 12-14
nutrition, 235
diet, 236-237
drinking, 237
energy bars, 238
post-match meals, 239
power drinks, 238
pre-game carbohydrates,
237
vitamins and minerals,
240
skin care, 240-246
recommended products,
242-243
sun protection, 244-245
sunscreen, 240, 242
heat (hard court
maintenance), 74
Heldman, Gladys, 348, 393
Hingis, Martina, 134, 393
hip replacements, tennis after,
335
hitting
slice shots
backhands, 183-185
forehands, 182-185
serves, 163
topspin shots with open
stance, 179-181
volleys, 167
backhand, 168
forehand, 167-168

Hoad, Lew, 32
to hold (tendere), 18
home practice techniques,
248-249
home workouts, 219-222
Hopman, Harry, 393
hospitality allowances, 19
human backboard player types,
strategies for handling, 282
Hunt, Lamar, 347

I

*Illustrated Introduction to the
Rules of Tennis*, 388
imagery (visualization),
262-263
indoor courts (surfaces), 73
injuries
3-minute play suspension,
95
ankle sprains, 232
groin pulls, 232
hamstring, 232
knee, 231
rotator cuff, 231
tennis elbow, 230
treating, 232
wrist, 231
Intercollegiate Tennis
Association, *see* ITA
International Tennis
Federation, *see* ITF
International Tennis Hall
of Fame, 384
international tours, 354-359
ITA (Intercollegiate Tennis
Association), 383
regulating racquets, 42
ITF (International Tennis
Federation), 322, 327, 383
circuit, 322
Ivanisevic, Goran, 394

J

Jaeger, Andrea, 394
jeu de paume (game of the
hand), 18
juggling, 248

407

ORDER TRISH FAULKNER'S
COMPLETE IDIOT'S GUIDE TO TENNIS VIDEOS

Two unique tennis videos that will take you from beginner to club champion in forty-five minutes.

These instructional videos include tips on clothing, racquets, shoes, and all the necessary equipment to turn you into the well-dressed player.

Trish will help you choose a club and a professional that is just right for you. She will take you through all the strokes, teach you the secrets of the pros and let you in on her personal training regime that has kept her the number one player in her age group in the United States. Learn how to play smart doubles with *The Complete Idiot's Guide to Tennis Doubles* video. Trish provides valuable information for all levels in both of these outstanding videos.

To order these special videos, call 1-888-234-4600.

You may also mail in the below form to receive a special *Complete Idiot's Guide* Book discount.

Each video is regularly priced at $24.95. *The Complete Idiot's Guide* discount price is $19.95 each, or $35.00 for both videos.

— —

Please send me *The Complete Idiot's Guide to Tennis* Video/*The Complete Idiot's Guide to Tennis Doubles* Video.

Name_____Phone_____

Address_____

City_____State_____Zip_____

Credit Card_____Amex_____Visa_____MC_____Other_____

Credit Card Number_____Exp_____

Check or Money Order Enclosed_____

Signature_____Date_____

Quantity (Tennis)_____ x $19.95   (Discount Price) $_____

Quantity (Tennis Doubles) x $19.95   Sales Tax (6% Florida Tax)   _____

Quantity (Both Videos) x $35.00   S & H $3.00 (for one) $ 6.00 (for both)

                                   Total Order $_____

Send this form with check, money order, or charge information to: Trish Faulkner, Triosports, 7100-39 Fairway Dr. #219C, Palm Beach Gardens, FL 33418. Or call 1-888-234-4600 to place your order.